A REBEL IN AUSCHWITZ

A REBEL IN AUSCHWITZ

The True Story of the Resistance
Hero Who Fought the Nazis
from Inside the Camp

JACK FAIRWEATHER

SCHOLASTIC
FOCUS
NEW YORK

ISBN 978-1-338-68695-1

10 9 8 7 6 5 4 3 2 1   23 24 25 26 27

Printed in the U.S.A.   37

This edition first printing 2023

Book design by Kevin Callahan

To David Booker,
who taught me to search for things,
not ideas

"Whoever loves much, does much.
Whoever does a thing well does much.
And he does well who serves
the common community
before his own interests."

—Thomas à Kempis

INTRODUCTION

Trucks rumble to a stop outside. Shouts and gunshots follow. The building caretaker bangs on the door of the apartment. "The Germans are here," he shouts. "Hide in the basement or get out through the gardens at the back."[1]

The man inside doesn't stir.

It's dawn on September 19, 1940, in Nazi-occupied Warsaw. The Germans invaded Poland the year before, plunging Europe into World War II. Intent on destroying Polish society by eliminating its professional class, they are arresting thousands of Polish people—doctors, teachers, writers, and lawyers—and either shooting them or interning them in camps. Three months ago, in June, the Germans opened a new concentration camp to hold some of the prisoners. Its name is Auschwitz. Little is known about what's happening inside.

The man has learned in advance about the morning's roundup and that those arrested would likely be sent to Auschwitz. That's why he's there. His mission, for the Polish resistance, is to infiltrate the camp, create an underground resistance, and gather evidence of Nazi crimes.

The door crashes open below and boots clatter on the stairs. The man is putting on his jacket when he notices that the three-year-old boy in the room opposite is standing up in his cot. His teddy bear has fallen to the floor. Fists pound on the door. The man quickly picks up the bear and hands it to the wide-eyed boy as the mother lets the Germans in. "See you soon," he whispers to the child.

Then, against every instinct he must have had, he steps into captivity.[2]

ONE YEAR EARLIER . . .

ONE

Witold Pilecki stood on the steps of his manor house, watching a car kick up a trail of dust as it drove down the lime-tree avenue toward him. It came to a stop beside the gnarled chestnut tree in the yard.

The summer of 1939 had been so dry that the peasants talked about pouring water on the grave of a drowned man or harnessing a maiden to the plow so that it might rain. Such were the customs of the Kresy, Poland's eastern borderlands. Finally, a massive electrical storm had come, flattening what was left of the harvest. But Witold wasn't worrying about their not having enough grain for the winter.[1]

The radio waves crackled with news about German troops gathering on the border with Poland. The führer of the Third Reich, Adolf Hitler, had threatened to reclaim territory ceded to Poland in 1918 at the end of World War I.

It was only by the "annihilation of Poland . . . and its vital forces," Hitler told his officers on August 22, that the German people could expand their territory. The next day, Hitler signed a secret nonaggression pact with the Soviet dictator Josef Stalin to divide Poland between them. If they succeeded in their plans, Witold's home and land would be taken and Poland reduced to vassalage, or destroyed entirely.[2]

A soldier stepped out of the dusty car with orders for Witold, who was a second lieutenant in the cavalry reserves. Witold had forty-eight hours to deliver his unit to the barracks in the nearby town of Lida, where they would board troop transports bound for the western border. Witold had done his best to train ninety volunteers, but most of his men were peasants who had never seen action or fired a gun in combat. Several of them didn't own a horse and planned to fight the Germans on bicycle. At least Witold had been able to arm them, with Lebel 8mm bolt-action rifles.[3]

Witold hurried into his uniform and riding boots and grabbed his Vis handgun from a pail in the old smoke room, where he'd hidden it after catching his eight-year-old son waving it at his little sister earlier in the summer.[4]

He took a moment to adjust his khaki uniform in one of the mirrors that hung in the hallway. The man in the reflection was thirty-eight years old, of medium build and handsome in an understated way, with pale blue eyes, dark blond hair brushed back from a high forehead, and a set to his lips that gave him a constant half smile.

As a young man, Witold had wanted to be an artist and studied painting at the university in Wilno (now Vilnius), only to abandon his schooling in the tumultuous years after World War I. Poland declared independence in 1918 out of the

Witold Pilecki and a friend in Sukurcze, c. 1930.

wreckage of the Russian, German, and Austro-Hungarian empires but was soon after engaged in a war with Soviet Russia. Witold skirmished against the Bolsheviks with his scout troop and fought on the streets of Wilno.

In the heady days that followed victory in 1921, Witold hadn't felt like painting. He worked as a clerk at a military supply depot and a farmers' union. Then, in 1924, his father fell ill, and Witold was almost relieved to have his destiny decided for him. He took on his family's dilapidated estate, Sukurcze, with its crumbling manor house, overgrown orchards, and 550 acres of rolling wheat fields.

Suddenly, he found himself the steward of the local community. Peasants from the local village of Krupa worked his fields and sought his advice on how to develop their own land. He set up a dairy cooperative to earn them better prices and founded the local reserve unit.[5]

Then, in 1927, he met his future wife, Maria, while painting scenery for a play at the school where she worked. He courted her with bunches of lilacs delivered through her bedroom window. They married in 1931, and within a year their son, Andrzej, was born, followed twelve months later by Zofia, a daughter. Fatherhood brought out Witold's caring side. He tended to the children when Maria was bedridden after Zofia's birth and taught them to ride horses and swim in the pond beside the house.[6]

The Pileckis' quiet home life was not cut off from the political currents sweeping the country in the 1930s. The newly independent country of Poland that reemerged in 1918 after 123 years of partition had struggled to forge an identity. Some politicians and church leaders called for a narrow

Witold, Maria, Andrzej, and Zofia, c. 1935.

definition of Polishness based on ethnicity and Catholicism.

The government suppressed groups advocating greater rights for minorities, such as Ukrainians and Belarusians. Jews, who comprised around a tenth of Poland's prewar population, faced discrimination in education and business as well as calls for them to emigrate. Some nationalists took matters into their own hands, boycotting and smashing up Jewish shops and attacking synagogues. In Witold's hometown of Lida, the main square was filled with shuttered shops belonging to Jews who had fled the country.[7]

Witold disliked the way politicians exploited differences. His family stood for the old order of the eighteenth century, when Poland had last been an independent nation and a beacon of culture in the region. That said, he was a man of his time and social class. He likely held a paternal view toward the local peasants and shared in some of the prevailing anti-Semitic views. But ultimately, his patriotism extended to any group or ethnicity that took up Poland's cause. They would all need to unite to repel the Nazi threat.[8]

The stable boy had readied Witold's favorite horse, Bajka (Polish for "fairy tale"), in the yard, and Witold galloped to Krupa, a mile away, where he likely called Maria from one of the few houses to have a telephone. She had taken the children to visit her mother near Warsaw, and he wanted them home. Next, he assembled his men and gathered supplies.

They received ammunition and emergency rations from the regimental headquarters in Lida but had to arrange the remaining provisions from the community: bread, groats, sausages, lard, potatoes, onions, canned coffee, flour, dried herbs, vinegar, and salt. Not everyone in the village was happy to contribute, having hardly enough for themselves, and it was a long day in the sweltering heat to load the wagons in the manor courtyard.[9]

Witold wasn't at home when Maria and the children finally arrived the following evening, hot and bedraggled, to find

Poland, 1939

SWEDEN

Baltic Sea

ESTONIA

LATVIA

LITHUANIA

Free City
of Danzig

GERMANY
East Prussia

• Wilno

Krupa •• Lida

• Berlin

Vistula

Ostrów
Mazowiecka •

Sochaczew • ⊙ **Warsaw**
• Łuków

GERMANY

Breslau
•

Piotrków
• Trybunalski

• Włodawa

POLAND

Kłobuck •

Prague
•

(Annexed by
Germany 1939)

Oświęcim • Krakow

CZECHOSLOVAKIA

Tatra Mountains

• Lwów

SOVIET
UNION

(Annexed by
Hungary 1939)

AUSTRIA
(Annexed by
Germany 1938)

HUNGARY

ROMANIA

N
W ⊕ E
S

| 0 | 50 | 100 | 150 miles |
| 0 | 100 | 200 km |

soldiers dozing in their beds. She was annoyed, to put it mildly. Witold was promptly summoned from the field and had to ask the men to leave.[10]

Maria was still upset the next day, but she put on one of Witold's favorite dresses for the send-off in Krupa and made sure Andrzej and Zofia were in their Sunday best. The children of the village gathered outside the school, and Krupa's single street was packed with well-wishers waving flags or handkerchiefs. A cheer went up as Witold led his column of horsemen down the street. He was dressed in a khaki uniform, with his pistol and saber strapped to his waist.[11]

Witold passed his family without looking down, but as soon as the column rode by and the crowd started to disperse, he came galloping back. He hugged and kissed the children. Maria, her unruly brown hair done up and lipstick on, was trying not to cry. "I will be back in two weeks," he told them. He could hardly say that in riding off on horseback to confront the most powerful military machine in Europe he would be lucky to survive the next few days.[12]

When Hitler invaded Poland, on September 1, 1939, his forces included an army of 3.7 million men—almost twice the size of Poland's—and he had 2,000 more tanks and almost ten times the number of fighter planes and bombers. Witold's unit was deployed outside a town called Piotrków Trybunalski, directly in front of the main thrust toward Warsaw of the German First and Fourth Panzer Divisions: more than 600 tanks moving faster than his horse could gallop. Witold witnessed the first waves of German Heinkel, Dornier, and Junkers bombers appear on the horizon, their

Witold on his horse, Bajka, on parade.

fuselages glinting in the morning light. The ground vibrated with the tremor of distant artillery.[13]

The Poles had no means of countering the blitzkrieg. Orders came for Witold to fall back to nearby woods as the German attack began but there was no escape: Artillery hit them in the forest, shattering the trees and blasting spears of wood into men and horses. They hunkered down as best they could, but then word spread that the panzers had broken through elsewhere, and the local Polish command began an urgent retreat along the main road to Warsaw.[14]

The panzers caught up with them as they queued to cross a bridge. The assault lasted only a few minutes, but by the end of it, Witold had lost most of his men—dead, injured, or captured. He headed for Warsaw with the survivors, knowing that all would be lost if they couldn't hold the capital.

The roadside was littered with corpses sprawled beside carts piled high with luggage and furniture—fleeing civilians who had been bombed and gunned down by the Germans: It was Hitler's stated goal to obliterate the Polish people as well as their nation.[15]

Witold arrived in Warsaw on horseback on the evening of September 6. He had no radio and no way of knowing the scale of the disaster. The Germans had cut through Polish lines at multiple points and were rapidly encircling the capital. Advance units were expected at any moment. The Polish government had fled, and while Britain and France had declared war on Germany, there was no sign of action.[16]

The only defenses Witold saw on his way into the city center were a couple of overturned tram cars that served as a barricade. Weary soldiers sat slumped on the sidewalks. It was clear

A girl kneels beside her older sister killed in a German air attack.

that Poland was about to lose its independence, and the question facing Witold—and every Pole—was whether to surrender to the Germans or to fight on. Witold could not accept the first option. He set off to find the military's headquarters, but it was retreating toward the border with Romania.

On September 13, at Włodawa, a town 150 miles east of Warsaw, Witold at last found someone who was preparing to take a stand: Major Jan Włodarkiewicz. They made for the woods, from where they could stage hit-and-run attacks and maybe find enough like-minded souls to plan a bigger operation.[17]

Over the following days, they attacked several German convoys and even a small airstrip, blowing up a plane. But

Witold knew that such attacks didn't achieve much. German checkpoints were springing up everywhere, forcing them to keep to the thickets and marshes and scrounge for food in the woods or from isolated peasants.[18]

At the end of September, they learned that Soviet forces had entered Poland from the east. Stalin claimed it was for the protection of Poland's minorities, but his intention was clear to most Poles: He had decided to seize his share of the spoils. Witold's home in Krupa was now under Soviet control.[19]

On September 28, Warsaw surrendered. The city had held out for another fortnight after Witold left, much to the fury of Hitler, who instructed his generals to darken the skies over Warsaw with falling bombs and to drown the people in blood. The aerial and artillery bombardment had left 40,000 dead and had destroyed or severely damaged a fifth of the city's buildings, including schools, hospitals, and churches. Tens of thousands of people squatted amid the debris, their homes in ruins.[20]

Witold heard only rumors of the city's devastation. Huddled with Jan in some woods near the town of Lubartów, dirty and unshaven, he realized that the fight to reclaim Poland would start in Warsaw. He and Jan ordered their men to dig holes and bury their weapons. Then they exchanged their uniforms for civilian clothes—Witold put on an old sheepskin jacket—and went underground.[21]

Before heading to Warsaw, Witold made a detour to Ostrów Mazowiecka, the town sixty miles north of the capital where his mother-in-law, Franciszka, lived. He hoped to find Maria and the children there. He set off through the

The Ostrowski family home.

fields and picked his way through the brush for several days until he reached the Bug River. The waterway was now the border between German and Soviet forces, and Russian troops patrolled Witold's side of the bank.[22]

He persuaded a local fisherman to ferry him across during a gap in patrols and found a way through the lines of barbed wire that the Germans had strung along the bank. When he got to the town, he found it eerily quiet. Half the 17,000 residents were Jewish, and most had fled to Soviet-occupied territory. Their shops had been looted and non-Jewish Polish families had moved into some of their homes.[23]

His mother-in-law, Franciszka, lived in a farmhouse on the outskirts of town. As Witold arrived, he saw German vehicles parked in the yard of the brewery near her home, which was now the headquarters of the German secret police, the Gestapo. He made sure to enter the farmhouse from the rear.[24]

Over the following days, Witold learned about the brutal new racial order the Nazis had imposed on the town. The Germans encouraged the ethnic Poles to abuse and beat the Jews and to point out their shops for looting. Most refused. The mayor hid a Jewish family in his basement, and Maria's parents did what little they felt they could—allowing fleeing Jews to take apples from their orchard.[25]

Each morning, Witold woke up praying for Maria to come walking through the door with the children, and each night, he went to bed fearing the worst. Eventually, he had to choose between waiting for his family and resuming the struggle against the Germans.[26]

His decision was clear: country before family. On the morning of November 1, he borrowed a bicycle and set off on the long ride to Warsaw. The main road was dotted with German checkpoints, so he stuck to country lanes, picking up snatches of news along the way. There was still no word of a British or French attack on the German forces, but he assumed one was imminent. Poland's best chance of driving out the Germans lay in staging an uprising to coincide with an Allied offensive.[27]

Witold approached the city on his clattering bicycle, unsure what he would find there or what form his resistance would take. As he joined the crowds crossing the Vistula by its last remaining bridge, the sight of Warsaw's broken skyline on the far bank must have startled him.

Collapsed buildings blocked the streets, and people made

pathways through the rubble. Glass from broken windows crunched underfoot. Hundreds paused at the intersection of Marszałkowska Street and Jerozolimskie Avenue to light candles in front of a giant mound of bricks and masonry that marked the city's largest mass grave.[28]

Witold made his way to a friend's apartment in the south of the city. His shock and dismay at the devastation were tempered by his practical need to understand Hitler's terrifying plans for the country. In September, Hitler had ordered that western Poland be annexed to the Reich and over 5 million

Polish Catholics and Jews were expelled to make way for German settlers.

The remaining territory, which included Warsaw and Kraków, was to become a German colony. Hitler made his former lawyer, Hans Frank, head of the "General Government" in charge of the region. Newspapers were censored, radios banned, and high schools and universities closed. Killing squads, known as the Einsatzgruppen, pre-empted resistance by shooting 50,000 members of the Polish educated and professional classes—lawyers, teachers, doctors, journalists, or simply anyone who looked intellectual. They buried their bodies in mass graves.[29]

Governor-General Frank had orders to impose a brutal

racial hierarchy. The Germans were the master race, as were any Poles who could prove German ancestry. They were given government jobs, property (much of which had been seized from Jewish people), and exclusive use of parks, public phones, and taxis. Ethnic Poles, as members of what the Nazis perceived to be the "weaker" Slavic race, were to serve as forced laborers.[30]

At the bottom of the pecking order were the Jews, whom Hitler considered to be a parasitic subspecies bent on destroying the German people. The occupation of Poland had brought 2 million Jews—ten times more than lived in Germany—under Nazi control. They were required to wear a Star of David on their sleeve or chest and were subjected to continual harassment.[31]

The Germans clearly intended to destroy Poland by tearing apart its social fabric and pitting ethnic groups against one another. When Witold made his way through Warsaw, he would have seen Governor-General Frank's official decrees plastered on lampposts around the city center, but no doubt he also saw encouraging signs of resistance: stickers declaring WE DON'T GIVE A DAMN and a giant poster of Hitler that had been given curly whiskers and long ears.

Poland was fighting back, and Witold knew what he had to do.[32]

TWO

On November 9, Witold contacted his coconspirator Jan Włodarkiewicz and arranged a meeting of potential recruits at his sister-in-law's apartment. That evening, he hurried through the rainy streets of the northern suburb of Żoliborz, trying to beat the 7:00 P.M. curfew. The area was relatively untouched by bombs, although the windows of most apartments were blown out and there was no electricity.[1]

Before that night, Witold had met his sister-in-law, Eleonora Ostrowska, only briefly. She was a charming, tough, thirty-year-old, with thin lips, pale blue eyes, and dark blond hair, which she wore pulled back into a bun. Her husband, Edward, a cavalry officer, had been missing since the start of the war. Witold couldn't be sure how Eleonora would respond to his call to arms, but she proved eager to help.[2]

She quickly showed Witold inside. Jan arrived next, wheezing and struggling up the steps. He'd taken a bullet in the

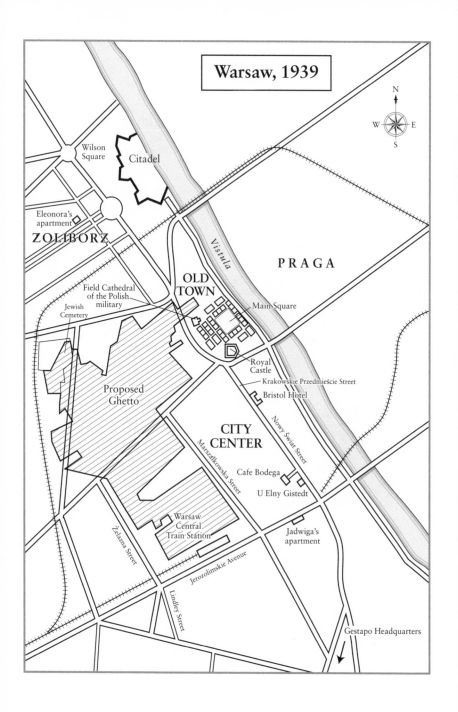

Warsaw, 1939

N
W E
S

Wilson Square
Citadel

Eleonora's apartment
ZOLIBORZ

Vistula

PRAGA

Field Cathedral of the Polish military
OLD TOWN
Jewish Cemetery
Main Square

Royal Castle
Krakowskie Przedmieście Street
Proposed Ghetto
Bristol Hotel

CITY CENTER

Marszałkowska Street

Nowy Świat Street

Cafe Bodega
U Elny Gistedt

Żelazna Street

Warsaw Central Train Station
Jadwiga's apartment

Jerozolimskie Avenue

Lindley Street

Gestapo Headquarters

Eleonora Ostrowska, 1944.

chest on his way to Warsaw that had somehow missed his vital organs, and he had been laid up at his mother's apartment recuperating. Half a dozen more coconspirators followed, mostly officers and student activists selected by Jan. Eleonora had put brown paper over the blown-out windows, but it was

Wartime image of apartment building at 40 Wojska Polskiego.

still cold inside the apartment, so they kept their coats on. They gathered around the candlelit living room table and talked strategy late into the night.[3]

Jan had reached some stark conclusions about the invasion and their country's double occupation by Germany and Russia. He believed that Poland's leaders were failing to harness the country's wellspring of Catholic faith against the invaders and that they must rebuild the nation on a foundation of Christian beliefs. Witold certainly shared Jan's anger at the Polish government, but he worried that an overtly religious mission might alienate potential allies. He was more focused on building a secret and effective resistance.[4]

They decided to call themselves Tajna Armia Polska—the Secret Polish Army. Jan would be the leader, Witold the chief recruiter. When the sun came up, they went to the Field Cathedral of the Polish Military, a baroque church on the edge of the Old Town, where, witnessed by a priest, they swore to serve God, the Polish nation, and each other. They left the church bleary-eyed but elated.[5]

Winter came early that year. The snow fell in flurries, and the Vistula froze solid. Witold began recruiting new members, seeking out those who shared his natural reserve and reticence. He was not always successful in judging temperament and constantly worried that an overeager member of his team would expose them all.

A hundred resistance cells had sprung up across Warsaw. Some, like Witold and Jan's group, were led by Polish army officers. Others were run by Communist agitators, by trade unionists, or by artists. There was even a group of chemists, who were planning biological warfare.

Witold and Jan's organization compiled a handbook of advice for new recruits that warned how "people had gone mad with resistance activity and were getting caught far too easily . . . If we want to have our revenge on the Germans, we have to survive long enough to get it."[6]

The very act of recruitment meant that Witold was placing his life in the hands of his recruits, and vice versa. At times, those whom Witold selected were surprised by his confidence in them. "Why do you trust me?" was a typical question.[7]

"Dear boy, you have to trust people," Witold would answer.[8]

Witold knew there was little his young army could do to directly oppose the occupation, at least not yet, but he thought they could serve as an effective intelligence-gathering operation. The organization had contacts in the Polish police—required by the Germans to continue work—and frequently knew about major operations in advance. They were able to warn those targeted that they were in danger. He did his best to nurture the group, which by December numbered nearly a hundred men. One soldier he recruited joked appreciatively that Witold was the group's "nanny."[9]

That winter, the SS stepped up deportations of Poles from the recently annexed provinces of western Poland. By January 1940, more than 150,000 Poles—Catholics and Jews alike—had been deported to make way for German settlers, and the SS planned to expel many more. Cattle trucks stuffed with people, frozen to the bone, arrived daily at the main train station in Warsaw. When the doors were peeled back, stiff corpses toppled to the ground like statues. The survivors had to sleep in the ruins of the city or else pack into the already crowded homes of friends and families.[10]

In areas of Poland occupied by the Soviet Union, the Communist secret police were rounding up thousands of Poles for transportation to work camps in Siberia and central Asia. That spring, Witold finally received word that Maria and the children were at her mother's farmhouse in Ostrów Mazowiecka. He rushed to see them, taking a rickety bus line that the Germans rarely inspected. Maria's account of their flight and the conditions in the Soviet-occupied east was harrowing.[11]

Maria had been tipped off before Christmas that she and the children were soon to be arrested and had time to pack up some clothes before escaping in a cart, leaving behind the family dog, Nero. For most of the winter, they'd hidden with family friends in Krupa. When the cold eased, they took the train to the new border between the Soviet Union and the Reich in the hope of reaching her mother's home.

They were stopped by the Russian police in the small town of Wołkowysk, twenty miles from the frontier, where Maria was led off for interrogation in a pigsty near the train station while the children waited overnight nearby. When she was finally released the following morning, minus her money and her wedding ring, eight-year-old Andrzej was catatonic with fear and cold.[12]

They made it to a cousin's house in a neighboring town, where they rested a week and tried again. A guide helped to sneak them across the border at night. It was subzero temperatures, and a full moon lit the wind-scourged no-man's-land. Halfway across, Andrzej stumbled and fell against a roll of barbed wire that snagged his sheepskin jacket. At that moment a German searchlight swept the area and caught them as they struggled to free him. They were rounded up but were lucky: The border guards who collected them showed little interest in their case and let them pass.[13]

They had arrived in Ostrów Mazowiecka to find it devastated by the unfolding German racial project. Maria was told that on November 11, the Germans had marched 364 Jewish men, women, and children into woods outside the town and shot them. The execution site was only a mile or so from her mother's house, and next to the family orchard where Andrzej liked to play. Despite being told not to go there, Andrzej did. He found a little boy's sodden cap among the trees. It was one of the first such massacres of Jewish families, but the Nazis had yet to make extermination their general policy.[14]

Witold did what he could to make sure the family were properly settled and then returned to Warsaw with a new urgency, only to discover Jan flirting with anti-Semitic views. Witold was worried that Jan's vision for their organization was too right-wing. The articles in their newsletter, *Znak*, "The Sign," spoke stridently about a Polish nation for Polish people—a truly Christian country. These views were disturbingly close to those of the right-wing ultranationalists who saw the Nazi occupation as a means of getting rid of the Jews for good.[15]

Witold explained to Jan, as tactfully as he could, that Poles must rally together in the face of mounting German repression, but his friend was adamant. Jan was clearly losing his way, and Witold felt compelled to go behind his back. He sought out the head of Związek Walki Zbrojnej (the Union for Armed Struggle), which had the backing of the newly formed Polish government-in-exile in France, to discuss a merger.[16]

Some of Witold's men saw the group as rivals, but he liked their inclusive approach. Its leader, Colonel Stefan Rowecki, had few illusions about what the underground could achieve against the might of the occupiers, but he felt that their resistance served the deeper purpose of rallying morale while they built up strength.[17]

Rowecki was also documenting Nazi crimes and smuggling reports to the West to put pressure on the Allies to act. So far, he had yet to stir them into action, although the Germans were embarrassed by some of the revelations. Witold was impressed by the quiet, secretive man and convinced of the need to submit to his authority.[18]

Jan immediately dismissed the idea and was taken aback

when Witold refused to fall into line. Several others in the group agreed with Witold, including the new chief of staff, a doughty colonel named Władysław Surmacki. Jan capitulated and agreed to accept Rowecki's leadership. It was a victory for Witold, but he knew that his partnership with Jan was ruined. "On the surface we agreed to keep on running the organization," Witold recalled, but there was no hiding the "deeper resentment."[19]

On May 10, 1940, Hitler's forces swept into Luxembourg, Belgium, and the Netherlands on their way to France. This was the moment the underground had waited for: when the combined might of the Allies would take on the Germans and either defeat them or distract them enough to make an uprising in Poland worthwhile. Jan's mother had an illegal radio in her apartment, and they gathered to listen, eagerly at first and then with increasing grimness, as the BBC reported that German forces had routed the British at Dunkirk and were sweeping into Paris.[20]

The governor-general of occupied Poland, Frank, realizing the foreign media's attention was elsewhere, ordered a mass roundup of military-age men. On June 20, 1940, 358 people were shot in the Palmiry woods, and thousands more were sent to concentration camps. The crackdown damaged Witold's network, and he was nearly caught himself when the SS raided Eleonora's apartment. He heard trucks outside and had just enough time to hide documents under the floorboards and slip out the door before they barged in. After that, he moved from safe house to safe house and started using the papers of another officer, Tomasz Serafiński.[21]

Shortly before dawn on the morning of July 3, the SS

dragged one of Witold's underground comrades, a doctor named Władysław Dering, from his apartment, along with his wife. The underground wasn't sure what had happened to him, but reports were emerging that the SS had opened a concentration camp in a former Polish army barracks outside the town of Oświęcim.[22]

Concentration camps were a feature of political life in Germany since Hitler's rise to power, and the Nazis had detained thousands of politicians, left-wing activists, Jews, homosexuals, and other so-called "social deviants" in half a dozen camps across Germany. The underground knew little about this camp beyond its name, Auschwitz; the fact that the Germans were dispatching more and more prisoners there; and that it was clearly a place of violence, as evidenced by the number of death notices the SS sent to the families of deceased inmates, sometimes accompanied by blood-splattered personal effects.[23]

A few weeks later, in August, Jan convened an emergency meeting. The heat in the room was stifling, and cigarette smoke hung in the air. Jan began by announcing the group's merger with the mainstream underground, just as Witold had urged. Then he turned to Witold. The tension between the two men was palpable. "A great honor has befallen you," said Jan.[24]

He explained: Auschwitz had come up in his discussions with Rowecki, who believed that as long as the camp remained shrouded in secrecy, the Germans could abuse prisoners with impunity. Rowecki needed someone to infiltrate the camp, to gain intelligence, and, if possible, to raise a resistance cell and stage a breakout.[25]

"I've mentioned your name to Rowecki as the only officer capable of doing this," said Jan.[26]

Witold struggled to hide his shock. He knew he was being punished for his refusal to support Jan's right-wing ideology.

Jan continued: The Germans were planning mass round-ups of military-age men for dispatch to Auschwitz. This was the perfect opportunity for the underground to get a man inside. There was also a chance that those caught and suspected of resistance work would be shot, so, given this risk, Jan said that he couldn't order Witold to take the mission. He needed him to volunteer.[27]

Witold's mind raced. Walking into a roundup was madness. Even if the Germans didn't suspect him of belonging to the resistance, what would happen after he got to Auschwitz? If the camp was as violent as the underground feared it was,

Witold and Jan, c. 1940.

the chances of forging a resistance group and staging a break-out were slim. If it was just another internment facility, then he might spend months or longer languishing in captivity away from the center of the action in Warsaw.

Witold weighed those risks against the knowledge that he had pushed Jan to accept Rowecki's leadership. How would it look if he balked at the very first request Rowecki made? He told Jan he needed time to think it over.[28]

A few days later, the two men met, and Jan confirmed that both Władysław Dering and Władysław Surmacki were in Auschwitz. Knowing that his comrades were in the camp might have been what decided Witold to accept the mission. He told Jan that he was ready to volunteer.[29]

Witold decided against telling Maria about his mission beyond the fact that he would be away for some time. It was better that she would be able to claim ignorance if the Gestapo came calling. He hoped the Tomasz Serafiński alias he planned to use would keep his family safe. On September 18, he packed his possessions into a knapsack and headed to Eleonora's apartment in the Żoliborz district, which the Germans were due to raid the following morning.[30]

There was the air of a last supper as he dined with Eleonora and her little son, Marek, that night. After the boy was put to bed, Witold double-checked the apartment to make sure there weren't any incriminating documents on hand and went over the plan again with Eleonora. If he made it to the camp, she would be his point of contact with Jan, who would pass on any intelligence he managed to send to the underground leadership.[31]

The following morning, Witold woke and dressed before dawn. He didn't have long to wait before he heard the

Witold and Marek, c. 1940.

rumble of the approaching trucks. A few moments later, there was a rap at the door. Eleonora, also dressed, opened it. The building's caretaker, Jan Kiliański, stood in the hallway, tense and fearful, and announced the Germans' arrival. He urged Witold to hide or escape.[32]

"Thank you, Jan," said Witold. He retreated to the bedroom Eleonora shared with Marek, who was standing up in his crib, wide-eyed.[33]

They could hear banging outside now and the barking of orders in German. That was when Witold noticed Marek's teddy bear on the floor and picked it up for him. Then the door to the building crashed open, and footsteps rang up the concrete steps, accompanied by shouts and screams.[34]

Witold and Eleonora working together, c. 1940.

Kiliański returned. "They're in the building. It's your last chance."

"Thank you, Jan," said Witold again, and stayed where he was.

There was a hammering at the door, and a soldier barged in, brandishing his weapon. "Up, up!" he shouted. Witold already had his jacket on and was calmly walking toward him. Soldiers and plainclothes police escorted him and the others onto the street. There must have been a hundred or more gathered there, some with bags and coats as if they were going on business trips, others barefoot and still in their pajamas.[35]

The soldiers marched them to Wilson Square, half a mile away, where their papers were checked. Factory and railway workers were released, and the rest were ordered into trucks and brought to a horse barracks where they were registered, relieved of their valuables, and ordered to lie down on the ground.[36]

Witold and a thousand other prisoners were held there for two days, during which time a few more were released or selected for labor in Germany. Early in the morning of September 21, they were loaded onto trucks and taken to a train station where a line of freight cars was waiting. Witold squeezed into one of the carriages with 60 other men. The guards gave them a single bucket to use as a toilet, but no food or water. Then the door to the carriage was slammed closed.

The slow rocking of the train and the hot, fetid air sent many to sleep, slumped against each other on the floor. A few kept watch at the chinks in the carriage walls, looking out for a clue as to their destination. The train stopped after dark, and they heard a door crash open somewhere up the track,

followed by shouts, screams, and the yelping of dogs.[37]

Next minute, the door of Witold's carriage was ripped open, and an intense light blinded the occupants. To shouts of "Out! Out! Out!" the men surged forward. Witold struggled to keep his balance. For a moment he was caught in the opening, dazzled by spotlights. He glimpsed the night sky and drizzling rain before he dropped down into the crowd below.

He hit gravel and stumbled as a club whistled past his head. Men with batons were laying into those who fell and were dragging stragglers from the train. Hands clutched at Witold, and he tore himself free to join the others, half running, half stumbling across a muddy field, guard dogs snapping at their heels.[38]

On either side of their ragged column, SS guards were smoking cigarettes and laughing among themselves. They ordered a prisoner to run over to a fence post. The confused man staggered off, only for the guards to gun him down. Then they dragged ten more out from the crowd and shot them too: collective responsibility for the "escape."[39]

Witold was so absorbed by the chaos that he barely noticed the barbed-wire fence looming out of the dark or the iron sign spanning the gateway that said ARBEIT MACHT FREI—German for "Work Sets You Free." Beyond the gate were rows of brick barracks, their windows unbarred and dark. They flanked a brightly lit parade ground, where a line of men was waiting.

Wearing striped denim blazers and rimless hats, the men had the word *kapo* emblazoned on their arms and were also carrying clubs. These so-called kapos ordered the newly arrived prisoners into ranks of ten, relieving them of any remaining watches, rings, and other valuables as they went.[40]

One kapo asked a prisoner his profession. A judge, the man replied. The kapo let out a hoot of triumph and struck the prisoner to the ground with his club. Some of the other Nazis joined in, striking at the man's head and body until all that was left was a bloody pulp. Then the kapo turned to the crowd, his uniform splattered with blood and gore, and declared, "This is Auschwitz Concentration Camp, my dear sirs."[41]

They singled out doctors, lawyers, professors, and Jews for beatings. Witold realized they were targeting the educated, which made sense, given the Nazis' stated aim of treating the Poles as mere chattel. The bodies were dragged to the end of each row. Then a strip of metal was beaten noisily, signaling roll call, and the new prisoners were addressed from a low

Washroom, *by Jerzy Potrzebowski, postwar.*

wall by the camp's deputy commander, SS-Obersturmführer Fritz Seidler.[42]

"Let none of you imagine that he will ever leave this place alive," Seidler announced. "The rations have been calculated so you will only survive six weeks. Anyone who lives longer must be stealing, and anyone stealing will be sent to the penal company, where he won't live very long."[43]

The speech was followed by more blows from the kapos' clubs, then the men were led off in groups of a hundred to a single-story building where they were ordered to strip, put their belongings into sacks, and toss any food in a wheelbarrow before entering the building one at a time. When Witold's turn came, he found a scrap of bread in his pocket and mindlessly threw it away.[44]

He joined a queue of naked men in a small whitewashed room and received his prisoner identification number on a little piece of fabric: 4859. In the next room, barbers were bent over a line of low benches shaving the heads, armpits, and pubic hair of prisoners, with blunt blades. Next was the washroom, where Witold took a blow to the face from a kapo's club because, the man said, he wasn't holding his ID card between his teeth. Witold spat out two molars and a mouthful of blood, and continued forward. Jewish prisoners, recognized by their circumcisions, were set upon with a special fury, punched and pummeled until they fell to the floor. Those Jews who survived the onslaught were kept separate from most other prisoners in a special penal unit that also contained Catholic priests.

In the last room, Witold received his prison uniform: a blue-and-white-striped jacket that buttoned up to the neck, pants, and a pair of wooden clogs. Shorn of hair and dressed in ill-fitting prison stripes or old army uniforms, the men hardly recognized one another. They sewed their numbers onto their shirts, along with a red triangle, which indicated their status as political prisoners.[45]

By the time Witold emerged from the building, the sky had lightened and he could see his surroundings more clearly. Some of the buildings around the square were plastered in white; others were ochre-red brick. Two sides of the parade ground were open: one to the field over which they had stumbled from the train, and the other to a road and a line of trees along what looked like a riverbank. There was a single line of barbed wire around the camp, with wooden guard posts every few hundred feet.[46]

In the Night, *by Jerzy Potrzebowski, postwar.*

The kapos continued to menace them, though in the pale light the wild men looked smaller than they had before. The prisoners were lined up once again and each assigned a block. Witold's was 17a, on the second floor of a barrack building facing the square. They packed in, 100 men to each room of 300 square feet, and, exhausted, placed thin jute mattresses on the floor and lay down.

Witold shared his mattress with two other men. They lay close together, like spoons in a drawer, using their clogs and stripes as pillows. Men groaned, snored, and cursed as they tried to shift position. Witold's shock had given way to a dull torpor. He had succeeded in getting into the camp. Now his work would have to begin.[47]

THREE

Witold had barely closed his eyes when a gong sounded, and the German kapo who ran the block charged in and laid into anyone not already on their feet. The prisoners hurriedly stacked their mattresses, collected soup tins, and pushed into the corridor while the kapo emptied the other rooms before rushing them all down the stairs to dress outside.[1]

Fog had rolled in from the river, turning the camp into a milky bowl. Witold followed the shapes of the others as they scurried around the back of the building to the latrine, an open trench over which a beam had been set. A kapo counted twenty men onto the beam and gave each group a few seconds to relieve themselves. Washing was compulsory, but the inmates had access to only one cistern in the yard, around which a scrum of men jostled and pushed.[2]

Breakfast was served back in the rooms. One of the kapo's

Washing under the Pump, *by Jerzy Potrzebowski, postwar.*

helpers dispensed ladles of a bitter-tasting liquid they called coffee. The men gulped it down, stacked their cups, and went outside. Prisoners from previous transports, thinner and grayer, clustered around the arrivals, asking for news. In return, the newcomers asked them about the camp. You'll need to have eyes in the backs of your heads, they were told.[3]

The kapo swaggered out of the building. His name was Alois Staller, a former construction worker from the Rhineland. Thirty-five years old, he had a long, thin nose and ears that jutted out at odd angles. He had been arrested in 1934 for putting up anti-Nazi posters in his hometown and detained indefinitely in the concentration-camp system. What spark of resistance he had once shown was long gone. He hated Poles with a passion and expected them to doff their caps and stand to attention in his presence.[4]

The daily running of the camp was carried out by kapos like Staller, who received extra food and were excused from hard labor provided they kept the other prisoners in line. The system had been well established in other concentration camps, but Hitler's stated desire to destroy racial enemies had added a murderous intensity to the hard labor and military drills the Auschwitz kapos forced on the prisoners. Kapos were under pressure to constantly prove how ruthless they could be. "As soon as we are no longer satisfied with him, he is no longer a kapo and returns to the other inmates," SS-Reichsführer Heinrich Himmler later explained. "He knows that they will beat him to death his first night back."[5]

Staller ordered the prisoners into ranks of ten, with the tallest men at the end of each row. The older inmates knew the drill and guided the newcomers. Each prisoner had to call out

Alois Staller, c. 1941.

his position in the row, in German, or be beaten. Staller singled out Witold and a couple of other German speakers and led them inside, where he lined them up, facing the wall.[6]

Then he instructed them to bend over to receive what he called "five of the best" and struck them hard with his cudgel. Witold had to grit his teeth to avoid crying out. They apparently met with Staller's approval because he told them they were to be room supervisors and would get their own clubs. The beating was "just so you know what it tastes like and just so you use your clubs like that, ensuring cleanliness and discipline on the block."[7]

Witold rejoined the inmates in the square for roll call. The bodies of those who had died overnight had been stacked at the end of each row. The numbers for each block were checked twice and then tallied by SS-Hauptscharführer Gerhard Palitzsch, a baby-faced German who was also the camp executioner. Witold and the others had to stand at attention until the count was done, and at the command "Caps off!" remove their caps if they had them and slap them against their thighs. Those without caps had to pretend. Few managed the drill neatly, and it was repeated until the deputy commandant, SS-Hauptsturmführer Karl Fritzsch, signaled that he was satisfied.[8]

Then, with a rasping voice, Fritzsch addressed the prisoners. "Your Poland is dead forever, and now you are going to pay for your crimes through work," he declared. "Look there, at the chimney. Look!" He pointed toward a building behind the row of barracks. "That is the crematory. The chimney is your only way to freedom." After the speech, a group of kapos dragged a prisoner from the crowd and pummeled him until

Karl Fritzsch, secretly drawn in the camp by Wincenty Gawron, 1942.

he was bloody and motionless. The gong sounded again, and the prisoners were dismissed.[9]

It was a Sunday, a "rest day," and the prisoners returned to their blocks to clean and shave. Witold, now a room supervisor, was allowed back onto the block as well, but the rest of the new arrivals were kept in the yard to practice military drills. Staller, club in hand, instructed them in how to stand to attention and remove their caps in unison. Mistakes were punished with "sport": push-ups, squats, jumps, and any other grueling exercises he could come up with.

Kapos from the other blocks did the same with their charges. Soon the yard was filled with dozens of prisoners running, hopping, tumbling, and swirling their arms like ballerinas. The kapos chased after anyone who was flagging, much to the delight of the guards in the tower, who watched the display, machine guns at the ready.[10]

Back in the block, Witold felt he had slipped into a dream. The world looked the same, but the people in it seemed strange—ghoulish even. He explored the block, which comprised half a dozen rooms off a central corridor, with Staller's private quarters at the top of the stairs. The prisoners in the other rooms paid him no heed. They were too caught up in their own affairs, squabbling over a couple of needles to repair their dirty clothes or else slumped against the wall. In one room, the block barber was shaving heads and bodies. He charged a scrap of bread in return for using a sharper blade.[11]

Most inmates underwent a personality change upon arriving in Auschwitz. The unrelenting violence broke down the bonds between the men, and they became "cantankerous, mistrustful and in extreme cases even treacherous," as one prisoner recalled. Some tried to secure protection by organizing themselves into small gangs, but that only seemed to escalate the violence. Prisoners frequently denounced one another to the kapos in the hope of a little more food. Jews who escaped initial detection were quickly ratted out and sent to the penal company.[12]

The camp's list of official regulations—and potential violations—was extraordinarily long. Offenses included talking at work, smoking, sluggishness, putting one's hand in one's pocket, walking too slowly, running without appropriate athletic poise, standing around, leaning on a freshly painted wall, wearing dirty clothes, imprecisely saluting an SS man, an impudent look, a sloppily made bunk, relieving oneself at the improper time and place.[13]

These offenses were all punished with beatings, and the sheer number of potential transgressions meant that, at any moment, prisoners were in danger of being disciplined. Survival of a sort was possible if you kept your head down and followed the golden rules: Don't expose yourself. Don't be the first in or the last out. Don't be too fast or too slow.

Avoid contact with the kapos, and, if contact was unavoidable, be submissive. "And if you're in for a beating," one prisoner wrote after the war, "always fall down on the first punch."[14]

Among the inmates, there was only one rule: Don't steal another man's food. Food was the camp currency: a spare button, a sliver of soap, a needle and thread, paper to write on, a packet of cigarettes—all were worth a portion of bread or more.[15]

The first few days were the hardest for newcomers, before they got their "camp skin." Inmates who couldn't accept the camp's subverted moral order were quickly finished off, like the prisoner who complained to an SS man about the violence of the kapos and was promptly beaten to death. Some lost the will to live and were preyed on by others. Others became twisted, like the kapos. Most adapted as best they could by narrowing their focus to the pursuit of food, safety, and shelter.[16]

Witold picked up the rules quickly, but he wondered how on earth he was going to connect with prisoners in such a desperate environment, let alone inspire them to join a resistance cell. Already he felt pangs of hunger and regretted tossing away his crust of bread the previous night.

As a room supervisor, one of Witold's tasks was to fetch and distribute the lunchtime soup, which was made in an open-air kitchen on the other side of the square. When the gong for lunch sounded after the noon roll call, he hurried across the parade ground with the other block supervisors, then they struggled back across the yard with the heavy kettles of thin barley and potato soup carried between them.[17]

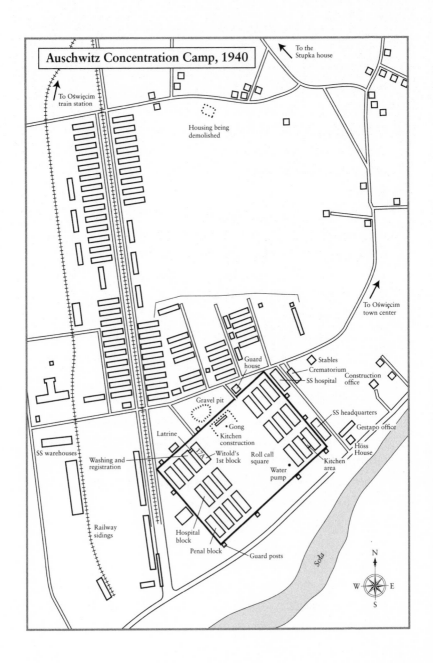

Auschwitz Concentration Camp, 1940

To Oświęcim train station

To the Stupka house

Housing being demolished

To Oświęcim town center

Guard house

Gravel pit

Stables
Crematorium
SS hospital
Construction office

SS headquarters

Gestapo office

Gong
Kitchen construction

Latrine

SS warehouses

Washing and registration

Witold's 1st block

Roll call square

Water pump

Kitchen area

Höss House

Railway sidings

Hospital block

Penal block

Guard posts

Soła

N
W E
S

The soup was served in the rooms. The old-timers, who had been so lethargic in the morning, jostled around the kettle, trying to be served first. They finished their portions quickly and got back in line to beg for more. Supervisors frequently had to use their ladles to smack hands and heads out of the way. The newcomers, sweaty and covered in dust after five hours in the square, looked disbelievingly at their paltry tins of thin liquid. As he ladled out the soup, Witold recognized that his position gave him a degree of power.[18]

The prisoners were allowed some freedom of movement on Sunday afternoons. Many stayed in their rooms, out of trouble. Others went to check on friends in the other blocks. Finally, Witold had a chance to look for Dering and Surmacki. He feared they might already be dead.

The camp comprised twenty buildings arranged along streets that led off the main square. In the far corner was the block reserved for the special penal company of priests and Jews. In the opposite corner, beside the open-air kitchen, was a small shed that belonged to a carpentry unit. The registration office was near the main gate and the guardhouse. The hospital, where Witold thought he might find Dering, was little more than a few rooms in a single-story block. The whole camp was fifteen acres in size, and a short walk in any direction led to the barbed-wire fence.[19]

To one side of a throng of internees, Witold spotted a handsome man sitting on a pile of stones. He wore dirty dress shoes and looked like he'd been nabbed at a dinner party. Another inmate, a thin, scrawny lad with an impish look, was examining the man's bruises.

"Those bloody kapos know nothing about military drill,"

Konstanty Piekarski, c. 1941.

the sitting man complained bitterly. "If they'd only let me take charge I could have the whole block marching like it was on parade—and without hitting anyone!"[20]

The idea was so preposterous that his colleague couldn't restrain himself. "Where do you think you are? In the military academy drilling cadets? Look at yourself! You look more like a bum or a convict than an officer. We must forget what we were and do the best with what is left of us."[21]

Witold approached them and asked if they were officers. The impish one introduced himself as Konstanty Piekarski, and said that he went by Kon or Kot, Polish for "cat." The bruised man was Mieczysław Lebisz. They were lieutenants in the horse artillery and had arrived with Witold the night before. Mieczysław had received his welts from a beating in the washroom after objecting to the kapos' treatment of a Jewish prisoner.

The three of them exchanged details, with Kon doing most of the talking. Witold was about to head away when the kapo who ran Kon's block, a heavyset German, lumbered into view. He wanted volunteers to stuff mattresses with wood chippings, and when none were forthcoming, he pointed at ten men, Kon and Witold included. It was an easy enough task and certainly an improvement on doing drills in the square, from where they soon heard the sounds of more beatings being administered.[22]

While they worked, Witold gently questioned the younger man about his career. "He spoke very softly, without authority," recalled Kon, "a man who preferred to listen rather than express opinions." He didn't realize that Witold was testing him out as a potential recruit.[23]

There was a final roll call before supper, where sick prisoners seeking to gain admission to the hospital were obliged to strip naked and parade before Deputy Commandant Fritzsch. Most were dispatched back to the ranks with a couple of blows; only those with broken limbs or severe exhaustion were allowed to go to the hospital. Then the day's dead were stacked, counted, and carried to the crematorium.[24]

The prisoners returned to their rooms for supper. It was Witold's job to divide loaves of dark, heavy bread into half-pound portions. These were served with a strip of pork fat and a cup of the bilgewater coffee. The older prisoners advised newcomers to save some of their bread for breakfast, but most were too hungry to resist eating it immediately.[25]

After they had eaten, Staller's assistant, Kazik, taught them the Auschwitz camp song. The kapo was very musical, Kazik explained, and he would be disappointed with a lackluster performance. In a reedy, plaintive voice, he sang the opening line: "I am in the Auschwitz camp, for a day, a month, a year / But I'm happy and I gladly think about my loved ones far away." They practiced singing for the rest of the evening, with Staller occasionally looming in the doorway, leaning forward with his hands clasped behind his back, as if enjoying himself.[26]

At last the gong for lights-out sounded, the mattresses were placed on the floor, and the prisoners lay down so Witold could count them and report the tally to Staller. The kapo then walked through the room, occasionally ordering an inmate to show him a foot so he could check if it was clean. Offenders were dealt a few blows on the buttocks. Then Staller turned the lights out.

After only one day in the camp, Witold knew that the idea of staging a breakout was naive. He needed to alert Warsaw about conditions and was certain that others would react with the same horror he felt. But who could he trust to help him get a message beyond the camp walls? He hoped Dering would have some answers—if he could find him.[27]

FOUR

The next morning, after roll call, Witold went to the hospital block to look for Dering. The kapos were calling out for the prisoners to form squads for work outside the camp. The newcomers milled around in confusion at the gate as a foreman screamed at them that he'd have them all flogged. But then Witold was surprised to see the man, a Pole, turn away from the SS guards and give the prisoners a knowing wink.

Witold joined the line of prisoners waiting outside the hospital. Those refused entry were deemed to be dodging work and sent to the square for "sport." Even so, dozens still queued each morning.[1]

Witold managed an excuse to get past the kapo. Inside, the hospital reeked of rot and excrement, and the sick lay in tightly packed rows on the floor. He found Dering on one of the wards. His friend was pasty and gaunt—scarcely recognizable. His legs were oddly swollen, and he was having difficulty standing up. Initially assigned to the road-building squad, one of the most brutal jobs in the camp, Dering was brought to the hospital semiconscious after a few days. He had recovered and gotten himself a job working as a nurse.[2]

Dering agreed with Witold's assessment that a breakout was inconceivable. Only a single prisoner had escaped. The SS had responded with a brutal twenty-hour roll call. Dering also advised Witold that while the kapos' clubs were lethal, they could be avoided with common sense and a little luck. The real killer, he said, was hunger.

SS-Obersturmführer Fritz Seidler had exaggerated only slightly when he told the prisoners they had six weeks to live. Even though they were assigned a daily ration of around 1,800 calories, pilfering of supplies and the fact that the kapos and their helpers ate as much as they wanted meant that most prisoners were on a rapid starvation diet of less than 1,000 calories a day. The SS later came up with a formula for calculating survival time: life expectancy in months = 5,000/deficit of calories.[3]

Hunger underpinned the entire camp system. A line of inmates queued most mornings and evenings outside the Gestapo office to betray their fellows to the SS in return for food. The other prisoners avoided these informers, but there was no telling who might reach his breaking point and join their ranks. Witold understood that if he was going to build a resistance, it would need to be capable of withstanding the crushing pressure of starvation. He had to be able to offer extra food—as incentive and reward. To his surprise, Dering told him that obtaining extra provisions might be possible.[4]

Their colleague from Warsaw, the underground's chief of staff, Władysław Surmacki, was still alive and working in

Helena Stupka and her husband, Jan, c. 1935.

the construction office on building projects outside the camp. He had made contact with a local family, the Stupkas, who lived near the railway station. Whenever Helena Stupka, a vivacious forty-two-year-old with bobbed hair and bright red lipstick, saw the inmates from Auschwitz approaching, she would invite in the SS guards accompanying them and ply them with food and vodka while the inmates visited the ground-floor toilet, where she had stashed food and medicine. The news offered a little encouragement.[5]

That evening, Witold watched the work squads returning to the camp. Columns of broken men dragged the fallen between them or pushed the dead in wheelbarrows, to be dumped in the square and counted. The inmates of Witold's block were lined up opposite the priests and Jews of the penal company—the Jews were distinguished by a yellow star on their dusty uniforms.[6]

These men did the hardest work of all in the gravel pits. Their kapo was an obese former barber from Berlin called Ernst Krankemann. Even the other kapos were scared of Krankemann, who had been committed to a mental asylum before the war. "He was a repulsive, horrible toad," one prisoner later wrote. "A giant chunk of meat and fat, endowed with unusual strength."[7]

Witold watched Krankemann move down a row of prisoners, stabbing with a knife those he determined to be out of line. Then he singled out one man and pummeled him to death. Witold had already witnessed a dozen murders by then, but this one seemed to jolt him out of his torpor. Looking down the line of inmates, he was sure they felt it too: a white-hot rage that cut through their collective fear and apathy. For the first time since his arrival, he felt he might succeed in rallying a force capable of fighting back.[8]

The flicker of hope didn't last long. Staller disapproved of Witold's ability to manage his room without brute force and

Ernst Krankemann, c. 1941.

told him he had to use more violence. One morning he exploded and kicked Witold out to work in the camp for three days. "Just so you see what it tastes like," said Staller, "and you appreciate better the comfort and peace you have here on the block."[9]

Witold was assigned to loading heavy wheelbarrows of gravel from a pit beside the main gate. He and the others then ran with their loads up a gangplank and along the camp fence, struggling to keep their balance on the track, which was muddy and treacherous in the drizzling rain. Rounding a corner, Witold saw the single dark column of the crematorium thrusting out of the ground, wreathed in smoke like a shroud. He had seen it before, but not this close. The horrifyingly sweet smell of cooked meat clung to his nostrils.[10]

The facility had a double-muffle, coke-fired oven capable of incinerating seventy corpses in twenty-four hours. It had been in service for only a month, but already the camp administration was worried about whether it could meet their needs. They had put in an order for a second oven and also wanted to increase the burn rate of the existing furnace by insulating the building's wall with a sloping rampart. This was what Witold was now helping to construct.[11]

After a couple of hours, he was shattered. By the end of the day, he could barely walk. The evening roll call in the rain felt interminable, and it took all his willpower to save some bread for the morning. By the third day, he knew it wouldn't be long before he faltered and the kapos set upon him. Then at lunchtime, Staller told him he could come back onto the block. "Now you know what work in the camp involves," Staller told him. "Take care with your work on the block, or I'll kick you back out into the camp for good."[12]

Crematorium oven.

But Witold wasn't going to start beating other prisoners for Staller, and it wasn't long before the kapo dismissed him for good. Witold knew he'd put his mission in danger, but how could he expect to be a leader for others if he allowed himself to be compromised? The squads had already left for the day, so Witold joined the invalids rejected from the hospital for punishment drills in the square.

It was cold after two days of rain. Some of the prisoners didn't have caps, or socks, or even shoes. They stood and shivered, and their hands and lips turned blue, but they didn't move. They stood at attention and waited for the kapos. After a few hours, a gang of kapos arrived to start the training.[13]

First, they ordered the prisoners to form a circle and hop, hop, hop like a frog. Witold immediately discovered that his ill-fitting clogs made this impossible. He had to hold his shoes in his hands and go barefoot on the rough gravel. The soles of his feet were soon lacerated and bleeding, and each hop tore them further.[14]

The only moment of rest came when someone fell and the kapos finished him off, joking about and mimicking the sounds of his death rattle. Witold suddenly remembered a scene from his childhood when a group of farmhands had tortured some animal they'd caught. It was screaming in fear, but they were laughing.

He'd been shocked by their cruelty but had dismissed the incident, choosing to believe instead that people were intrinsically good. Now he thought of that poor animal and realized how naive he'd been. His childhood self had seen humans for what they really were: carnal and vicious.[15]

In the afternoon, the penal company joined Witold and

The Regular Roller Squad, *by Jan Komski, postwar.*

the others in the square. The camp had a giant road roller, designed to be pulled by four pairs of horses. Fifty Jewish prisoners had been harnessed to the draw bar. A second, smaller roller was pulled by twenty priests.

Riding triumphantly atop the former was the quivering mass of Krankemann. He held his club aloft like a scepter and every now and then brought it crashing down on an inmate's head. Back and forth he rode across the square, and if someone fell from his blows or from exhaustion, he insisted on driving over them. The savage exercise didn't stop until evening roll call, when Krankemann dismounted to inspect the flattened bodies. Then the day's survivors were dismissed.[16]

Otto Küsel, c. 1941.

By the third morning of "sport," Witold was certain he would not survive the day. He was standing with the others in the circle, his back to the gate. Some instinct made him look over his shoulder, and he saw the kapo in charge of squad assignments running toward them. The kapo's name was Otto Küsel, a thirty-one-year-old drifter and petty thief from Berlin. Instinctively, Witold stepped forward to meet him.[17]

"You're not by any chance a stove fitter?" Küsel asked.[18]

"Yes, sir. I'm a stove fitter," Witold lied.[19]

"But are you a good one?"

"Of course I'm a good one."

Küsel told him to pick four others and follow him. Grabbing the nearest men, Witold chased after him to receive buckets, trowels, brick hammers, and lime. Küsel must have forgotten to form a work squad—hence his haste and readiness to believe Witold.[20]

Witold could scarcely believe his luck as he found himself marching through the open countryside with the rest of the squad and two SS guards. The Germans had claimed the

Postcard of Oświęcim, c. 1930s.

territory around the camp and were clearing out the locals. The finer homes near the train station and along the river had been appropriated for the families of SS officers; the rest were demolished and the raw materials used for other building projects.[21]

The old town of Oświęcim occupied a low bluff on the opposite bank of the Soła, about a mile from the camp. Its skyline was dominated by a fourteenth-century castle used by the Haberfeld family, a major vodka and liqueur producer, to store their schnapps and flavored spirits. Half the town's population was Jewish, and on one street were half a dozen synagogues and religious schools. The Germans were disgusted by these residents and the conditions of the town, which gave "an impression of extreme filth and squalor." They had burned down the Great Synagogue and had plans to deport the Jewish population to a nearby ghetto.[22]

Witold's work detail was brought to a town house and introduced to the SS officer who lived there. He was civil with them, almost normal. His wife was coming, the officer explained, and he wanted to renovate the kitchen. Could they move the ceramic tiles to a different wall, and the stove to a different room?

He didn't need so many workers for the task, said the officer, as if embarrassed, but he didn't mind if some of them just tidied the attic, provided the work was done well. And with that he left. Because the two guards had stayed outside, the prisoners were left to their own devices.[23]

Witold turned to the others to check whether any of them knew a thing about stoves, which, of course, they didn't, so he set them to work on other tasks while he focused on dismantling the range and the flues. His life might depend on doing the work properly, but at least there was no immediate threat of a beating.

From one of the windows, he could see backyards and lines of laundry. He heard children playing nearby and church bells ringing. Suddenly, he felt as though he might cry at the sharp reminder that life continued, indifferent to their suffering. Knowing that his own family was in relative safety was no comfort now that he knew this abhorrent world existed and that, at any moment, Maria might be caught in a roundup and brought to Auschwitz or a place like it.[24]

Then he thought of the SS man whose home they were renovating, how he had talked excitedly about his wife's arrival, no doubt imagining her joy when she saw her new kitchen. Outside the camp, this SS officer appeared to be a respectable man, but once he crossed its gate, he became a sadistic murderer. That he could inhabit both worlds at once seemed most monstrous of all.[25]

The rage that coursed through Witold now was a desire for revenge. It was time to start recruiting.

FIVE

Witold worked on the stove for several days, figuring things out as he went, painstakingly removing each valve and duct and memorizing its position. He knew that if he made a mistake, his lie would swiftly be revealed, but in his weakened state, he couldn't be sure he'd gotten it right.

The evening before the stove was due to be tested, Witold turned in desperation for help from the winking foreman he'd spotted at the gate. Witold's instincts proved correct: The foreman agreed to slip him into another work detail. He introduced himself as Michał Romanowicz, a Polish army captain, and Witold decided to trust him with his true mission. Michał agreed without hesitation to swear an oath to serve Poland and the underground.

The next morning, instead of reporting to the stove fitters, Witold marched out the gate with another squad. He heard the

Rudolf Höss and family, wartime.

kapos searching for him among the melee of prisoners but didn't look back. His new squad was laying out a garden for a villa near the crematorium, which he soon learned belonged to the camp commandant, Rudolf Höss. The Nazi leadership had started to develop plans for the colonization of Eastern Europe, which called for the enslavement or expulsion of its Slavic population. Höss saw Auschwitz as a test case for future colonial rule.[1]

The squad worked to level the land, raise beds, and crush

brick for paths—all according to the commandant's design. It rained hard that day, and the next. There was no chance to dry off, so they went to bed with wet clothes. At the end of Witold's second day in the garden, Michał again came to his rescue.[2]

He explained that he would be taking charge of a twenty-man detail to unload trains bearing supplies to the camp's warehouses and that he could handpick the squad himself. It was a prime opportunity to convene and assess underground recruits. Michał had some names in mind, and Witold suggested his mattress mate, Sławomir "Sławek" Szpakowski, with whom he'd been arrested in Warsaw.[3]

The warehouses had a reputation for finishing off prisoners, but Michał had no intention of actually working there. The next morning, he marched his squad over to a warehouse kapo and informed him that he had orders to demolish one of the farmhouses in the fields opposite. It sounded plausible enough, given the SS clearance operation around the camp, and Michał was waved away.[4]

The farmhouse he selected was on the grounds of a manor that had already been reduced to a shell. Where the orchard had once stood was a tangle of broken limbs, mottled-gray apple trees, and a shattered pear tree. Michał set a watch and made sure two stretchers were loaded with debris, ready to be carried outside if a kapo approached.[5]

The team worked on the house as slowly as they could, just enough to stay warm, making sure to keep the roof intact until the inside was gutted. It gave Witold and Michał plenty of time to discuss the creation of the first underground cell.

Witold knew he would have to weigh carefully whom to

trust. Someone who had been a decent operative or even a decorated officer in Warsaw might become a Gestapo informant as readily as anyone else. The camp had a way of revealing a man's true personality. "Some slithered into a moral swamp," Witold wrote later. "Others chiseled themselves a character of finest crystal."[6]

To break the power of the kapos, they needed to prove that goodness could endure. Witold would home in on prisoners who showed signs of altruistic behavior—the sharing of a piece of bread or the nursing of a sick friend—then gently probe them about their motivation.[7]

He also drew some harsh conclusions: Not everyone could be saved, either physically or spiritually. Some prisoners embraced the camp's hierarchy and competed with one another to earn the kapos' admiration; others gave up almost at once and refused to be rallied. Then there were those, like the priests and Jews, who were kept apart in the penal company and completely unreachable.[8]

Witold began by tracking down two more of his former Warsaw colleagues, Jerzy de Virion and Roman Zagner, whom he knew he could trust. At Dering's suggestion, he also vetted an exuberant twenty-year-old named Eugeniusz "Gienek" Obojski, who worked in the hospital morgue. Together with Dering and Surmacki, they formed what Witold called a "five." Using the same principles Witold had employed in Warsaw, the men knew each other but they didn't know anyone in any subsequent cells Witold created. Dering was in charge of the hospital; Surmacki, outside relations; and Witold was recruiter in chief.[9]

Witold next tried to broaden the reach of the organization

Evening Market, *by Jerzy Potrzebowski, postwar.*

by selecting men in different work squads. The best time to conduct his operations was in the evenings, between roll call and curfew, when the SS guards withdrew to the towers, leaving the kapos in charge and the prisoners free to move around the camp. Witold liked to walk the strip between the barracks and the fence closest to the river, which had become the camp's unofficial promenade.[10]

He would lead a potential recruit out of earshot and quietly tell him he'd been selected for the resistance. Most accepted immediately, but a few were reticent—like Kon, Witold's acquaintance from his first day in the camp. Kon had lost his pluckiness and was covered in welts and bruises after two weeks spent unloading freight trains at the warehouses.[11]

Witold took him to one side. "What I have to say to you, Kon, is in great confidence," he said. "You must swear on your honor as an officer that you won't mention it to anyone without my consent."[12]

Area used for prisoner promenade.

"If it is such an important secret then you have my word," said Kon cautiously.[13]

Witold explained that he'd come to Auschwitz voluntarily.

"You must be nuts!" exclaimed the younger man, but he was clearly impressed. "Who in his right mind would do such a thing? Don't tell me you asked the Gestapo if they'd be so kind as to send you to Auschwitz for a couple of years?"

"Please don't joke," Witold replied. He explained that the underground considered Auschwitz the center of the German effort to crush Poland and that it was vital for a resistance cell to function there.[14]

"If what you say is true," Kon replied, "you're either the greatest hero or the biggest fool." He looked like he thought the second option more likely. He doubted Witold's ability to rally an underground force and wasn't convinced what a camp underground could achieve, given the risks that surrounded them.

Witold explained that they were starting small. "The first and most immediate purpose is to help the weaker among us survive the camp," he explained.

Kon looked startled at the suggestion that anyone might survive. He had accepted the German promise that his death was inevitable. Now, suddenly, he wasn't so sure. At last he said, "I may be as nutty as you are, but let's give it a try."

Witold hugged him impulsively. "We'll call on you," he said.

*

The first snow of 1940 fell that October in fat, wet flakes that lingered on the skin. Witold's squad were stripping the roof from the farmhouse, and he worked with his back to the icy gusts that came howling off the Tatra Mountains in the distance. The camp was expanding fast, with transports bringing in hundreds of prisoners each week. Work had begun to add stories to existing blocks, and foundations were being dug in one corner of the roll-call square for new barracks.

It was painful to watch the new arrivals being broken in.

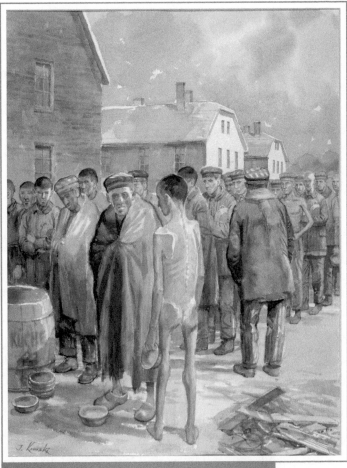

Queuing at the Barrel for Food, *by Jan Komski, postwar.*

"Remember, do not try to comfort them," the old hands advised. "For then they will die. Our task is to try and help them adapt." The newcomers reminded veterans like Witold of what they were becoming.[15]

As Dering had predicted, the prisoners who'd arrived at the same time as Witold had started to starve, and Witold could feel his own body changing. In the mornings, he woke to gnawing pangs of hunger and odd chills in his feet. His joints ached, and his skin scaled off in yellow flakes. He shivered incessantly and found it increasingly hard to focus on resistance matters.

He and his mattress mate, Sławek, talked compulsively about food, savoring the words as if they had flavor. Witold's favorite treat was young cucumbers from the garden dipped in the amber honey from his clover fields. Sławek dreamed about potato pancakes, fried in butter until they were toasted at the edges, topped with tangy sour cream. He promised to cook them for Witold when they got out. In the meantime, they scavenged for mangelwurzels, a variety of beets, which farmers had grown for their animals. They gnawed on them raw, but the roots did little to satisfy their hunger.[16]

Witold was trying to figure out how to send a report to Warsaw, one that would provoke an international outcry. The camp authorities coerced prisoners into writing home twice a month, in German, saying that they were fine and doing well. The censors in the mailroom carefully checked all outgoing letters. Witold sent two messages to Eleonora this way. "Auntie feels good, she is healthy and she greets everybody," Witold wrote in one. And then, a short while later, "Auntie plants trees that grow really well."

Even that level of contact felt dangerous, and he decided

that these would be his only letters. His contact outside the gates, Helena Stupka, couldn't help pass on a report to Warsaw either: She had no links to the capital nor fake papers that would allow her to travel. He needed to find another way.[17]

The camp authorities occasionally set prisoners free, after their families paid a hefty bribe or pulled the right strings with the authorities. They were sworn to secrecy on pain of return to Auschwitz if they told anyone what they had witnessed there. For most, that was enough to ensure compliance. Michał knew a young officer, Aleksander Wielopolski, who was due to be released and who might carry a message. It was too dangerous for Aleksander to carry a written document, so they prepared an oral report for him to memorize.[18]

The prospect of making contact with his underground colleagues in Warsaw gave Witold a boost of energy. But what should he include in his message? He'd compiled a mental list of the crimes he had witnessed, although the details seemed inadequate to describe the enormity of the Nazis' brutality. He needed facts, especially the crucial statistic—the death toll—which was a closely guarded secret.

Then one day, it dawned on him that this information was hidden in clear sight: in the numbers sewn onto the prisoners' shirts. Every inmate in the camp was given a number in the order in which he arrived. The latest arrivals, in October 1940, were in the six thousands. But the number of prisoners at roll call was only around 5,000. In other words, 1,000 men had died in little more than four months.[19]

The grim figure made the hopelessness of their situation clear. Witold wondered whether they would be better off if the British simply bombed the camp and brought an end to their suffering. The moment of despair passed, but over the following days, he gave the idea more thought. It wasn't as crazy as it first seemed.

Witold had learned from Kon that the SS unloaded weapons and ammunition at the warehouses. If the British bombed those buildings, some of the prisoners might be able to get away in the chaos. Many would surely perish, but at least their "monstrous torture" (as he phrased it in the report memorized by Aleksander) would be over. At the time, pilots relied on charts and landmarks for navigation, so Witold included in the report instructions for finding the camp by following the river.[20]

Just before Aleksander was due to leave, the camp was subjected to a dreadful ordeal. At noon roll call on Monday, October 28, the numbers didn't tally. This in itself was not unusual—the SS men often stumbled over their arithmetic. But this time a prisoner really was missing. The camp siren wailed, and a furious Deputy Commandant Fritzsch announced that no one would move until the escapee was found.[21]

The pots of soup at the kitchen went untouched. The drizzle turned to sleet, and the wind picked up from the northwest, driving sheets of ice against the men in the front row. Witold tensed and released his muscles to keep warm—in vain. Soaked through and ankle-deep in slush, the men swayed and shook. Hours later, darkness fell and a blizzard set in, and men began dropping one by one.[22]

Dering was at the entrance of the hospital when the men of the penal company, working as stretcher bearers, started bringing in stricken inmates. "It was terrible to see these

Evening Roll Call, *by Jan Komski, postwar.*

men," he recalled. "Comatose, half-conscious, crawling, reeling like drunks, babbling incoherently and with difficulty, covered with spittle and foaming at the mouth, dying, gasping out their last breath."[23]

Regulations required that every new admission be washed, so the men were stripped and sprinkled with water, then lain on the floor in one of the wards and covered with thin blankets. When the ward was full, the nurses put the men in the corridor. And still more came. It wasn't until 9:00 P.M. that the "escaped" prisoner was found, dead, behind a pile of logs in a work yard, and Fritzsch finally released them.[24]

The whole shivering mass of prisoners descended on the hospital, and the orderlies had to hold the door shut as the sick tried to force their way in. The kapo, enraged, ran to get his club and flung the door open to charge the mob, which rapidly dispersed back to the blocks. By the next morning, eighty-six men had died of hypothermia.[25]

Witold endured the cold well enough, but Michał had developed a cough. Insisting he was fine, he took up his usual position as lookout beside the building they were knocking down. The storm had cleared, the sun shone fitfully, and Witold's gloom lifted with the news that Aleksander had been released. Soon, Warsaw would know the truth. Soon, surely, something would be done.[26]

It should have been a moment to savor, but Michał's cough continued to get worse. He was racked with dry spasms and started spitting blood. He put on his usual show of shouting and swearing in front of the other kapos, but by that evening, he was drained.

After a week he was so unsteady on his feet that he had to lie down on the floor of the cottage for most of the day, coughing and shuddering. Witold took him to see Dering, who diagnosed pneumonia and made sure Michał was admitted to the hospital. Dering had made himself so useful around the wards that the kapo had given him the job of inspecting prisoners. Choosing who would live or die each day was a hellish job, but it gave Dering real power to help the underground.[27]

Under normal circumstances, Michał would have taken a course of antibiotics and might have recovered in a few weeks. But Dering had nothing to give him. He died a few days later, and his body was laid on the parade square to be counted with the others who had died that day. An SS man drove a

Marching to work.

spike through his chest to make sure he was dead, then his corpse was tossed onto a wagon.[28]

After Michał's death, and without his protection, Witold and the rest of the squad went to work at the warehouses, unloading trains under the kapos' glare. Trains arrived at the railway sidings every day bearing iron bars, bricks, piping, tiles, and hundred-pound sacks of cement. Everything had to be unloaded on the double.[29]

Witold had been conserving his strength for weeks, but now he was burning through his last reserves. His body ached, his skin was shiny and translucent and sensitive to the touch, and his fingers, ears, and nose had turned blue from poor circulation. His legs and feet were so swollen, it was almost impossible to get his trousers and clogs on in the morning. He found that his thoughts were often jumbled, and sometimes he lost consciousness walking back to the camp. He somehow always managed to keep marching until his brain slowly reengaged and he realized with a jolt how close he'd come to stumbling.[30]

Dering was alarmed by Witold's condition. Once, in late November, he arranged to meet Witold at the hospital but found it hard to identify him among the crowd of bone-thin stinking wretches pressing against the door to get in. Casting an expert eye over his friend, Dering offered to admit him and perhaps even arrange a job on a ward.[31]

Witold insisted that he was fine. Most of his men were in worse shape than he was, he said. "How would it have looked if just once I had complained that I felt bad . . . or that I was weak . . . and that I was so overwhelmed with work that I was looking for anything to save myself?" he wrote later. "It was obvious that then I would be unable to inspire anyone else or require anything of them."[32]

But as Christmas approached, and snow began drifting in the roll-call square, Witold had to act to save himself. One of his agents, Ferdynand Trojnicki, was employed in the carpentry workshop. The kapo was an ethnic German from Poland named Wilhelm Westrych, who wasn't as violent as the others. Ferdynand said he could arrange an interview with Westrych, but Witold would have to impress the man with something other than carpentry skills.

Witold took the bold step of saying that he was in the camp under an alias and that he was in fact one of the wealthiest

Carpentry workshop.

aristocrats in Poland—a gentleman, who would reward Westrych for a good deed. Westrych seemed to buy the story, and Witold landed the carpentry job. Shortly afterward, he found another spot in the workshop for Sławek.[33]

After the ordeal of the warehouses, Witold spent his first few days with the carpenters in a state of delayed shock. He was issued a coat, cap, and socks. The workshop was clean, and there was a stove. He had to do some woodworking, but Westrych shielded him from the scrutiny of the other kapos.[34]

With his newfound comfort, Witold could appreciate the news that electrified the camp a few day later. The latest arrivals informed them that the Warsaw underground had published a full report about Auschwitz in its main newspaper and that people were talking about the camp's horrors. Aleksander had made it; his call for action would surely reach the Allies soon.[35]

SIX

On Christmas Eve, the prisoners returned from work to find a massive fir tree installed beside the kitchen. It's branches were festooned with colored lights that danced as the wind shifted. For a joke, the SS had stacked under the tree, as if they were Christmas presents, the bodies of the prisoners from the penal company who had died that day.[1]

After roll call, SS-Hauptscharführer Palitzsch the executioner mounted a small podium that had been erected beside the tree, accompanied by three kapos: one with an accordion, another with a guitar, and a third to lead the singing. They played the opening chords of "Silent Night," and, en masse, the assembled ranks of prisoners joined in. Then they returned to their blocks without a word.[2]

The weather turned bitterly cold a few days later. The snow crusted over to form sheets of ice, and the square was a frozen sea of ruts and troughs. Witold's kapo, Westrych, sent him

and a colleague to the hospital for a carpentry job. By this time, the hospital had expanded to four barracks to cope with the increasing numbers.

The job was in the block reserved for the so-called convalescents, where the patients were packed into five small wards, a hundred in each room. Most were little more than skeletons with grotesquely swollen legs. Some had abscesses the size of dinner plates, or broken and unset limbs splayed at awkward angles. They moaned and whimpered beneath their soiled rags. Lice, which now infested the camp, crawled over their bodies. The stench of excrement was overwhelming.[3]

The hospital kapo set Witold and his colleague to work constructing a wooden walkway in each room. It wasn't long before the other carpenter started to complain about feeling unwell. The next day, he was coughing and unsteady on his feet, and then he was laid up in one of the wards with pneumonia. The following morning, he was dead.

Witold felt the sickness touch him and slowly settle inside his body. At first it was a warm, lugubrious sensation. He felt

A hospital block.

an overpowering urge to rest but knew he had to avoid lying down on one of those dirty mattresses at all costs. Then the chills began. He started to shake violently, his joints ached, and the light hurt his eyes.

He made it through the next few roll calls without collapsing and thought he might recover, but then the SS announced that every prisoner in the camp would have to take a shower that evening and have his clothes deloused. Witold's block was ordered to the storehouse and told to strip.[4]

Their showers didn't last long, but it was hours before their clothes were returned. One of the rooms in the block had been converted into a primitive delousing facility by sealing the door and window with strips of paper and installing a fan. The clothes were stacked inside the room and a pesticide introduced.

The Germans used a cyanide-based disinfestation agent known by its trade name: Zyklon B. It came in the form of

Tin of Zyklon B.

blue pellets that turned to gas upon contact with the air. It was extremely toxic, so inmates wore gas masks to scatter the pellets around the hanging clothes and then aired the room before collecting the garments afterward. Day was breaking by the time the clothes were returned, tinged with blue and smelling of bitter almonds.[5]

Witold managed about a dozen steps into the street before he collapsed. He was dragged to the hospital, where he was stripped down again, doused in cold water, and had his number written on his chest in indelible ink. Then he was given a soiled hospital gown and underpants and taken to the very room where he'd been building a gangplank, where he was tossed onto the infested matting.

Too sick and exhausted to move, Witold looked down at his blanket and was horrified to see that it was heaving with lice. He killed dozens, but it was futile. He didn't have the strength to continue and didn't know if he even wanted to. He asked for a paper and pencil from one of the nurses and wrote a note. "If you don't get me out of here at once," he managed to scribble, "then I will use up all my reserves of strength fighting lice. In my present condition I am rapidly approaching the crematorium chimney." He added his location and asked the nurse to take it to Dering immediately.[6]

A couple of hours later, Dering and another nurse appeared. "What's wrong with this fellow?" Dering said, stopping beside Witold. "Can you look him over?" Despite his increasing influence in the hospital, he still had to be cautious. Dering diagnosed Witold with pneumonia of the left lung and said he would take him away for tests at the dispensary.

They helped Witold to his feet and half carried him over to another block, where an upstairs room had been fitted with beds and new, lice-free, mattresses. Witold had a bed to himself. He stretched out and fell into a deep and boundless sleep, all thoughts of resistance gone.[7]

For ten days, he fevered in bed, dreams looping with waking thoughts, certain only of the passage of light to dark and back again. Occasionally, he felt the window open or a rough sponge against his body, or hot soup pressed to his lips. On the tenth day, the fever passed and he began to slowly regain his strength. Eventually, Dering judged him well enough to be transferred to the convalescents' block, where Witold helped the nurses where he could.[8]

The doctor in charge of the hospital, SS-Hauptsturmführer Max Popiersch, was generally only around for the first hour or so. He left the running of the hospital to SS-Unterscharführer Josef Klehr, a cabinetmaker from Austria who liked to think of himself as a doctor. Klehr used to arrive at the hospital on his motorcycle and expected one nurse to buff the paintwork and another to remove his boots and wash his feet at his desk.

Josef Klehr, 1962.

A third gave Klehr a manicure while he puffed on his pipe "like a pasha," as one prisoner recalled.[9]

One evening, Dering brought Witold into Popiersch's office in the main hospital block. A few weeks earlier, Dering had suggested to Popiersch that he install a phone line between his office and one of the new hospital blocks, and then he had the inmate electrician who installed the line bundle in a radio wire. Popiersch was delighted with the results, as was Dering, though for very different reasons. Dering had arranged for a radio to be stolen from the camp's electrical workshop and hidden under some floorboards.[10]

When Dering led Witold into Popiersch's empty office that night, the radio had been taken out of its hiding place and was on the desk. It was probably one of the Telefunken models that were popular with the SS: a varnished wooden chassis with art deco curves, and knobs on either side of the speaker's grill for dialing in the frequency.

Dering flipped the switch and waited for the radio's tubes to warm up and for the speaker to hum. He turned the dial, the signal whined and crackled, and suddenly the two men were overwhelmed by sounds from the outside world: songs, jingles, and voices that spoke in German, Italian, Slovak, and Greek. Dering searched for the BBC, which, unlike the tightly controlled German broadcasts, was by and large a reliable source for news.

At last he caught four drumbeats: three short and one long—Morse code for the letter *V*, for *victory*. Then the electrifying greeting in German: "Here is England . . . Here is England . . ." They didn't dare listen for long, but they were back again the next night, and the night after that.[11]

Władysław Dering, c. 1941.

The news was bad. Britain had staved off the threat of German invasion and had become a shelter for all those resisting the Nazis, including the Polish government-in-exile. But the Germans continued to bombard British cities and seemed poised to capture Egypt and the Suez Canal. Crucially, America remained on the sidelines. It would have been clear to Witold that the British were too pinned down to attack Auschwitz.[12]

In fact, Witold's first message from the camp had reached British officials by early 1941 only for the Royal Air Force to conclude that an attack on Auschwitz would be costly and symbolic at best, and decided to hold off.[13]

Witold distributed what little nuggets of good news there were among the other prisoners for the purpose of raising morale. Gaggles of prisoners gathered in the square to excitedly discuss a U-boat that had been sunk in the mid-Atlantic, or an Italian defeat in the highlands of Ethiopia. "People were living on this," recalled one prisoner. "From this news we took fresh energy."[14]

By the end of February, Witold had nearly recovered from

Karol Świętorzecki, c. 1941.

his illness. He found a set of prisoner stripes to replace his patient gown and was able to move around the camp on underground work while still officially a hospital patient. He carried his old toolbox with him for cover. Such a ruse would have been impossible even a short while ago, but after six months in the camp, Witold knew the kapos' daily routines and which parts of the camp to avoid.

The underground had grown in size to more than a hundred men stretched across most work details, and they were making an impact. They exhorted prisoners to work together and leaned on those they felt might turn to the Germans. Witold encouraged his agents to moderate the behavior of kapos with small bribes—a stick of margarine stolen from the kitchen or a loaf of bread that had been smuggled into the camp—and to seek positions of power within their squads.

As the camp grew, there were more and more openings for kapos and foremen and not enough German prisoners to fill the roles. One of the underground's agents landed the kapo job on a new block; another ran the stables. They were able to shelter others, secure a little extra food, and exert a measure of control over the camp.[15]

Most days, Witold visited his man in the stables, Karol Świętorzecki, to give him the latest radio news. In return, Witold would get a mess tin of wheat bran mixed with water and sugar—the rarest of treats. The camp had received a delivery of sugar for the horses, and though it was contaminated with salt and charcoal, Karol discovered that if he added water, the salt dissolved faster than the sugar and could be poured off. There was still charcoal in the mixture, but this was good for diarrhea.

The resulting blend made the "finest cake," recalled Witold, especially when washed down with a glass of milk. Karol had persuaded the SS that their prize stallion needed a bucket of milk every day, and he was careful to daub a little milk foam around the horse's mouth. Apart from that, it never got a drop.[16]

Karol had his own news for Witold one day in early March, when the camp was on lockdown for the visit of an unknown German official. The entourage had visited the stables, and Karol had recognized SS-Reichsführer Heinrich Himmler himself. What Karol didn't know was that the Nazi security chief had come to order a major expansion of the camp from 10,000 to 30,000 prisoners, which would make it one of the biggest concentration camps in the Reich.

Over the following days, Witold learned more about Himmler's intentions from his comrade Władysław Surmacki, who worked in the SS construction office. There were plans to build eight new blocks in the roll-call square and to add additional floors to existing buildings, vastly increasing the camp's capacity.[17]

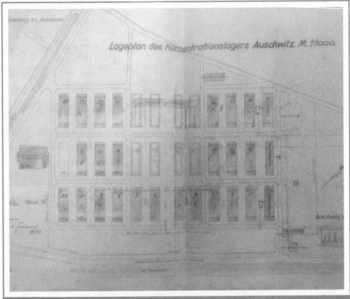

Lageplan des Konzentrationslagers Auschwitz M. 1/1000.

SS plans for camp expansion. Original image shows center blocks shaded in orange to highlight new barracks.

Transports of Polish prisoners began arriving daily that spring. Witold took advantage of the influx to step up recruitment. His force had grown to several hundred men, a size that was influential enough to provide security for its members but also one that made secrecy increasingly difficult to sustain.[18]

The camp authorities had begun to suspect the existence of an underground, but they had no idea of the scale of Witold's organization nor the fact that it was affiliated with the resistance movement in Warsaw. Instead, they assumed that the prisoners had segregated themselves into gangs, as was common in other camps.[19]

Witold made sure he was the only person who knew

everyone in the network and kept a low profile by issuing orders and information through confidants such as Karol. But there was no doubt he was becoming known around the camp. Occasionally, the Gestapo would sift through their files looking for prisoners with a prior record of underground work. Then, at morning roll call, they would summon a half dozen or so, and execute them. Witold lost several agents that way.[20]

One evening, Witold and Karol were walking through the crowds of new arrivals, appraising them for potential recruits, when someone shouted Witold's name—his real one, not the alias he had been using. He turned to see a friend from Warsaw rushing toward him.[21]

"There you are!" the man exclaimed. "The Warsaw Gestapo chopped my arse into little pieces asking what had happened to Witold." Witold did his best to remain calm and nonchalantly led the man away before swearing him to secrecy. Even so, several prisoners had noticed the reunion.[22]

The next morning, Witold's number was read out at roll call, along with twenty or so others. They were marched to the records block and lined up in the corridor as their numbers were checked. Then Witold was singled out and led to the mailroom. Several SS censors poring over prisoner letters for suspicious content looked up from their desks. One beckoned him over. "My dear boy," he said. "Why are you not writing letters?"[23]

Witold suddenly realized why he'd been summoned, and he almost laughed out loud. It was true he hadn't been sending any letters, for fear of drawing attention to Eleonora or to Maria and his children. However, he'd anticipated this might

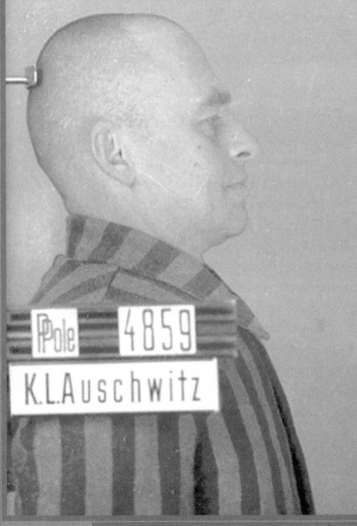

Witold's mug shot.

get him into trouble with the SS and had stashed a bundle of letters falsely stamped "rejected" by an underground recruit in the censorship office.[24]

"I do write," he told the man. "I can prove it."

"Well I never! He has proof!" the German declared, and a guard escorted Witold back to his block to get the letters.[25]

Any satisfaction Witold might have felt at escaping punishment was tempered by the sound of gunshots as the other prisoners whose names had been called out with his that morning were executed.[26]

Spring made the prisoners restless. On Sundays, the kapos had boxing matches behind the kitchen, which was partially hidden from the view of the guard towers. One Sunday afternoon in March, Witold and some other inmates were in the yard when a prisoner ran over, flushed with excitement. Walter Dunning, the kapo from the abattoir that provided meat for the SS officers' tables, was offering to fight anyone who dared take him on. For bread.

"I've heard that some of you can box," the prisoner said.[27]

Everyone looked at Tadeusz Pietrzykowski, who was sitting, shirt off, atop a pile of bricks. "Teddy," as he was known, was a recent recruit to the underground. He had trained as a bantamweight in Warsaw, although he was hardly in fighting shape now.

One of the men warned him that it was crazy to take on Dunning, who was a former middleweight champion and known for breaking jaws. Teddy just shrugged and jogged through the puddles in the square toward the kitchen, where a crowd jostled for a view.[28]

Weighing two hundred pounds, and muscled with it,

egitymacja członkowska WF ~~lub P~~

Nr

uprawnia łączn
z zaświadczenie
do korzystania
ulg na kolejac
pańs wych
przejazdy w cela
WF i PW

W a ż n a

do dn. 193

(podpis właściciela)

(nazwisko i imię)

(miejscowość i data wystawienia legitym

Tadeusz Pietrzykowski, 1939.

Kitchen area where the fight took place.

Dunning stood shirtless in the center of a makeshift ring. At the sight of little Teddy, the crowd chanted, "He's gonna kill you! He's gonna eat you!" Teddy's hunger overcame his fear. He entered the ring, and someone gave him a pair of workman's gloves. He held them out for a tap, Dunning raised a single nonchalant fist in return, and the referee shouted, "Fight!"[29]

The German came in fast, trying to finish Teddy off, and didn't bother keeping his fists up. Teddy was able to land a left jab before ducking out of the way. Dunning came at him again, swinging wildly. Teddy skipped inside and landed another blow. The pattern repeated, until the roll-call gong was sounded for the end of round one.

"Beat the German!" came the cries of a few emboldened Poles in the crowd. Teddy quickly held up his glove, calling for them to stop. As soon as the next round started, he landed a left hook that bloodied Dunning's nose, and the prisoners started chanting again. This time the referee grabbed his stick and started laying into the noisiest section of inmates. He was quickly joined by Dunning, who had blood dripping down his chest from his nose.[30]

The prisoners scattered, except Teddy, who was still standing in the ring, fearing the worst. Dunning marched over to him and threw down his gloves. Then he shook Teddy by the hand and led him over to his block. "When did you last eat?" he asked on the way.[31]

"Yesterday," said Teddy.[32]

Dunning gave him half a loaf of bread and a piece of meat. "Very good, young man, very good" was all he said. Teddy ran back to his block to share the rewards. Shortly afterward, he landed a prized job in the stables. The camp buzzed with stories about the fight over the following days, which grew with each retelling.

In the square, Witold started to hear talk about uprisings and breakouts from a group of colonels who had arrived in the camp with the new influx of prisoners. Most evenings they could be found marching up and down the riverside promenade as if on parade. The walkway had recently been planted with an avenue of silver birches and given a street name, Birkenallee.

From what Witold could gather, the colonels' plan was for

one of their number to attack the main gate and escape to rally what forces he could in a nearby town. Another colonel would hold the camp until backup arrived. Witold thought the plan ill-conceived and premature, given that each colonel had recruited only a few men.

He held back from contacting them, concerned about their indiscretion and fearing that they might try to pull rank on him. But he needed to keep an eye on them in case they launched an attack that led to a crackdown. His own thinking about a breakout remained unchanged: The majority of prisoners were too weak to make it very far, and the SS would surely exact a terrible revenge on the hundreds if not thousands who were left behind.[33]

Witold wanted guidance from Warsaw about how to handle the colonels, so around April he started work on his next report. Karol was due to be released after his family pulled the right strings in Warsaw. Witold was happy for him even though it meant he would be losing a trusted lieutenant. Over sugar cake, they took stock of the underground's achievements: the continuing expansion of the organization and its ability to sustain lives, the smuggling network, and Dering's radio listening post.

These successes they measured against the mounting death toll. More than 15,000 prisoners had entered Auschwitz since it opened, and less than a year later, only around 8,500 were still alive. Security had been tightened. What had been a single line of barbed wire around the perimeter was now a double row of electrified fences, and Commandant Höss had instigated a grim new form of collective punishment for escapes: Ten prisoners were chosen at random from the escapee's block and made to starve to death. Witold included these details in the report he asked Karol to memorize.[34]

It's probable that Karol also carried a message for Witold's family that under no circumstances were they to try to obtain Witold's release. The number of prisoners being released from the camp—over 300 since it opened—raised the prospect that Maria would try to secure his freedom. And the truth was that Witold didn't want to leave, not with his work just beginning.

Contrary to his fears about being removed from the center of the action in Warsaw, he had come to see Auschwitz as the center of the Nazis' quest for domination and felt that he was standing right at the point of opposition. It felt strange to admit, but he'd almost started to feel happy. "The work I had begun completely absorbed me since it was beginning to pick up speed in line with my plan," he wrote later. "I really began to worry that my family might buy me out, like some of the other fellows, and interrupt the game I was playing."[35]

Witold found an opportunity to be near the gate to see his friend off. Karol was wearing the same dress suit he'd been arrested in, complete with cuff links. The actor Stefan Jaracz was being released at the same time. He had tuberculosis and had suffered frostbite so deep that his finger bones had been exposed. Both men were layered in powder to hide their wounds from the medical inspection and their cheeks had been touched up with beet juice. They looked as if they were off for a final turn on the stage. As Karol was about to leave, he looked over at Witold and saw him lost in thought for a moment. Then Witold looked up and winked.[36]

A few days later, Commandant Höss showed up at the

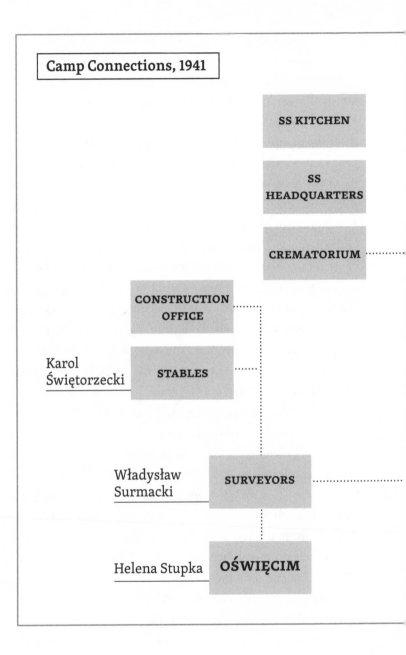

Camp Connections, 1941

SS KITCHEN

SS HEADQUARTERS

CREMATORIUM

CONSTRUCTION OFFICE

Karol Świętorzecki

STABLES

Władysław Surmacki

SURVEYORS

Helena Stupka

OŚWIĘCIM

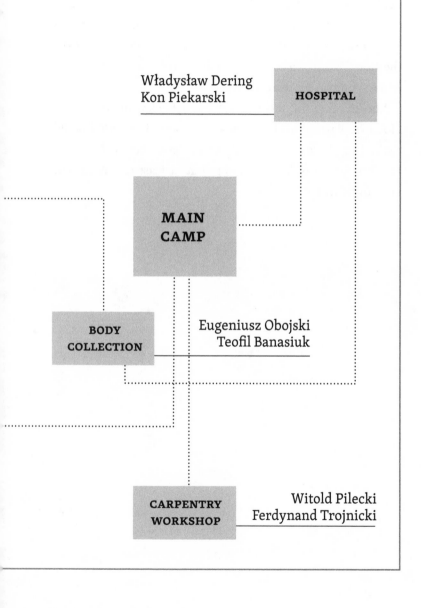

Władysław Dering
Kon Piekarski

HOSPITAL

MAIN CAMP

BODY COLLECTION

Eugeniusz Obojski
Teofil Banasiuk

CARPENTRY WORKSHOP

Witold Pilecki
Ferdynand Trojnicki

stables. It was his wont to take a horse and ride it around the fields surrounding the camp, surveying his domain. Teddy the boxer had taken the opportunity to place a button under the horse's saddle, and no sooner had Höss swung his leg over the horse, then it took off at a gallop and the commandant had to cling on for dear life.

Shortly after, the horse came trotting back without its rider. Höss was carried to the hospital on a stretcher with a badly twisted leg. Teddy and the others had a good laugh about that afterward. It wasn't an uprising, but at least one Nazi had been overthrown.[37]

CHAPTER SEVEN

A t roll call on the morning of June 22, 1941, Witold picked up on a strange new mood. The guards seemed downcast, almost fearful. The kapos didn't beat the prisoners as much as usual. Word spread quickly: Germany had invaded the Soviet Union.

The idea that the Germans would open a second front seemed incredible. Witold sought out Dering to discuss the news on the radio, and the BBC confirmed that in the early hours of the morning, Germany had attacked the Soviet Union with the largest army ever assembled: over 3 million men and 500,000 motorized vehicles spread across a thousand-mile front.[1]

Witold saw the invasion from a military perspective, and it filled him with hope. The Germans would struggle to fight on two fronts and surely would be defeated. Poland would reclaim its independence. His confidence was shared by the

Edward Ciesielski, c. 1941.

other men. That evening, he saw a jubilant crowd gather in the square around one of the colonels, who sketched out Germany's downfall in the gravel.[2]

But within days came reports of German advances through the Soviet-occupied eastern provinces of Poland. Brześć Litewski fell, then Białystok, Lwów, Tarnopol, Pińsk. The Red Army collapsed so quickly that the BBC reports started to sound like Nazi propaganda. A few weeks after the invasion began, several hundred Soviet POWs arrived in Auschwitz. They were immediately and brutally beaten to death in the gravel pits by kapos armed with shovels and picks.[3]

Despair swept through the camp as the German victories mounted that summer. Most days began with a prisoner rushing at the fence to die, whether by the 220-volt charge or in a hail of bullets. The SS left the bodies sprawled on the ground or strung out on the wires like broken scarecrows until evening roll call.[4]

Witold's youngest recruits were particularly affected.

"I can see that you surrender to bad moods," Witold said

gently to Edward "Edek" Ciesielski, a baby-faced nineteen-year-old with a dimpled chin. "Remember, we are not allowed to break down mentally in any circumstances. The victories of the Germans only postpone their final defeat. But it must happen, sooner or later."[5]

"I count only on you, sir," said Edek, wiping away his tears.[6]

Privately, Witold had his doubts too. What if Germany prevailed? Maybe it was better to rise up and die fighting. And why had there been no Allied response to his reports? He waited and waited for a reply to his report from the underground in Warsaw and listened intently to the BBC for any mention of the camp. But there was nothing. The weather

Camp orchestra, c. 1941.

turned warm and balmy. Off-duty SS men sunbathed in their gardens and played with their children down by the Soła River. A camp orchestra made up of inmates had become a daily fixture at the gate, playing military marches for prisoners as they departed for work and returned in the evening.[7]

The warm July weather also delivered the camp's first outbreak of typhus, which was spread by the endemic lice. The illness began with flu-like symptoms and red spots on the torso and arms and rapidly progressed to feverish hallucinations, narcosis, and a catastrophic immune response as bacteria colonized the linings of the blood vessels and major organs. There was no cure, and survival rates were low, but those who pulled through were immunized against reinfection.[8]

"A ward full of typhus patients in the second week of the disease bears more resemblance to an acute mental ward in an asylum than to a hospital ward," one doctor wrote. Patients often had to be strapped down so they could not attack staff or throw themselves out windows or down flights of stairs. The camp's four hospital blocks were packed with patients whose delirious cries kept the camp on edge.[9]

Siegfried Schwela, a newly arrived SS doctor, wondered what was the point of keeping so many sick prisoners in the hospital? "A doctor's duty is to heal patients, but only those who can be cured. The others we should prevent from suffering," he declared. And so SS medical staff started to experiment in what they called euthanization, or "mercy killing," injecting patients with various substances such as hydrogen peroxide, gasoline, evipan, perhydrol, ether. They discovered that a shot of phenol administered by syringe straight to the heart was quickest and routinely murdered a dozen patients a day using this method.[10]

Delirious Dreams, *by Stanislaw Jaster, c. 1942.*

Dering and the other nurses came under increasing pressure to take part in the killings. One day, Dering was working on a sedated prisoner when a German doctor brought his attention to a syringe filled with a yellowish-pink fluid. It's a glucose shot, said the man. His eyes betrayed a flicker of excitement. Dering picked up the syringe, knowing it was phenol.[11]

"I'm sorry, I cannot do it," he said softly, and returned the needle to the table. The German appeared more disappointed than angry and instructed someone else, probably Klehr, to inject the man. The patient shuddered and died, a pink spot blossoming on his chest. Dering was ordered confined to his block for two weeks.[12]

A few weeks later, Commandant Höss made a curious announcement at morning roll call. "All ill or crippled can report themselves for a visit to a sanatorium," he said. "Everyone will be cured there." Witold watched with concern as a motley crowd staggered to the storeroom block to put their names down.[13]

Dering told him that he had been assured by the hospital kapo that the invitation was genuine, but also that the hospital staff had been ordered to draw up a list of "incurables." He promised to find out more.[14]

A few weeks later, on July 28, a medical commission arrived at the hospital for a further selection. It was a warm day, so Popiersch set up in the street. SS-Sturmbannführer Horst Schumann, the neatly coifed director of the supposed sanatorium, also took a seat at a table. The first inmates hobbled forward. Those selected were sent to the clothing block to be deloused and given fresh stripes and blankets. "Lucky guys," the other prisoners murmured.[15]

Over the course of several hours, patients went to increasingly desperate lengths to get on the list, faking coughs and limps and bribing the nurses with bread. "Take me, take me," cried one inmate, Aleksander Kołodziejczak, raising his hand to show a missing thumb from an old injury. Schumann nodded kindly and added his name to the list, which grew to 575 patients, around a fifth of the hospital.[16]

Those who had been selected were on their way to the waiting train when one of the SS doctors let slip to Dering the truth. They weren't going to a spa at all but to a medical center outside Dresden.

The facility was part of the T4 Euthanasia Program that had

been established in 1939 as part of the Nazi project to eliminate German citizens deemed mentally or physically unfit. The program had served as a laboratory for developing ways of killing large groups, and its doctors pioneered crowding people into airtight rooms and flooding them with carbon monoxide. The murders were meant to be secret, but it came to

Horst Schumann.

public attention when, over the course of the next two years, tens of thousands of people, many of them children, were killed. SS chief Himmler saw the T4 program as a possible model for clearing "non-productive elements" from his concentration camps, which had seen a huge increase in the number of sick inmates over the winter of 1940.[17]

Dering watched in horror as the inmates traipsed through the camp to the train, which the SS had supplied with mattresses, pillows, and pots of coffee to maintain the illusion of a spa holiday. The sight of the patients eagerly boarding and getting settled down was too much for the hulking kapo Ernst Krankemann.

He blurted out that they were all going to be gassed. In the ensuing panic, Deputy Commandant Fritzsch drew his pistol and ordered Krankemann be hanged by his own belt.[18]

Days later, one of the SS doctors confirmed to Dering that the prisoners had been gassed with carbon monoxide. The news stunned the nurses. "From then on we realized that the SS might do anything," recalled one orderly. A few weeks after the transport, Schwela demanded a second list of incurables, and rumors spread that another train was being organized.

Witold started a campaign warning prisoners not to volunteer, while Dering worked to release any patients capable of walking. Hundreds were still trapped on the wards. Dering redoubled his efforts to coach patients on how to play down their illnesses. To his frustration, some didn't believe him, preferring to put their faith in Schwela's promise of a spa holiday. Eventually, Dering gave Schwela a list of a dozen of the sickest prisoners, in the hope that would satisfy him.[19]

Dering and Witold assumed that the SS would send another transport of prisoners to Dresden, but there were signs that the Germans had a different plan in mind. The penal company was relocated, and the half-sunken windows of the basement levels on their old block were sealed and filled in with dirt. Some prisoners thought that the Germans were building an air-raid shelter against an impending Allied offensive. Others were not so sure.[20]

In fact, now that the logic and efficacy of gassing prisoners en masse had been established, the SS planned to carry out the next round of executions inside the camp. What was more, they were expanding the program to deal with an anticipated influx of Soviet POWs. Himmler had reached an agreement with the German military to transport 100,000 Soviet POWs to Auschwitz. He hoped to put most of them to work as forced labor, but any Communist agents or Jews identified in their ranks would be eliminated.[21]

One morning in early September, Schwela and two other doctors swept into the hospital to announce that the selection was beginning. Schwela set up a desk and instructed the prisoners to come forward. A "small, bulbous, gingerish-blond with a good-natured face," according to Dering, Schwela smoked and smiled benignly, his cigarette ash gathering on the floor beneath him as Klehr ticked off the numbers.

Dering was able to make the case for a few, but Schwela was looking to fill a quota. Practically the whole block of tubercular patients was selected, and there were no reprieves for infectious diseases. Nearly 250 prisoners were added to the list, until at midday, Schwela pronounced himself satisfied.[22]

The nurses started transporting the sick patients to the basement of the penal block—supposedly to wait for the train. Many were unable to walk the distance of a hundred yards, so the nurses carried them on stretchers as far as the basement steps, and then on piggyback down to the cells below. "You could see from their terrified faces that they were guessing they were going to die," recalled Konrad Szweda, a priest and one of the stretcher bearers.[23]

The rest of the prisoners were ordered to stay in

Basement of the penal block.

their blocks. Tense and nervous, no one could sleep that night. Witold sat in the gathering dark, waiting. Then he heard the sound of heavy diesel engines. Those who had the nerve to peek out the windows described seeing a convoy of trucks, which unloaded prisoners wearing soiled uniforms and *ushanka* hats. Soviets, perhaps 600 in all. SS men escorted them into the closed courtyard of the penal block. Then the trucks pulled away, leaving the camp in wakeful silence.[24]

Just after midnight, Witold heard a scream from the penal block. Not a single voice but many voices, roiling up and down the octaves. On and on it went, the same anguished sound. Then silence.[25]

The next day, a Saturday, the camp was filled with rumors. One prisoner had seen SS men in gas masks. Another had heard a German say that the Soviets had gotten what was coming to them. On Monday, after evening roll call, there was another block lockdown and further activity at the penal block. The day after that, a nurse named Tadeusz Słowiaczek tracked down Witold. Tadeusz was shaking and wild-eyed as he spoke.

The screaming from the other night was the sound of 850 men being gassed, he explained. The patients they'd brought into the block and the Soviets who came afterward were all dead. Tadeusz and the other nurses had spent most of the night carrying out their bodies. His account was terrifying. Commandant Höss had summoned the nurses and sworn them to secrecy. Next, he had led them to the basement of the penal block, put on a gas mask, and descended the steps. He emerged a few moments later and signaled them to follow him inside.[26]

The cell doors were wide open, and by the dim light of a single bulb, they could see into each room. The dead were pressed so tightly together that they were still standing, eyes bulging, mouths gaping, teeth bared in silent screams. Wherever skin was exposed, it had a dark bluish hue.

Every doorway framed a similar scene. Farther down the corridor were the hospital patients, in less-crowded cells. It looked as if they had guessed what was coming. Some had stuffed rags into their mouths and nostrils. Scattered on the floor were blue pellets, which some of the nurses recognized as the delousing agent Zyklon B.[27]

Several of the orderlies vomited on the floor, but Gienek Obojski, the morgue worker, remained calm and directed the others to start with the bodies of the patients, who were less tangled than the Soviets. They carried them up to the washroom, one corpse held between two men, until they found it was quicker to simply drag the bodies over the floor.

The patients were already naked, but the Soviets had to be stripped. Clothes, cigarettes, and keepsakes were gathered in a pile. Occasionally, an SS man would slip some bauble into his pocket when he thought no one was looking. The dead suffered the final indignity of having their mouths pried open and any gold fillings removed with pliers. Then the corpses were loaded onto wagons and carted off to the crematorium. The nurses worked all night, but they barely got through half the rooms.[28]

Tadeusz was almost incoherent by the time he finished telling Witold his story. "Don't you see?" he said. "This is just the beginning. What's to stop the Germans from gassing us all now that they realize how easy it is?"[29]

Witold couldn't fathom the Nazis' intentions. The gassing of the incurables in Dresden had at least conformed to the logic of eliminating those who couldn't work. It made no sense for the SS to kill off the Soviets without first extracting their labor. One thing he was certain of was that the killings represented an unprecedented new evil that might shock the Allies into understanding the importance of the camp. When one of the nurses, Marian Dipont, was released from the camp on September 14, it is likely he was carrying with him the first eyewitness account of the gassing.[30]

Underground leader Stefan Rowecki was unsure what to make of this development. It certainly contravened international law, but it seemed to be a one-off. Rowecki's colleagues

Rollwagon, *by Władysław Siwek, postwar.*

theorized that the gas was a new weapon being tested for use at the front. He still had Witold's report written up for dispatch to London, but it was one of many horrors the underground was reporting at the time: In Warsaw, the Germans had packed the city's 400,000-strong Jewish community into the cramped streets of the ghetto. Thousands died each month due to shortages of food and medical care. Elsewhere, the Germans were committing mass shootings of Jews in what was now Nazi-occupied eastern Poland. Neither Rowecki nor the British officials who read the report were able to connect the Nazis' capacity to kill in Auschwitz to their genocidal policies elsewhere.[31]

A week later, Witold's block was repurposed as a delousing facility, and he was moved to a barracks along the perimeter, facing the crematorium. The weather turned cold, and a sharp wind whipped down the streets. One day, he was hurrying to roll call when he saw SS guards using their rifle butts to herd a long column of naked men into the crematorium. They must be Soviets who had arrived the night before about to be issued underwear and clothes, Witold figured, though he did wonder why the crematorium would be used for that purpose.

That night he learned that the SS had emptied tins of Zyklon B onto the heads of the screaming men through holes specially drilled in the flat crematorium roof. There was a sinister logic behind murdering the Soviets in the crematorium rather than the penal block basement: corpses no longer had to be hauled through the camp for disposal. Also, the morgue's ventilation system meant that the fumes could be cleared quickly.[32]

Witold surmised that the Soviets had been killed because no accommodation was ready for them. His conclusion was reinforced a few days later when several blocks in the camp were fenced off and designated the "Soviet POW camp." Then in October 1941, the prisoners were again confined to their blocks as the first of a dozen freight trains carrying thousands of Soviet POWs arrived. It was a bright and cold day, and the first frost had come, lining the block windows with ice.

The Soviets were forced to strip and then jump into a vat of foul-smelling disinfectant before being chased into the camp. Witold caught a glimpse of them, crouched outside, naked and shivering. They were left outside all day and overnight, howling in the cold.[33]

One of Witold's friends from the carpentry shop went to check on them. "They're going to finish these people off," he reported on his return. "The kapo says they will be outside until the evening."[34]

"Those who kill prisoners of war can never win the war," observed one inmate. "When the other party finds out about it, it will be a fight to the death."[35]

Despite the Soviet Union's role in the destruction and occupation of Poland, Witold's beloved country, he recognized that the German atrocities against the Soviet soldiers needed to be reported to the Allies too. He prepared another oral report on the gassing experiments and the sudden influx of Soviet POWs, which was likely carried out of the camp on October 22 by released prisoner Czesław Wąsowski, and then sent on to London.[36]

Transports of Soviet POWs arrived every few days, and by

early November, the Soviet contingent in the camp stood at 10,000—almost equal to the number of Poles. They were put to work building a new camp two miles away. The SS planned to construct 174 brick barracks over 81 hectares of water-logged terrain to house an expected 100,000 POWs. To begin with, they demolished the small village near the site, which was in an area of marsh and silver birch that gave the place its name: Brzezinka, or, in German, Birkenau.[37]

Witold could only guess at what the purpose of the completed camp would be. Its size meant that the Nazis must be planning to make it a central collection point for Soviet POWs, and Witold likely surmised that they would be worked to death. The existing Soviet prisoners limped back from work each day, pulling carts stacked with the corpses.

The crematorium couldn't cope with the numbers, so the SS had the bodies buried in the woods around Birkenau. When the ground froze, they kept them in one of the Soviet blocks in the main camp, filling up the basement first, then the next two floors, as the dead replaced the living.[38]

Witold was determined to uncover the numbers dying and placed an agent in the camp's records office, where some of the prisoners worked as clerks. According to his source, 3,150 Soviet POWs had died in roughly a month—more than the total number of Poles who had perished in the camp's first year. Witold could not have known the direction the camp was taking—the Nazi leadership itself had yet to decide—but he saw that the horrors were mounting and that he needed to provoke an Allied response.

His next messenger, the carpenter Ferdynand Trojnicki, was released in mid-November with news about Birkenau

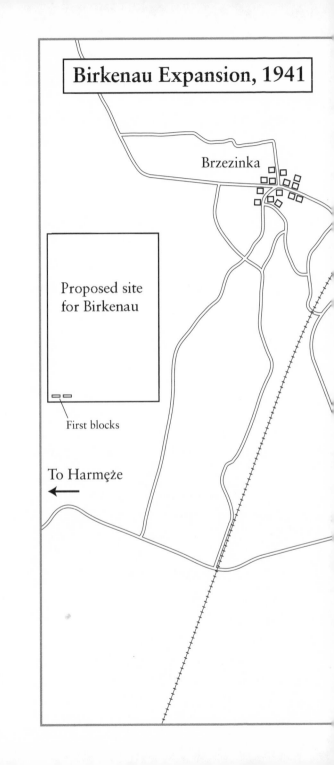

Birkenau Expansion, 1941

Brzezinka

Proposed site
for Birkenau

First blocks

To Harmęże

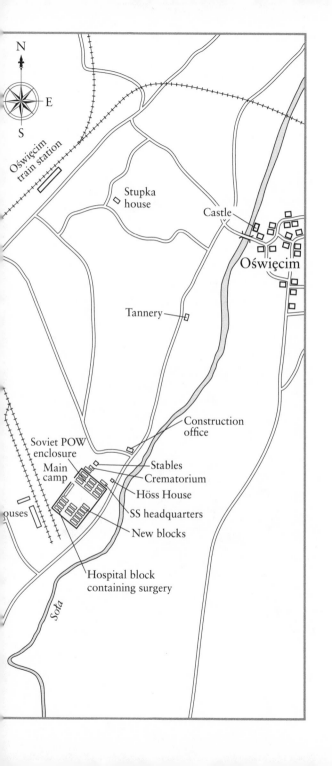

and the latest figures. The inmate surveyor Władysław Surmacki left a few weeks later, bearing a similar report. On each occasion, Witold took the men aside and made them repeat his message over and over until he was certain they had memorized the details and understood how to use the facts to make a case for action.[39]

Meanwhile, Witold began to reluctantly consider an uprising. The odds hadn't changed. In fact, the garrison had doubled in recent months to around 2,000. Many if not most of his men would be killed in a fight. But the Nazis' new ability to kill on an industrial scale had raised the possibility they might one day liquidate the camp, in which case, Witold felt

Auschwitz SS garrison.

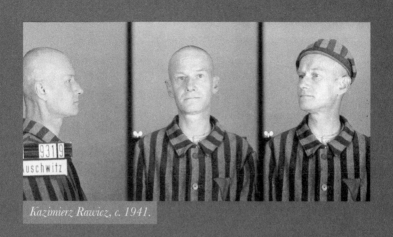

Kazimierz Rawicz, c. 1941.

they had nothing to lose. To make the Germans pay, he would need the Polish colonels. He had been monitoring them for months with growing respect as they developed their own cells and avoided detection. Altogether they might number almost 1,000 men—enough to inflict some damage and even enable some to escape.[40]

Military etiquette required him to cede control of a combined underground to the superior ranking officer. He had come to admire one above the rest, a slight officer named Kazimierz Rawicz. The two men met one frigid November evening by the hospital block.

Rawicz agreed with Witold that their combined force could destroy at least some of the camp and the nearby train lines while creating a window of opportunity for prisoners to escape. He suggested they send word of their plan to Warsaw for approval.[41]

Even though Witold knew the uprising could take months to plan and that organizing an army of that size was fraught with danger, he felt a renewed sense of purpose. At that time, he had a position at an old tannery complex, outside the camp, where the SS employed several hundred skilled workers: leather workers, locksmiths, blacksmiths, and tailors. One of his agents had fashioned a hideaway in the main hall of the tannery complex. The room contained a dozen deep pits for holding chemical solutions, and the tanners had kept one of the pits dry, its opening covered with strips of drying leather. It was the perfect place to discuss underground matters.[42]

They also had a treat on offer: a bath in a large tank of warm water for soaking skins. "I took a bath and felt as I had once felt as a free man," Witold recalled. Such moments couldn't last, nor would he have wanted them to, with the uprising approaching and death all around.

Tannery buildings.

At roll call on November 11, Armistice Day and the anniversary of Polish independence after the Great War, the SS called out the names of 151 prisoners and marched them off to the courtyard of the penal block, where they were shot, one at a time. There was so much blood, it oozed under the gate onto the street.[43]

A few days later, Witold noted to a recent tannery recruit, Wincenty Gawron, that the number of SS men guarding the tannery had been reduced to only twenty. Wincenty, a thirty-one-year-old wood engraver from the hills outside Kraków, had become a trusted confidant, and Witold saw something of himself in the charming and oddly vulnerable younger man.

Then, one day in December, Witold noted there were barely a dozen guards on duty. "Do you see?" he whispered to Wincenty. "We could easily overpower them, dress in their uniforms, and surprise the camp."[44]

Wincenty wanted to laugh, but Witold had a look in his eye. "It's doable in theory," the younger man ventured.[45]

The next stage had begun.

EIGHT

I t worried Witold that he had received no word from Warsaw since he arrived in the camp. Were his messages getting through? Had he failed to convey the horrific nature of the crimes he had witnessed? The Americans had finally joined the war effort after Hitler had rashly declared war on them in December 1941 following Japan's attack on Pearl Habor. The BBC reported on an upcoming conference to condemn Nazi war crimes, held at the behest of the Polish government-in-exile. But when it came to action, British prime minister Winston Churchill and US president Franklin D. Roosevelt appeared to be concerned only with preparations for a major offensive against the Germans. Somehow, Witold needed to make them see that Auschwitz represented the heart of the Nazis' evil.[1]

So, as Rawicz finalized plans for the revolt, Witold turned his attention to the German plans for the rapidly expanding camp. He was intrigued to learn from his men that they had

Stanisław "Stasiek" Dubois.

bumped up against another resistance cell running its own intelligence-gathering operation. Its leader was a well-known left-leaning activist and parliamentarian named Stanisław Dubois, who'd been jailed before the war for his opposition to the government's right-wing policies.

Stanisław—Stasiek to his friends—could be found most nights outside his block defiantly puffing on a cigarette. Witold made contact with him, and the two men agreed to coordinate efforts.[2]

All the various resistance leaders gathered together on Christmas Eve. It was minus 13 degrees Fahrenheit at roll call that night, the snow was coming down in crystal shards, and the SS guards were all eager to be inside. The prisoners returned to the barracks for soup and bread, and the kapos left them in peace.

Wincenty had smuggled a small fir tree into one of the rooms and decorated it with angels, stars, and an eagle carved from root vegetables. Professor Roman Rybarski, a right-wing politician, gave a speech and handed out smuggled

Drawing of an eagle wearing a crown, Poland's national emblem, that adorned the Christmas tree in 1941, by Wincenty Gawron, postwar.

Christmas wafers. He then embraced Stasiek, a former political adversary, much to Witold's quiet satisfaction. As they returned to their blocks, they heard a German guard in one of the watchtowers whistling "Silent Night."[3]

The SS records office presented Witold and Stasiek with a trove of information. A ledger known as the stärkebuch, or "daily count book," noted new arrivals, transfers, releases, and deaths—the evidence the underground needed to fully document the Nazi crimes.

Until then, Witold had forbidden keeping written records because of safety concerns, but he realized that the full extent of the atrocities could be accurately preserved only on paper and agreed to a change in policy. And so Witold's and Stasiek's agents in the records office started making a copy of the stärkebuch. There was no chance of doing this during the day, but sometimes the clerks had to work through the night with little or no supervision. The copied papers were then brought over to the storage block where another member of the underground collated the information and hid the documents.[4]

They calculated that, by March 1942, 30,000 Poles had been registered in the camp, of whom 11,132 were still alive. The initial figure included around 2,000 Polish Jews, most of whom were dead. Of the 12,000 Soviet POWs who had arrived in the camp, only around a hundred were alive.[5]

Stasiek prepared written reports to be taken out of the camp by the inmates who worked as surveyors in the construction office. They hid the documents in map cylinders or in the hollowed-out components of the surveyors' measuring tools and arranged for them to be left in various pickup points in the fields around the camp, to be collected by Helena Stupka.[6]

The Stupkas had been evicted from their house near the camp, and now lived on the other side of the river. Helena used her six-year-old son, Jacek, to deliver and collect messages. The boy would wait by the bridge for the inmate surveyors to march past, and he knew to approach them only if they were singing a certain tune, which meant the SS men had been bribed. One time he mistook the tune, and a guard picked him up by his ears and carried him back over the

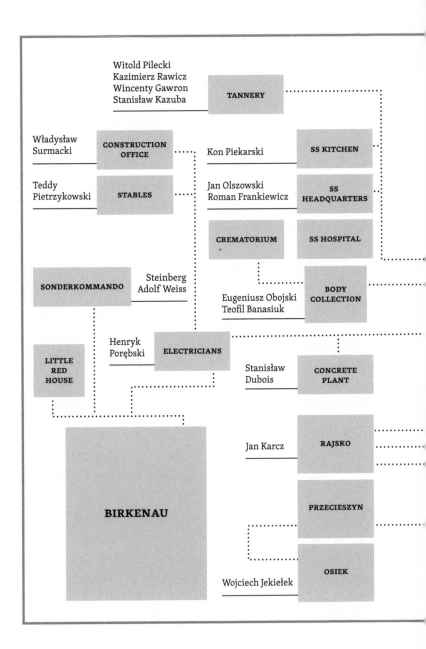

Witold Pilecki
Kazimierz Rawicz
Wincenty Gawron
Stanisław Kazuba

TANNERY

Władysław
Surmacki

CONSTRUCTION
OFFICE

Kon Piekarski

SS KITCHEN

Teddy
Pietrzykowski

STABLES

Jan Olszowski
Roman Frankiewicz

SS
HEADQUARTERS

CREMATORIUM

SS HOSPITAL

SONDERKOMMANDO

Steinberg
Adolf Weiss

Eugeniusz Obojski
Teofil Banasiuk

BODY
COLLECTION

Henryk
Porębski

ELECTRICIANS

LITTLE
RED
HOUSE

Stanisław
Dubois

CONCRETE
PLANT

BIRKENAU

Jan Karcz

RAJSKO

PRZECIESZYN

OSIEK

Wojciech Jekiełek

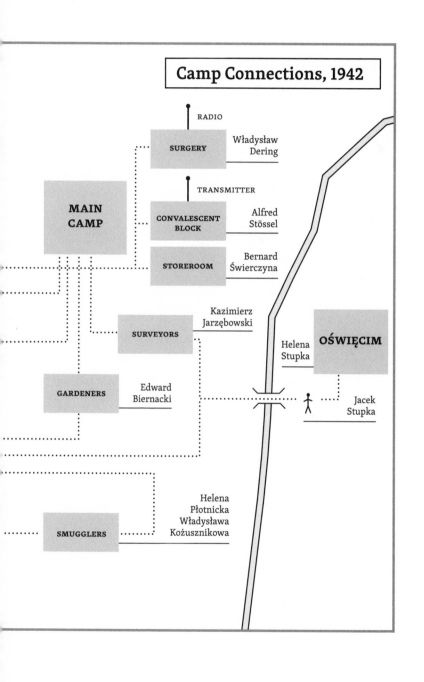

Camp Connections, 1942

RADIO

SURGERY — Władysław Dering

TRANSMITTER

CONVALESCENT BLOCK — Alfred Stössel

MAIN CAMP

STOREROOM — Bernard Świerczyna

Kazimierz Jarzębowski

SURVEYORS

OŚWIĘCIM

Helena Stupka

GARDENERS — Edward Biernacki

Jacek Stupka

Helena Płotnicka
Władysława Kożusznikowa

SMUGGLERS

Jacek Stupka, wartime photo.

bridge, tearing his earlobes in the process—a lucky escape all the same.[7]

Other families in the area also helped smuggle reports at huge personal risk, such as Helena Płotnicka and Władysława Kożusznikowa, who carried food and medicine for the prisoners that they deposited near the camp while collecting messages from inmates in return. They'd almost been caught on several occasions, and Commandant Höss had written to the local police complaining about Polish women seen "laden with sacks and packages" nearby.

While the underground prepared its reports for smuggling out, Witold found a more direct method for contacting the outside world. There was one area of the camp that the resistance had yet to penetrate: the SS headquarters' radio room, from where the camp authorities communicated with Berlin. Inmates were forbidden to approach the radio room, but one of Witold's agents, an engineering student named Zbigniew Ruszczyński, worked in the construction office, which had a storeroom for spare radio parts. Zbigniew believed it contained everything they needed to construct their own transmitter.[8]

The radio would be a simple device for relaying Morse code. All Zbigniew needed was a battery with a switch to create a current, a couple of vacuum-tube valves to boost the

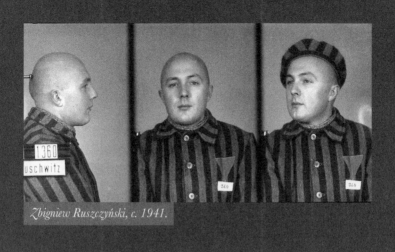
Zbigniew Ruszczyński, c. 1941.

frequency, and several meters of copper wire, a section of which, wound into a coil, would conduct the signal to the antenna. If Zbigniew was right, their creation would be heard in Warsaw and beyond.[9]

Witold volunteered himself for the mission and tapped Kon to join him. The young recruit had established a reputation as one of the most brazen thieves in the camp, assisted by his repertoire of magic tricks. Kon had landed a job in the SS kitchen, preparing food for the guards, after impressing the German kapo who ran the squad with his ability to disappear loaves of bread. The kapo, nicknamed Mamma, saw the value in having someone with thieving skills on his team and roped Kon into stealing sausages and smuggling them into the camp under his shirt. Mamma paid off the guards with a portion, took his own cut, and left Kon a little to share around.[10]

A day before the radio operation was to begin, Witold led Kon out of the block to talk. It was bitter outside, the snow piled in drifts around the buildings. "I have to ask you to make a big sacrifice for the organization," Witold began, and explained the mission. Kon seemed unfazed by the task but was unhappy about leaving his job in the kitchen.

Witold assured him that he could go back after the task was complete. He'd already asked Mamma, and Otto in the labor office had approved the transfer.

"It appears I have no choice," said Kon.[11]

The next day, Witold and Kon joined a dozen inmates in the construction office, where they found the camp's chief architect, SS-Hauptsturmführer Karl Bischoff, scrambling to modify the plans for Birkenau. The slow pace of construction had obliged Bischoff to switch from building brick barracks to using prefabricated horse stables for rapid assembly.

The SS had at first planned for Auschwitz to house an influx of Soviet POWs captured in the wake of victory in the east. But Germany now faced a war of attrition against the combined might of Britain, America, and the Soviet Union, and the lack of Soviet POWs for Birkenau meant that Himmler had an empty camp.[12]

Himmler proposed to Hitler that he fill Birkenau with Jews, and in early February 1942, he told the Auschwitz hierarchy to expect transports of Jews from Slovakia and France. Historians once believed that Hitler delivered a single order to kill Europe's Jews, but in fact the program of extermination we have come to call the Holocaust came into being in the winter of 1941 through the acceleration of murderous processes already occurring at all levels of the Nazi state.

The T4 Euthanasia Program had developed gassing trucks that pumped carbon monoxide into their cargo bays to kill patients. Himmler subsequently deployed the trucks to occupied Russia to assist SS death squads mass murdering Jews. They were also used at a camp outside the village of Chełmno in territory annexed from Poland to kill Jews in the region, the first of four such purpose-built death camps.[13]

Then, in January 1942, senior Nazis and state officials met in the Berlin suburb of Wannsee to discuss plans to deport Jews from the rest of Europe to the occupied East, either to be murdered immediately or worked to death in labor gangs. They called this secretive program the Final Solution.[14]

Witold had no knowledge of the Nazis' plans for the exploitation and mass murder of Jews. It's possible he overheard the SS architects discuss the incoming Jewish workers, but the news would have fitted in his mind with the existing Nazi practice of exploiting Polish and Soviet labor.

Witold found a moment to slip away from his desk in the construction office and scope out the single-story building, which had several rooms off a central corridor. The storeroom with the spare radio parts was at one end and strictly out of bounds.

After a week of careful pilfering, Witold and Kon had gathered the pieces Zbigniew needed to assemble a transmitter. All the parts were in a box in a bathroom stall. Witold approached Kon's desk with a flushed face and told him that they had to be moved immediately.[15]

"Let me look at it," Kon replied.[16]

A few minutes later, Witold heard a crash in the corridor, then Kon shouting: "Where do you think you're going? Out you go, you swine dogs."

Kon reappeared in the room, looking nonchalant. He'd almost been discovered by a couple of prisoners as he stashed

Construction office staff.

the box in a supply cupboard in the corridor. Luckily, they ran away when he shouted at them.

The new hiding place was an improvement on the bathroom, but it was temporary. The conspirators discussed their options that evening outside the blocks. The only way to bring the box to the camp undetected was by wagon. Gienek's morgue cart was the most likely to escape inspection at the gate.

Gienek agreed to pick up the box if they could place it in a garbage pit around the back of the construction building. That left the problem of how to get the box to the pit, two hundred yards from the building in a wasteland beside the main road. Witold said they should sleep on it, but the next day, they were no closer to an answer, and Witold spent the morning worrying that someone would find the box.

It wasn't until evening approached that he struck on a plan. The kapo informed them that they would have to work late and that soup would be served in the office. When they had finished eating, Witold asked to go to the toilet.

"Go," the guard replied, "but don't try anything stupid or I'll fill you full of holes."[17]

The guard opened the door to the corridor and stood at the doorway. Witold came back shortly after. He'd noticed that the bathroom window had no bars and faced the garbage dump. One of them might be able to climb through with the box, deposit it in the garbage pit, and rush back again.

"How can you take that huge radio from the cupboard in full view of the SS guard?" asked Kon.[18]

"I'll pretend I have diarrhea and go to the toilet every fifteen to twenty minutes," said Witold. "During one of these trips you start performing your magic tricks for everybody. Get the guard sufficiently involved to keep him away from the door. When you think there's enough time for me to get the radio out, say loudly: 'Now, watch very carefully!' That'll be my signal."

Kon smiled. "All right," he said.

Witold began to groan, holding his stomach, while Kon tried to get his neighbor's attention by making a coin dance over his knuckles. The kapo wasn't impressed. "No funny business there!" he shouted. "Get back to work!"[19]

Witold was allowed to go to the toilet, but he was only gone a minute when the guard grew suspicious and came to check on him.

Later, the kitchen cart arrived with acorn coffee, and during the break, Kon started up his tricks again, this time quite openly. One of the German guards had a deck of cards in his pocket, and he challenged Kon to show him what he could do.

Kon picked a couple of cards from the deck. "Watch very carefully!" he said, and started a simple monte trick where one card transformed into another. He performed the trick over and over until the guards were demanding to know how it was done.

Witold requested the toilet, and this time the guards waved him away. In the corridor, he forced the supply cupboard's doors open, eased the box off the shelf, and shuffled to the bathroom, where he stacked the box on the window shelf.[20]

Kon went to the toilet next, and Witold waited nervously. After a few minutes, he heard a crash outside and guards shouting. The SS men in the room looked up. He had to do something. "Toilet!" he shouted, and he rushed into the hallway and started banging on the door.[21]

"Get out of there!" he yelled. "Don't you see that I'm going to do it in my pants?" It was the only way he could think to hide the commotion outside. He heard someone scrambling back through the window. "How can you just sit there and let me suffer?" he continued to shout.

Kon instantly got the ruse and shouted back, "You've camped here already for half the night! You'll get your turn soon enough!"[22]

Kon emerged a moment later and gave Witold a thumbs-up before returning to the room. On the march back to the camp, Kon revealed that he had fallen into the garbage dump, and the commotion had alerted some nearby SS men.

Fortunately, he'd managed to make it back to the building before they could spot him.

Gienek picked up the box some time later. Witold arranged for the transmitter to be set up in the basement of the convalescent block, where few SS men went for fear of catching a disease. Zbigniew just needed one or two more parts, but he knew where to get them.[23]

NINE

Spring came early in 1942. The sun warmed the leafless trees, and the first swallows appeared. At the start of March, the surviving Soviets were moved to the newly completed barracks in Birkenau, which the inmates called Paradise, possibly because being sent there meant death.

The Soviets' blocks weren't empty for long. There were rumors among the kapos that soon women would be arriving in Auschwitz. The prisoners dismissed these as gossip, but on the afternoon of March 19, a shout went up: "They are coming!" Witold was back working in the tannery, and everyone there rushed to the windows to watch the five SS trucks carrying Polish female political prisoners as they arrived.[1]

A carpenter named Kluska hurried in a short while later. Incredibly, his fiancée, Zosia, was among the women. She was wearing her favorite brown fur coat. Their eyes had locked. "From now on, from this moment, I've a purpose in life," Kluska told the men in the tannery. "I will take care of her. I will give her my food, I will feed her."[2]

"They will be treated like the men," Witold told Wincenty quietly.[3]

That evening, the prisoners were marching back to the camp when an SS officer headed off their column. He said something to the kapo, who turned pale. Sounding almost panicked, the kapo ordered the prisoners to start running and to keep their eyes firmly turned in the opposite direction as they passed the crematorium. "Whoever doesn't will be shot!" he yelled.[4]

They broke into a trot and did as they were told, but Wincenty managed to steal a glance. The gate to the crematorium was open, revealing the stacked bodies of women and girls. One of the corpses was wearing a fur coat.[5]

Jewish women from Slovakia arrived later that month. Their heads were shaved, and they were given the dirty, bloodstained uniforms of the dead Soviets to wear. The only concession to their femininity was that they were allowed to wrap their roughly shaved scalps with scarves and scraps of cloth.

The next day, they were formed into work squads. Wincenty and his block mates crowded around their window to stare at the women as they passed. His friend had fallen for one: "Rózia, there goes my Rózia. Look at her! What a figure. With what style she has tied that scarf on her head!"

Such yearning didn't last long. The women's health rapidly deteriorated, and Witold noted that "the girls quickly lost the sparkle in their eyes, their smiles and the spring in their step."[6]

The arrival of the women heralded other changes. There were rumors that Jewish men had started to arrive in Birkenau.

Female Jewish prisoners, 1944.

Henryk Porębski, c. 1941.

Inmate electricians from the main camp were working on powering the new fence there. One of them, Henryk Porębski, was a recruit for the underground. Henryk reported that transports of around a thousand Jewish men were arriving daily from Slovakia and that one had come from France. The Jewish prisoners were assigned the same murderous tasks as the Soviets: digging ditches and laying roads.[7]

Witold confirmed the information with some French Jews who were brought to the main camp in April. He was becoming aware of the European-wide scope of the Nazis' actions, although he still had no inkling of their plans to mass murder Jewish people.

The Frenchmen had come from the Drancy internment camp in the Paris suburbs and a facility outside the town of Compiègne. They had been told that they would be working in factories in the east. Compared to the Jews in Birkenau, the Jews registered in the main camp were being treated well, and the SS asked them to write letters home attesting to that fact. Witold guessed that the SS would use those letters to trick other Jews in France to board transports and warned the Frenchmen they were being manipulated, but they ignored him. Later he called them "foolishly stubborn." As soon as their letters were written, the Jewish kapo in the penal block murdered them, using a spade.[8]

The rush of developments convinced Witold that he needed to send another report to Warsaw. However, the Germans were no longer freeing as many inmates who might take word to the resistance for him. Then one of his agents in the Gestapo office shared with him that the German army's high command had ordered a halt to collective punishments for escapes because of fears that German POWs might receive the same treatment from their captors.[9]

Witold understood at once the significance of this information: He could arrange for breakouts for his couriers without endangering the lives of others beyond the underground. The risks were still inordinately high. There had been around two dozen escape attempts in 1941, and all but a couple had ended in death. Most were impulsive dashes for freedom by prisoners on work details outside the camp that had ended in a hail of bullets, but even the better-organized attempts required luck to evade the search parties and their dogs. Those who did get away were still in danger of being picked up by the police.[10]

Witold had identified a promising escape point: a nearby farm called Harmęże, where the SS were using inmate labor to expand fish ponds and to breed Angora rabbits for wool. The farm was several miles away from the main camp, and security was reportedly lax at the mansion where the prisoners were housed.[11]

His fellow underground leader, Kazimierz Rawicz,

Stefan Bielecki, c. 1941.

opposed the idea of an escape. He probably didn't trust that there would be no reprisals and feared what would happen if the courier was caught and forced under torture to betray them. Witold tried to reassure him about the route and the courier he'd selected, Stefan Bielecki, whom he knew and trusted from the underground in Warsaw. Furthermore, Stefan had been arrested by the Gestapo when he was in possession of a firearm, which meant the SS might execute him at any moment in one of their periodic culls. Rawicz remained unconvinced, but Witold decided to go ahead. The information he wanted to send about the massive influx of Jews to Birkenau was too important.[12]

Using his labor-office contacts, Witold arranged for Stefan's transfer to Harmęże. He also continued to gather evidence about the Jewish arrivals. In April, one of his recruits, Jan Karcz, was sent to the penal squad in Birkenau. Jan managed to register as a patient in the camp's rudimentary hospital, and he reported back via the electricians that he was forming a cell.[13]

In early May, a transport of Jews was unloaded from cattle cars near the warehouses. Instead of being brought straight to Birkenau, they were marched into the main camp—men, women, and, for the first time, children. The camp was put on lockdown, and Witold and the other prisoners were ordered to lie on the floor in their blocks.

Teddy the boxer managed to hide in a manger by the window of the stable facing the crematorium and watched the column of around 600 Jews, led by a rabbi wearing a yarmulke, his prayer shawl around his shoulders, enter the courtyard of the crematorium. An SS guard struck the rabbi in the face with his rifle, sending his skullcap flying. Then the courtyard gates closed behind them.[14]

SS-Untersturmführer Maximilian Grabner, the Gestapo chief, appeared on the crematorium roof and spoke to the people gathered below, telling them that they were going to be disinfected because, he said, "we don't want any epidemics in the camp. Then you will be brought to your barracks, where you'll get some hot soup. You will be employed in accordance with your professional qualifications." He picked out one man from the crowd and asked him, "What is your trade?" When the man answered, Grabner continued: "A shoemaker? We need them urgently. Report to me immediately after!"[15]

The first families stepped through the blue-painted doors of the crematorium. SS men went in with them, joking and reassuring. When the morgue inside was full, the SS officers slipped out. Panic set in as the door was screwed shut, and angry voices could be heard through the vents in the concrete roof.

Grabner was joined atop the building by SS men wearing gas masks and carrying small tins. They positioned themselves

Maximilian Grabner, c. 1941.

beside the openings. Someone inside must have caught a glimpse of a masked face, because it was then that the screaming began. Grabner made a sign to the driver of a truck parked nearby, who turned on his engine and revved the throttle to drown out the noise. But the cries were still audible. Then Grabner gave the order, and the men in gas masks opened their tins and emptied them into the vents. A few minutes passed, and the cries grew weak. Then there was silence.[16]

The ventilator was turned on and the room unsealed. The SS ordered a detachment of Jews from the penal block to strip the corpses of clothing and to check for valuables. The clothes were stuffed into bags, and any jewelry, watches, and cash stored in a box. The mouths of the dead were pried open, and gold fillings and dentures were removed. Finally, the corpses were stacked for burning and the room was scrubbed down.[17]

A few days later, another trainload of men, women, and children was gassed.

And another a few days after that.

The killings marked the start of the systematic mass

Drawing of crematorium in the main camp, by Tadeusz Iwaszko, 1984.

murder of Jews in Auschwitz. The first victims were taken mostly from nearby towns, and it seems that the Nazi leadership initially saw Auschwitz as part of a network of regional killing centers being set up in Poland that spring, which mostly targeted Eastern European Jews.

Witold heard the details from the prisoners who worked the ovens. He recognized that the killings were a terrible new development. When the Soviets were gassed, he had assumed it was because there was no space for them in the camp. This theory seemed plausible because the gassing stopped after the construction of Birkenau. When Witold heard that Jewish corpses were being stripped of their clothes and valuables, his first thought was that the Nazis must be killing Jews for plunder. He struggled to believe that the Nazis were slaughtering Jewish people simply because they were Jews.[18]

The crematorium team could hardly keep up. The ovens overheated and the chimney cracked. The camp's fire-engine crew sprayed the outside of the building with water, causing huge clouds of steam to rise into the air. The remaining bodies were loaded onto trucks and driven to a secluded area of Birkenau, where they were dumped in pits.[19]

The cracked chimney seemed to signal the end of the mass murder, but it didn't take long for Witold to find out that the gassing had merely shifted to Birkenau. Henryk the electrician reported that a facility had been prepared in woods near the new camp—a redbrick farmhouse to which a 220-volt electric cable had been installed. The house was small and the plot empty save for a couple of apple trees just coming into blossom.

The SS brought in German contractors to brick up the windows and reinforce the doors and ceiling. In early May, the first groups of Jews were marched to what became known as the "little red house," disappearing into the woods between the stands of birch and pine.[20]

Henryk befriended several members of the so-called Sonderkommando, or "special work squad," which the SS created to assist with running the new gas chamber. These Jewish workers were kept isolated from the other prisoners, though they could interact briefly with them at the water pumps. The Sonderkommando confirmed to Henryk that groups of Jewish families were being gassed. The SS had refined the operation by having their victims undress themselves before entering the

Area around Birkenau where pits were dug.

chamber. The Sonderkommando ushered the families inside, and afterward they removed the bodies, checked the teeth for gold, and hauled the bodies off to the pits.[21]

Witold activated his escape plan in mid-May, when Stefan Bielecki had been in position in Harmęże for several weeks. Witold asked his artist friend Wincenty to join him. Ever since he witnessed the massacre of the female political prisoners, Wincenty had been broken in spirit. On one occasion, Witold found his friend preparing to commit suicide by charging the electric fence, and Wincenty confessed to Witold that he couldn't last much longer.

Just as Witold hoped, the prospect of freedom gave

Wincenty Gawron, c. 1941.

Wincenty a burst of energy. He threw himself into preparations and, over the following days, obtained some extra bread and a set of civilian clothes.[22]

On May 15, a Friday, Wincenty tracked down Witold to tell him that everything was arranged for his departure the following morning.

"You need to pass on the information about how the Germans treated the Soviet POWs," Witold told him. "But the most important thing is the mass killing of Jews." Wincenty was to alert headquarters that children and the elderly were being gassed upon arrival in the camp, while others were being worked to death. The Germans were bringing Jews to the camp under the pretext of working in the war industry, but their real intention was to systematically rob and murder them. It was vital that the underground inform London at once so the world would come to the Jews' assistance.[23]

The next morning dawned bright and clear. The kitchen buggy bound for Harmęże was already waiting for Wincenty, and he clambered into the seat beside the kapo, who handed him the reins. At the gate, Wincenty's order papers were checked and his transfer to Harmęże confirmed. An SS guard joined them, and they trotted off. The route took them over the railway tracks, and they soon reached the edge of Birkenau. It was the first time Wincenty had seen the place, and its blank rows of barracks scared him.[24]

The cart pulled up outside a stolid mansion. The prisoners slept on the second floor and were locked in every night, behind barred windows. The ground floor contained mostly workshops, and there were no grills on the windows. A low fence surrounded the building, which had no barbed wire. Wincenty suspected that escaping might be even easier than he had thought.[25]

First, he had to find Stefan Bielecki, who returned to the house for midday roll call with the eighty or so other prisoners. Stefan, a wiry, intense man with a lopsided face and a lazy eye, recognized Wincenty as one of Witold's confidants. As soon as roll call was over, he seized him by the arm, hissing, "Why have you come here? Don't you know that all the men in this barracks are to be replaced with women in two weeks?"[26]

"Don't worry, I'm planning to escape long before that," replied Wincenty.

"If so, then that's quite another matter," said Stefan, smiling. "How about tonight?"

"I'm in," said Wincenty.[27]

They shook hands and collected their lunch of rutabaga soup and three baked potatoes, then Stefan explained his plan. After supper, the doors upstairs were left open for

Mansion in Harmęże from which Wincenty and Stefan escaped.

fifteen minutes so prisoners could use the toilets. The latrine was to the rear of the building, at the edge of thick bush that led down to the Vistula River. It was the obvious escape route, which was why Stefan intended not to use it. His plan was to break out from a window at the front of the building and head in the opposite direction—toward the fish ponds and the fields. The terrain was more open, but if they cut across the ponds, that would confuse the dogs.

As evening approached, Stefan became more and more tense. He pointed out the window in one of the ground-floor rooms used for carpentry. It was missing a pane, leaving an opening large enough for them to squeeze through. "Our window to freedom," he said. He'd made a habit of tidying up the room every evening during the fifteen-minute toilet break, so the guards were used to seeing him in there.[28]

"Won't the guard be suspicious if I show up too?" asked Wincenty.

"That's what I'm afraid of," Stefan replied.

They had an hour before the two of them would have to make their move, and their sense of the risks was growing. Dinner was a piece of bread, a spoon of marmalade, and some bitter tea. Wincenty and Stefan were so agitated, it was hard to eat. Then there was nothing for it but to try their luck.

Stefan walked past the two SS men and into the carpentry workroom, Wincenty right behind him. The Germans didn't look up. Stefan quickly closed the door and grabbed a heavy ax from a workbench. He was breathing hard as he stood there, frozen, waiting to see if a guard was going to follow.[29]

Wincenty climbed onto a desk beneath the window. He slipped through, with Stefan following immediately after. They scaled the fence and started sprinting down the road, trying to stick to the cover of the willow trees that lined the route. It was almost dark now, and the frogs were croaking all around.

They reached a bend a couple of hundred yards from the house, and Stefan pointed to a small dike that ran perpendicular to the road toward a large pond shining in the gloom. Just as they cut off the road into the surrounding field, they heard a shout and saw the two SS guards burst out of the front door of the house and run around the back toward the Vistula, as Stefan had predicted they would.

The two fugitives stumbled across the field and had

Lakes along Wincenty and Stefan's escape route.

reached the reeds of the lake's shoreline when, to their horror, they saw another SS man bearing down on them from the opposite direction on a bike. "For God's sake," Stefan gasped, and plunged into the water. Wincenty followed. What else could they do?[30]

The lake was dark and cold. Wincenty held his breath for as long as he could, knowing they'd surely been spotted, and when he finally poked his head out of the water to claw in a breath, there was the SS man, not fifteen yards away, peering at him in the half-light. "Jesus and Mother Mary," Wincenty muttered, plunging back underwater, waiting for the end.[31]

When he surfaced again, a few moments later, he was stunned to see the man back on his bike, cycling away from them toward the house. He'd forgotten his gun. Stefan came up gasping for air, saw the retreating guard, and immediately set off through the shallow water to the opposite bank.[32]

Wincenty turned to the camp for a moment, shouted, "Up yours!" and followed Stefan.[33]

They crossed the stone-gray Soła River just before dawn, holding hands to steady themselves against the current. Once on the other side, they stripped off their wet clothes and waited, naked, in the woods until nightfall. For the next few days, they moved only at night, sticking to the forests and staying in peasant homes when they could.[34]

Wincenty brought them straight to his sister's place in the village of Limanowa, where he was reunited with his family. He later ecstatically recalled the details of their first meal: sausage, traditional circular cake, and a glass of home brew to celebrate their return from "the other world."

Stefan left for Warsaw a few weeks later, to find the underground and deliver his report.[35]

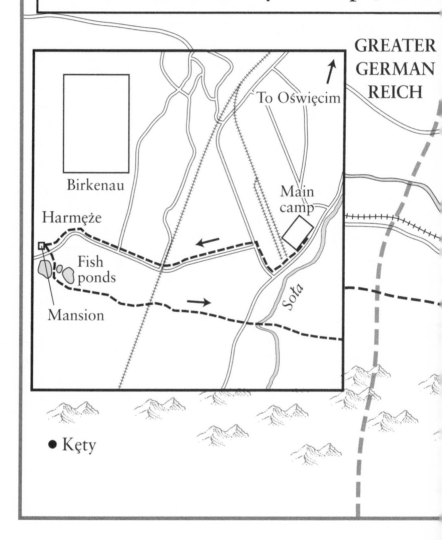

Stefan and Wincenty's Escape, 1942

GREATER
GERMAN
REICH

To Oświęcim

Birkenau

Main
camp

Harmęże

Fish
ponds

Mansion

Soła

● Kęty

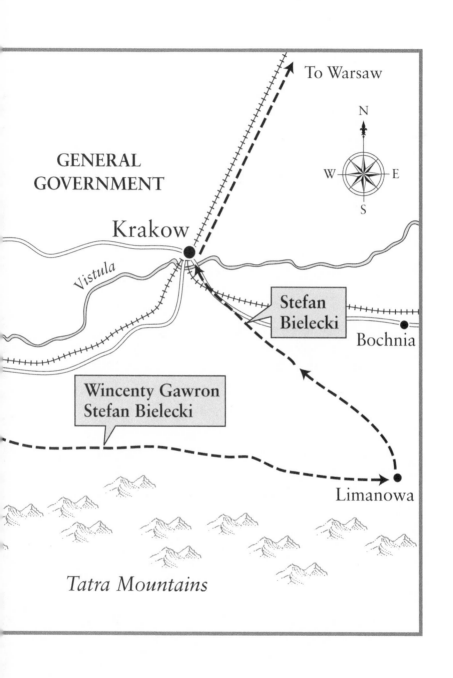

Witold heard the siren on the night of Wincenty and Stefan's escape. Had they been caught? If so, would they inform on the resistance? He had no way of knowing. At least there were no reprisals following the escape.

That didn't mean he was safe. For most of Witold's eighteen months in Auschwitz, the Germans had considered the underground to be little more than a collection of prison gangs, but it seemed now that the SS suspected there was more to it. The first sign of trouble was the mailbox on a block wall near the camp entrance, in which prisoners discreetly posted tip-offs in exchange for food. The box was locked. Witold ordered one of his men in the smithy to forge a skeleton key, which they used to remove from the mailbox anything that might betray the resistance.[1]

Then one afternoon, an ashen-faced Kon pulled Witold aside to tell him it was likely that one of the new recruits in the tannery was a Gestapo agent. Kon's source had shared a cell with the man in Kraków. The SS had always seemed to know what was being discussed in the cell, and several prisoners had been shot.[2]

Witold confirmed with an inmate clerk working in the Gestapo office that the recruit was working on "special assignment." Even though Witold had given the recruit only an outline of the underground's mission, there was no getting around the fact that he had been exposed. The only question was whether the man had been able to make a report to the Gestapo.

Every moment was vital. Dering suggested dosing the enemy agent with croton oil, a fast-acting purgative, which would get him to the hospital, where Dering would try to trick the SS doctors into selecting him for a phenol injection. The operation risked exposing more members of the underground, but they had no other choice.

That afternoon, the tannery crew cooked up a stew and served the spy a portion laced with the oil. He was clearly unwell by roll call, and as soon as they were dismissed, he made a dash toward the main gate. Witold's men intercepted him and marched him over to the hospital, where he was registered as suffering from acute meningitis. An SS doctor approved his euthanization with only a cursory inspection.[3]

Witold was still afraid that the man had given his number to the Gestapo, and it was not until a few weeks later that he realized his secret was safe—but for how long? The Gestapo continued randomly executing prisoners because they had a record of being in the resistance or because they held an officer's rank.

One morning in May, Rawicz was called in for interrogation. He persuaded the Gestapo that they had mistaken him for someone else, but he was shaken and decided that the time had come to launch the uprising.[4]

The challenge facing their rebellion remained daunting: The SS garrison had expanded that spring to 2,500 men that now included a rapid response unit capable of deploying in thirty minutes. Rawicz calculated that even if a third of the garrison was on leave or off duty at any given time, the underground's 1,000 men would still be badly outnumbered and outgunned.[5]

Their one advantage lay in surprise. If they struck in the evening when the squads were returning from work and the camp was in maximum flux, they might have a precious few minutes for one group to overpower the guards at the gate and in the sentry towers while a second group seized the reserve arms stored in the construction office and distributed weapons to the main camp's 9,000 prisoners.

Rawicz hoped the rest of the prisoners would follow their cue and join them. They would then deploy to the town of Kęty, twelve miles south of the camp. Rawicz thought that a small contingent of prisoners could seize the town while the rest escaped into the woods.[6]

Witold feared the plan would end in slaughter and that even if they succeeded, the Germans would exact revenge on those left behind. A least a quarter of the prisoners were confined to the hospital block and in no shape to move. Then there were the several thousand prisoners in Birkenau, two miles distant, to consider. The only way to prevent a bloodbath, he believed, was to coordinate their uprising with a diversionary attack by underground forces outside the camp.[7]

Rawicz agreed but made it clear they couldn't wait indefinitely, not when scores of men were being shot each day. The plan Rawicz sent to the underground leadership in Warsaw in May 1942, via a released prisoner, carried with it an ultimatum: The camp was prepared to go it alone if they didn't hear back from Warsaw by June 1, less than a month away.[8]

As they waited, the tensions and the death toll mounted. There was yet another outbreak of typhus, which prompted the SS to euthanize up to a hundred sick patients a day. Word spread that the hospital was to be avoided and that the sick should stay on the blocks for as long as possible, which accelerated the spread of the fever.

The underground fought back using the one weapon they had that would escape detection: the infected lice. The simplest method was to empty a jar of lice onto a jacket or coat. Teddy the boxer emptied a vial of lice under the collars of several jackets in the cloakroom of the SS hospital, which was used exclusively by officers and their families. The first German cases of typhus were recorded soon after.[9]

One of Dering's targets was Schwela, the SS doctor who oversaw the phenol injection program. Schwela was soon complaining about a temperature and sweating profusely under his uniform. He stopped showing up at the hospital, and Dering learned he had taken to bed, covered with red spots. Two weeks later he was gone. It was possible that Schwela had been accidentally infected, but the underground swore they'd gotten their man.[10]

Dering also went after the camp executioner, Gerhard Palitzsch, and dumped infected lice in the beds of hated kapos. The campaign boosted morale but did little to ease the rising anxiety as the date of the uprising approached. The weather became hot, the skies were clear, and a jasmine tree near the entrance filled the camp with the scent of its blooms.[11]

At morning roll call on May 27, the SS called out the numbers of 568 prisoners. Of those, 168 were marched straight to the penal block for immediate execution. The other 400 were sent to the penal company in Birkenau. Fear rippled through the crowd, and there was talk on the blocks of rising up that very night.[12]

Witold urged patience, but he found the waiting intolerable. They had been ready for weeks. *How soon before we can attack?* he thought as he marched past the guards and the orchestra at the gate. June 1 arrived with no word from Warsaw. Some men muttered darkly about the underground's leadership.[13]

The pressure only mounted: Witold's source in the Gestapo office told him that the 400 men who had been sent to Birkenau were to be shot—in small batches to avoid provoking unrest. Twelve were executed on June 4. Two days later, nine more were killed.

The remaining men sent Witold a warning that they planned to fight back. "I inform you that since we must soon become nothing but puffs of smoke, we shall try our luck tomorrow during work," one of them wrote. "We have little chance of success. . . . Bid my family farewell, and if you can and if you are still alive, tell them that should I die, I do so fighting."[14]

Witold felt for the men, but he also saw the bigger picture. An attempt to break out of Birkenau would almost certainly lead to a campwide crackdown at the very moment that authorization might be coming from Warsaw. Rawicz agreed that

Stables in Birkenau.

the men in Birkenau needed to wait for Warsaw and on June 9 sent instructions that the operation was to be called off.[15]

Some of the Birkenau men were relieved to hear Rawicz's order, but the majority insisted that it was better to die fighting than wait to be shot. They decided to go ahead the next day regardless.

It was damp and overcast the following morning as the condemned men started work on a drainage ditch. Few ate lunch as they waited for a sign. It started to rain torrentially. Word spread that they would rise up when the whistle sounded to return to camp.[16]

But then the guard blew early—at only 4:30 P.M. Did that signal the end of work or a break? Some of the inmates made a dash for it; others remained rooted to the spot. One young prisoner, August Kowalczyk, raised his spade to hit the nearest guard, but the man had rushed off after another escaping prisoner. August took the opportunity to scramble up a nearby causeway, then dashed over open ground to a patch of trees he knew was close to the Vistula. With bullets flying around him, he ripped off his prison stripes, and upon reaching the riverbank, plunged into the gray-green waters.[17]

August was one of only nine to get away. The rest were brought back to their barracks and kept under heavy guard. SS-Hauptsturmführer Hans Aumeier, the new deputy commandant, showed up to demand the men name the ringleaders. When no one answered, he walked down the line shooting men in the head and pausing only to reload.

He killed seventeen in total. His deputy killed three more. The remaining men were ordered to undress, and their hands were tied behind their backs with barbed wire. Then they were led through Birkenau to the little red house in the trees to be gassed. More than 200 prisoners were shot on June 14; another 120 were shot a few days later.[18]

Details of the men's fate filtered back to Witold in the main camp. Morale plunged. Each morning at roll call, more numbers were read out. Each night, the prisoners prepared farewell messages for their loved ones and discussed whether it was better to die by bullet or gas or phenol injection. Witold wondered whether he'd be able to rally the underground even if Warsaw approved an uprising. At that low point, one of the prisoners slated for execution, Eugeniusz Bendera, decided to take matters into his own hands.[19]

Eugeniusz worked as a mechanic in the SS garage and

regularly serviced a Steyr 220 sedan. The black, six-cylinder, 2.3-liter car was the fastest vehicle in the camp, and Eugeniusz fantasized about stealing it and speeding away to freedom.

He shared his dream with his friend Kazimierz "Kazik" Piechowski, who pointed out that he wouldn't make it past the checkpoint unless he had an SS uniform and could speak German. As it happened, Kazik was fluent, and he knew where the Germans' spare uniforms were kept.[20]

When Witold learned of the idea, he thought it so preposterous that it just might work. He arranged for one of his men, twenty-one-year-old Stanisław Jaster, to join Kazik and Eugeniusz and had Stanisław memorize his next report. Witold stressed that the Allies must be made aware of the Birkenau revolt and the gassing of Jews and be convinced to attack the camp at once.[21]

The escape was set for Saturday, June 20, at lunchtime, when the warehouse and garage were likely to be empty. Student Józef Lempart also joined the attempt. Kazik arranged for them to take a wagonload of kitchen waste to

Stanisław Jaster, c. 1941.

the camp dump beside the main road. The guards at the gate duly waved them through. No sooner were they out of sight than they changed course for the warehouse, entering via a coal chute.[22]

Inside, Kazik quickly located the storeroom where the uniforms were kept and took a senior sergeant's getup and a gun. As they stripped and changed, all four men agreed that if they were stopped, rather than allow the SS to capture them, Kazik was to shoot them and then himself. Eugeniusz left to fetch the car from the garage, returning a few minutes later to pick the others up at a side door to the warehouse. Wearing the uniform with the highest rank, Kazik took the passenger seat. They pulled out onto the road.[23]

When Eugeniusz saw the barrier, 300 yards away, he eased his foot off the pedal and slowed down. A hundred yards out, there was still no movement from the guards at the gate. Kazik flipped open his holster and placed his hand on the gun. At 50 yards, they could practically see inside the guard post. Eugeniusz brought the car to a stop.

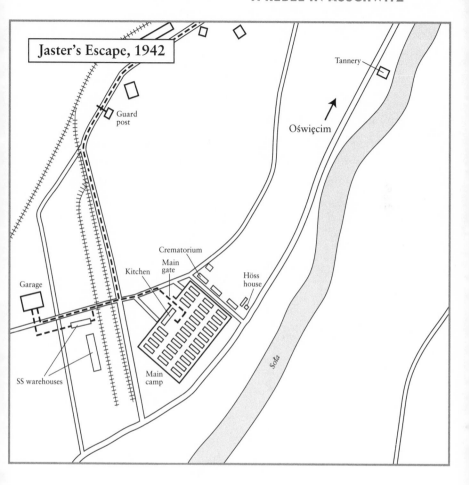

Jaster's Escape, 1942

"Kazik, do something," Jaster whispered hoarsely from the back seat.[24]

Kazik leaned out the window and yelled in German for someone to open the gate. A sheepish-looking guard appeared and casually jogged over to the metal barrier, which he hoisted upward. Eugeniusz resisted an urge to floor the pedal and instead drove sedately through.

They passed Deputy Commandant Aumeier riding his horse and gave him a "Heil Hitler." Aumeier returned the salute. And then they were free.

Witold waited anxiously for the siren to sound. Each passing moment gave him hope.[25]

The SS didn't work out that the four men were missing until evening roll call. Deputy Commandant Aumeier let out a tirade of abuse at the assembled inmates when he realized he'd been duped. Then he threw down his cap and burst out laughing.[26]

ELEVEN

S till no word came from Warsaw. In early July, the
Germans transferred Rawicz to another camp. His
departure meant that Witold was once again de facto
leader of the underground, and the decision about the uprising fell to him. The failed attempt in Birkenau confirmed
Witold's fears that a revolt in the main camp without outside
help would end in slaughter. They would have to wait, even if
that meant enduring more executions.[1]

Meanwhile, the Germans were transforming Auschwitz
from a regional killing facility into the central hub of the
Final Solution. Poland's ghettos were to be liquidated and
their inhabitants gassed at extermination sites like Treblinka,
including the majority of the 400,000 Jews trapped in
Warsaw. Auschwitz was to exterminate Jewish communities
from Poland and the rest of Europe.[2]

That summer of 1942, the SS prepared to deport 125,000

Jews to the camp from Slovakia, France, Belgium, and the Netherlands. This time, entire families would be sent and a selection made upon arrival: workers would be registered in the camp; everyone else—mothers and their children, the infirm and the elderly—were to be gassed. A second farm-house in the woods of Birkenau had been repurposed as a gas chamber in June, which meant the SS now had the capacity to exterminate an entire transport of around 2,000 Jews at once.[3]

The first transport to be subjected to selection arrived from Slovakia on July 4. The unloading ramp at the railway line, a mile from Birkenau's main gate, was tightly guarded. The thousand Jews on board were taken from the train, stripped of their possessions, and lined up for inspection. SS doctors judged that 372 were fit for work. The rest were sent to the woods.[4]

Witold's agent in Birkenau, Jan Karcz, was soon reporting on the almost daily arrival of transports from across Europe. Witold immediately grasped the sheer horror of the project. "One wonders what the SS men were actually thinking," Witold wrote later. "There were a great many women and children in the wagons. Sometimes the children were in cradles. They were all to end their lives here together. They were brought like a herd of animals, to the slaughter!"[5]

He talked about a "new nightmare" and saw the crime in existential terms as a crisis for mankind. "We have strayed my friends, we have strayed dreadfully . . . I would say that we have become animals . . . but no, we are a whole level of hell worse than animals."[6]

As the mass murder escalated that July, Witold appears to

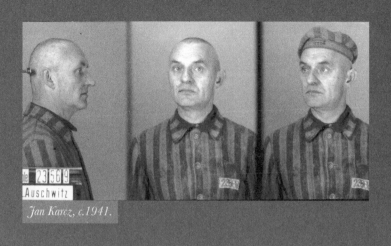

Jan Karcz, c.1941.

be the author of a letter to the outside world describing the Nazis' systematic program of murder. The letter began with a description of the failed breakout attempt by the penal company and the daily executions that followed. Then it turned to the mass gassing of Jews. "In Birkenau the SS cannot keep up with all the dead they're creating. The bodies are stacked up outside the gas chambers for burial in pits."[7]

The letter described the mood of despondency among the prisoners. "Life in the camp is very difficult at the moment. People are prepared for the worst. People are saying that if we have to die, let's not die like sheep; they say we should do something." The imperative for action was clear. A camp revolt "would echo greatly around the world," the letter concluded.

Stasiek also completed a major report about prisoner mortality to accompany Witold's letter. This report included a monthly breakdown of Polish and Soviet deaths and highlighted that 35,000 Jewish people had died in Birkenau over the past two months. Transports arrived every few days

(Above) Separation of Families *and (below)* To the Gas, *by anonymous artist.*

carrying Jewish families for gassing, and 3,500 people could be disposed of in two hours. Auschwitz had become a "death camp."[8]

In mid-July, the underground arranged for the letter and report to be smuggled out of the camp with the devastating news. A few days later, the prisoners in the main camp were suddenly issued clean uniforms and allowed to wash. On July 18, the healthier looking of them gathered in rows in the bright, early-morning sun.

The orchestra's trumpet struck up the first notes of Verdi's "Triumphal March" from *Aida*, a black sedan pulled up at the gates, and SS-Reichsführer Heinrich Himmler emerged from the vehicle, blinking in the sun and smiling. It was

Heinrich Himmler during his visit to Auschwitz, July 17–18, 1942.

Himmler's second visit to Auschwitz. He wanted to see the extermination process in Birkenau for himself, and a transport of Jewish people from Holland had been specially kept for his arrival.

He watched as the Jewish families disembarked, were stripped of their belongings, and then processed. A group of 449 men, women, and children were selected for gassing in the little white house. Himmler followed them there to observe the undressing and the sealing of the doors, and then he listened to the screams and then to the quiet. "He did not complain about anything," recalled Commandant Höss.[9]

That evening, Himmler attended a dinner party in the nearby city of Katowice, hosted by the local Nazi governor. There he indulged in a cigar and a glass of wine and revealed to the select group Hitler's plan to completely exterminate Europe's Jews, confident that the camp's secret—perhaps the greatest secret in Nazi officialdom—was safe.[10]

In fact, the information about the mass murder had by then reached Warsaw via Witold's messengers, where it was dispatched to London with the devastating news that the Germans had begun to liquidate the Warsaw Ghetto. Reports had also started to reach London and Washington, DC, of the massacre of Jews in former Russian territory and elsewhere. The British had even cracked radio messages from German units in Russia that recorded the numbers shot at the start of the invasion. Despite the evidence, some officials refused to believe what they read, while others betrayed a genteel racism by suggesting that any attempt to draw attention to the suffering of Jews might provoke anti-Semitism at home. No action was taken. The Allies claimed they did not want to divert resources from the main task of defeating Hitler.[11]

In the meantime, train after train trundled up to the railway sidings near Birkenau. On August 1, a couple of weeks after Himmler's visit, 1,007 Dutch and German Jews from the Westerbork transit camp arrived. Of the group, 200 were gassed immediately, and 807 were admitted into the camp. The next day, 1,052 French Jews arrived from Pithiviers; 779 were gassed. Then a second train came, with Polish Jews from the Będzin Ghetto. Nearly 1,500 were gassed. Two days later, another train of 1,013 Jews from Westerbork arrived, and 316 were gassed.[12]

Witold used a rough method to keep a tally of the slaughter in the tannery where he worked. Every day, a truck pulled into the courtyard, loaded with leather goods: braces, belts, handbags, shoes, and suitcases bearing name tags. These were to be sorted and either burned or sent for distribution to German families.

Pairs of shoes formed ghostly lines in the yard: polished brogues and well-worn loafers, elegant heels and baby booties. The prisoners knew what the shoes meant. Some reacted with dread; others made a point of showing they weren't affected.[13]

Often, valuables were hidden in the heels of boots and suitcase linings: gold ingots, purses of precious stones, thick rolls of banknotes in various currencies. Soon the camp was awash with loot, and money lost all meaning—a loaf of bread on the black market went for $1,000.[14]

The SS had orders to crack down—valuables were meant to be handed over for the coffers of the Reich—but the guards

Warehouse of items taken from Jewish victims.

wanted their share of the spoils too. Commandant Höss also wanted a cut. He started making regular trips to the tannery, ostensibly to have his boots shined, but Witold watched from an observation post in the workshop attic as the commandant picked through the goods. "[Höss] took gold, jewels, valuables," recalled Witold, which meant he had to "turn a blind eye to his subordinates' infractions."[15]

Witold refused to touch the plunder. He understood that the owners were dead, but he couldn't overcome his distaste for things he considered "stained with blood." Food was another matter: chocolates, Dutch cheeses, strings of figs, lemons, sachets of sugar, and little tubs of butter were all calories that meant the difference between life and death.[16]

Since the disappointment over the uprising, Witold had struggled to maintain his mens' spirits. Warsaw's silence meant that there was no imminent prospect of a revolt, but Witold refused to give up on the plan. The truth was, they needed to believe that they had some control over their fate.[17]

Then, one morning in August, Stasiek's prisoner number was read out at roll call. Witold feared the worst, but it turned out that Stasiek had simply received a package of food—Höss had recently relaxed the rules on political prisoners in the main camp getting parcels.[18]

That evening, Stasiek happily shared the tins of sardines he'd received with his friends, who quizzed him on how it had felt to have his number read out. "I wanted to go out with my head held high," he told them, "because I knew you'd all be watching!"

The next day, the Gestapo picked up Stasiek. The parcel's

arrival had reminded them of Stasiek's presence in the camp. He was shot half an hour later.[19]

Witold had lost one of his closest collaborators. He hit back in the only way he knew how: with resistance work. After months of scavenging, his radio expert, Zbigniew Ruszczyński, had finally gotten the parts he needed to finish assembling the shortwave transmitter.

To broadcast a signal was to risk revealing their position to the German tracking vans that patroled the area, so the messages were intentionally brief. No record of the transmissions survives, but it's likely that they included data collected by Stasiek. In addition to the 35,000 Jews gassed in Birkenau that summer of 1942, around 4,000 inmates had died from typhus and a further 2,000 from the Nazi executions and phenol injections.

Witold had no way of knowing whether anyone heard the broadcasts, but they needed to know that someone beyond the fence might be listening.[20]

Witold redoubled his efforts to ease the suffering of the sick by smuggling ever-increasing amounts of medication into the camp. The inmate gardener Edward Biernacki estimated that over the summer he had collected almost two gallons' worth of glucose shots, antibiotics, and painkillers, as well as enough typhus vaccine to treat seventy prisoners.[21]

At Witold's request, Dering also cultivated the friendship of one of the new SS doctors, SS-Hauptsturmführer Friedrich Entress, helping him improve his surgical skills in return for exempting Dering's patients from selections.[22]

The sight of Dering on seemingly good terms with an SS doctor led to concerns among some in the underground about

Friedrich Entress, c. 1946.

his loyalties. The matter came to a head over the use of smuggled medicines. Dering used some of the underground's morphine to bribe a construction kapo to tile and paint the operating theater. Another day, Gienek, the morgue worker, found a German kapo mixing glucose supplements into his tea. He stormed off to confront Dering, declaring that he no longer trusted him.[23]

And yet, Dering's German contact saved lives. At the end of August, Dering learned from Entress that a hospital-wide selection was planned to tackle the typhus epidemic. Dering went to warn Witold, and the two men set to work removing as many people from the hospital as possible. The paperwork to discharge each patient took time, and, as a result, they were able to rescue only a fraction of the total. Dering estimated that he extricated 112, but 756 were still gassed—almost a quarter of the total hospital population, and everyone on the convalescent block. It was yet another shattering blow for the underground.[24]

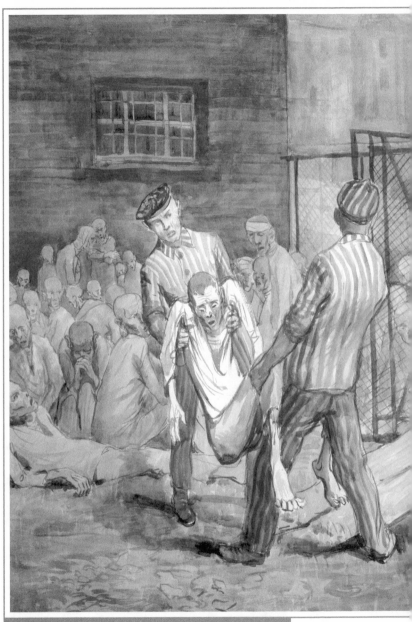

Taking Away Ill Prisoners, *by Tadeusz Potrzbowski, postwar.*

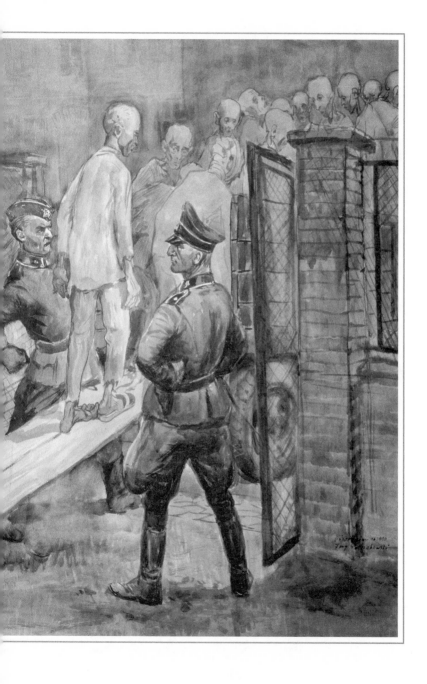

TWELVE

few days after the hospital gassing, Witold started feeling light-headed. He had arranged a job for himself painting a mural of camp life inside the block, but the pigments swam before his eyes, his joints ached, and he had a raging thirst that no amount of water could quench. He suspected he had typhus.[1]

He woke up the next morning with his skin on fire and his mattress soaked with sweat, and he had to force himself to get up for roll call. Even though the weather was warm and muggy, he shivered convulsively. After roll call, his block leader agreed to let him stay in his room, and Witold lay in his bunk, too weak to move.[2]

Suddenly, Dering appeared. He checked Witold's pulse and lifted his shirt. Witold's torso was covered in red pustules: typhus. Dering helped Witold to his feet, put his arm under his shoulder, and together they staggered to the hospital.[3]

For the rest of the week, Witold drifted in and out of consciousness. On the first night, he heard shouts and felt a deep throbbing in his ears. "Air raid!" someone was yelling. "Air raid!" Witold struggled to organize his thoughts. Could it be true? Were the Allies attacking the camp? *There wasn't time to launch the uprising!* He wanted to sound an alert but felt as if a vast weight was pinning him to the bed.

The ground shook with the first explosion, which sounded like it came from near Birkenau. Were they targeting the gas chambers? Another dull thud. Somewhere, flames were lighting the night sky. Witold struggled to stay conscious, but he found himself floating away in a dream.[4]

Dering gave him injections to reduce his fever, and a nurse spooned him lemon juice mixed with sugar and helped hide him during selections. Then a week into the fever, Witold's temperature plummeted, his blood pressure dropped, and he was on the verge of cardiac arrest. He struggled to breathe, and it seemed to him that the air was filled with smoke, black and choking, as if the flames from the furnace inside him had spread and the whole camp was on fire.[5]

The nurses mopped his brow and pressed a sponge to his lips; there was little else they could do. When the fever finally broke after ten days, Witold's only thought was to get out of the isolation ward. He pulled himself to his feet and staggered against the wall, inching his way along, until one of the nurses coaxed him back into bed.[6]

Dering brought him up to speed on the bombing raid: Soviet planes had indeed attacked fields near Rajsko for unknown reasons but had not returned. Witold's dreams about smoke had also been real. The mass graves in Birkenau

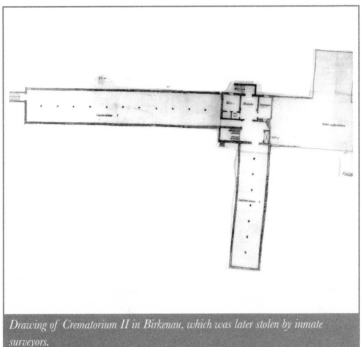

Drawing of Crematorium II in Birkenau, which was later stolen by inmate surveyors.

were contaminating the groundwater, and the stench was alarming citizens outside the camp. Two new crematoria were planned, but they were months from completion, so the SS had ordered giant pyres be lit to burn the bodies. The fires raged around the clock, lighting up the night sky and emitting huge clouds of smoke, which drifted past the camp as Dering and Witold spoke.[7]

Witold returned to work a few days later, but his resolve was faltering. He had been a prisoner in Auschwitz for two years, and over the past year, he had lost almost a hundred men to executions, phenol injections, and sickness. Many of them, like Stasiek, had been his close collaborators. Morale was low, and petty rivalries and squabbles had surfaced as the underground's sense of purpose slipped away. Witold wasn't sure how much longer he could hold them together.

Witold was standing in the square with a few men one November evening when he heard someone calling his name. He turned to see one of Rowecki's staff from the Warsaw underground, a man named Stanisław Wierzbicki, making his way toward them. It was Witold's first contact with someone from Rowecki's inner circle since entering the camp. Witold wanted to know how his reports had been received. How had the world responded to news of the mass gassings, the phenol injections, the vast piles of goods plundered from the Jews?[8]

Stanisław could confirm that Witold's messengers had made it to Warsaw, their reports written down and then smuggled to London. But no decision had come of it. Stanisław explained that few people gave much thought to Auschwitz, which was true: The Allies were planning to issue a public statement condemning the mass murder of Jews but considered war crimes a matter to be dealt with after Hitler's defeat. The underground leadership in Warsaw was itself preoccupied with the eastern front, where Soviet forces had started to roll back German gains and were approaching Polish territory. Witold nearly laughed in shock. The men standing with him looked as though they had been punched. Their reports, the atrocities, *their lives*— dismissed with a shrug.[9]

Despite now knowing that his reports would likely be met with indifference, Witold continued to gather intelligence on Nazi crimes. What else could he do? With spirits so fragile, he worried the underground would fracture entirely.[10]

One inmate, Bernard Świerczyna, compiled a list of every

prisoner death and probable cause in the main camp. It contained 16,000 names. At the same time, Witold's intelligence-gathering operation began to reveal the full scale of the mass murder of the Jews. The Birkenau victims were never officially registered, so they based their estimate of 502,000 Jews gassed on the number of trains pulling into the camp. (The number was some way off the actual figure, at this time, of around 200,000.)[11]

Witold helped engineer a brazen escape to deliver the documents to Warsaw. His courier was Mieczysław Januszewski, a twenty-four-year-old naval officer who worked in the labor-assignment office. Mieczysław was joined by Otto Küsel, the friendly German kapo from the same office who helped underground agents switch work squads when required, and two other men.

On December 29, the escapees drove a horse-drawn cart loaded with furniture from the carpenters' workshop, ostensibly for delivery to an SS man's home nearby. The Germans found the cart abandoned, along with the prisoners' stripes. A note in one of the jackets implicated head kapo Bruno Brodniewicz in the escape. Witold admired the escapees' flair in doing so—Brodniewicz was subsequently sent to the penal block for interrogation.[12]

However, Witold's sense of satisfaction was short-lived because the SS immediately stepped up its efforts to stamp out resistance. Rumors spread that SS chief Maximilian Grabner's informers had finally uncovered a plot to seize the camp and that mass executions were imminent. They were all jittery that winter, listening to the screams emanating from the Gestapo office. Among those shot were the morgue worker Gienek Obojski, radio expert Zbigniew Ruszczyński, and the Birkenau cell leader Jan Karcz.

Witold ordered everyone to scale back their activities and to be wary of new arrivals in their squads. He began to think of escaping himself. *Perhaps,* he thought, *only he could persuade the Allies to attack Auschwitz.* The odds of success were as small as ever. There had been around 170 breakout attempts in 1942, and only a dozen or so had been successful, and Witold had played a hand in ten of those. But now he struggled to think of a workable scheme.[13]

One evening, Witold came upon a group of a dozen men,

Fugitives Mieczysław Januszewski, Jan Komski, Otto Küsel, Bolesław Kuczbara after the escape, with resistance members Andrzej Harat and his daughter Władysława, c. December 1942.

Prisoners constructing a new crematorium in Birkenau, c. 1943.

women, and children standing outside the main camp's crematorium. The main gassing operations had moved to Birkenau, where four new gas chambers were being built to increase the SS's killing capacity to more than 4,000 people per day. However, the morgue of the old crematorium was still used for executions of political prisoners or Jewish families caught locally.

It was cold, and the sun had set long ago. A small boy of perhaps ten, the same age as Witold's son, Andrzej, looked around expectantly. Then the gate to the crematorium opened, and he and the others disappeared inside. Witold lay awake that night thinking of the boy and was overwhelmed with guilt. For all his talk of uprisings, he'd failed to act on behalf of a single child.[14]

His shame was underscored by the fact that the treatment of prisoners in the main camp had actually improved a little. The Nazi leadership, facing massive labor shortages, now sought to employ camp inmates in war production. Dozens of small factories and satellite camps sprang up around Oświęcim, and prisoners in the main camp served in an increasing number of administrative jobs.

Bathrooms were installed on the blocks, and morning roll call was abolished—prisoners now had time to wash and shave. Because of uniform shortages, many began wearing civilian clothes with only a red stripe painted on the arm or back to mark their status. Commandant Höss even issued an instruction to stop mistreating inmates. The kapos still used their clubs, but it was almost as if they did so to remind anyone watching that they were still in a concentration camp. Witold thought the inmates marching to work each morning in suits and blazers looked like office workers.[15]

Portrait of Witold, drawn by Stanisław Gutkiewicz, c. early 1942.

He feared he was becoming inured to the suffering around him, but the camp had not lost its capacity to shock. In early February 1943, Witold's colleagues in the tannery came across piles of clothes that unmistakably belonged to Polish peasants: clogs, farmers' smocks, and a few simple rosaries. The news was confirmed that evening: A transport of Poles had arrived from the Zamość district in eastern Poland, and half of them had gone straight to the gas chamber. It was one of the first times that ethnic Poles had been treated to the same extermination process as Jewish people, and Witold must have wondered if he and the other Polish prisoners were about to face the same fate.[16]

Thirty-nine boys from the Zamość transport were separated from their families and brought to the hospital on February 23, where they were stripped and put in the washroom. Several of the children guessed they were going to die and started crying. The hospital orderlies gathered around them. They brought soup and sang songs, and the children quieted down.

One of the nurses, Stanisław Głowa, began to weep. "So we're going to die," one of the older boys said. A few hours later, two men injected the children with phenol. The hospital echoed with the cries of "Mummy, Daddy, help me!" and "Dear Jesus, why do we have to die?"[17]

"We had already seen many mountains of corpses in the camp," recalled Witold, "but this one . . . made an impression on us, on even the old inmates." A week later, eighty more Polish boys were injected.[18]

Witold had to get out. But how?

"Blasted world," Witold was muttering to himself one afternoon in the parcel office when a young prisoner, Edmund

Zabawski, interrupted him. They fell into conversation, with Edmund doing most of the talking. Witold liked the earnest young man. Over the course of several conversations, Edmund revealed that one of his friends was planning to escape from a bakery outside the camp.[19]

Witold knew Edmund's friend by sight: a six-foot-four primary-school teacher called Jan Redzej who'd arrived in Auschwitz at the same time as Witold. Jan worked in the squad that delivered bread around the camp. Edmund arranged for them to meet. It was drizzling that night, and Jan's balding pate glistened in the rain. He flashed them a grin as they arrived in the square and let Witold in on his plan.[20]

The bakery where Jan collected bread was in the perfect place for an escape: a mile from the camp and in sight of open fields. Prisoners operated the ovens around the clock. Jan hoped to join the night shift—he had already befriended the baking kapo—to then slip away under the cover of darkness. Edmund had suggested he then hide at his family's home in Bochnia, sixty miles away from the camp.

The obstacles to simply exiting the bakery were formidable. The guards locked and double-bolted the door during working hours, and it was also latched from the outside by the departing shift. There were no other entrances, and all the windows were barred.[21]

Jan thought it might be possible to steal a door key. One hung from a guard's belt at all times, but a copy was kept in a glass box. The problem was that even if they could acquire the second key and unlock the door, they'd still be stumped by the outer latch. That "damned latch" made the escape impossible, concluded Jan. Witold was encouraged and

Jan Redzej, c. 1941.

suggested that Jan switch to the baking unit and look at the problem more closely.[22]

A few days later, Jan reported that the latch rested on a hook that was bolted through the door and secured by a nut on the inside. If they could unscrew the nut, they would be able to free the latch. Jan had even made an imprint of the nut with a piece of dough, which Witold handed over to a metalworker friend to find him a wrench that would fit it. The key was trickier, but Jan managed to remove the copy from its box while the guards' backs were turned to make another dough imprint. Witold had a cast made, which Jan tried in the lock. It worked.[23]

The final details came together. Civilian clothes were stashed in the bakery, as well as money and a pocketknife, plus tobacco to throw on their trail and put the dogs off their scent. Witold would also have to bribe the baking kapo into allowing him to join the unit; he arranged for apples, jam, honey, and a bottle of spirits, plus potassium cyanide capsules—suicide pills—in case things went wrong. As Witold had recently joined the camp's postal unit, he was concerned that changing to the baking unit might attract attention. Instead, he planned to feign sickness first to enter the hospital and then try to switch from there. He would have a window of only a few hours before his ruse was discovered.[24]

The Saturday of Easter weekend, April 24, 1943, dawned warm and clear. As soon as he arrived at his job at the parcel office, Witold began complaining of a headache. That afternoon, he stayed in his block and made sure the kapo overheard him talking about pains in his joints and calves—classic symptoms of typhus. The kapo ordered him to report to the hospital at once. The nurses gave him a few wry comments when he arrived at the hospital claiming to have typhus, pointing out that he'd already had the disease and was innoculated against it. But they didn't push.[25]

Edek helped register him without an inspection. The next day, Witold explained his plan and asked Edek to help arrange his release. "Edek, let's not beat about the bush," he said. "I'm getting out. Since you got me into the hospital avoiding the usual formalities and you're going to arrange for my release, who are they going to nab after I escape? You. Therefore, I suggest you join me."[26]

"I count on you, sir," said Edek, without even asking about the plan.[27]

Witold informed Jan of Edek's inclusion when he visited the hospital that afternoon. Jan grimaced. It was going to be hard enough to find a slot for Witold with the bakers, let alone one for a second person. Witold said he'd made the decision. "Well, that's that then," Jan said, shrugging. He slipped the baking kapo the alcohol, and then introduced him to Witold and Edek by calling them a pair of chumps who thought they'd have it easy on the unit. Jan promised to work them hard. The kapo, who had already had a glass or two, chuckled and gave his assent.[28]

A storm was approaching from the south as the men passed through the gate the next evening, April 26, on their way to the bakery. The sun was dipping beneath the clouds, and its orange light caught the letters of the sign ARBEIT MACHT FREI. The old crematorium chimney at the gate was smoking: thirty-three corpses had arrived that day for disposal. In Birkenau, the SS had recently completed two new crematoria and gas chambers. That evening the fires were being stoked for 2,700 Jews from Thessalonika, Greece.[29]

"Under no circumstances must I walk back through that gate again," thought Witold.[30]

THIRTEEN

They reached the bakery just as the sky opened and it began to rain. Three of the guards accompanying the bakery night shift had peeled off at the bridge leading into town, probably heading off for some holiday drinking. That left two SS men to supervise them.

The prisoners from the day shift emerged coated in flour and complaining about the downpour, and Witold and the other night-shift workers entered the building. A guard locked the heavy studded door after them, and they heard the latch being fitted from the outside.

The main bakery hall was a long rectangular room with a line of open-faced ovens at the far end. Witold's job was to mix dough in a large electric mixer and then shape the loaves onto baking trays. He was soon drenched in sweat and struggling to keep up.[1]

Edek shoveled coal into the oven for the first batch of

around 500 loaves and then cleaned out the oven for the next bake. Picking up a large plank with loaves, he let out a cry and fell to the floor, pretending to have hurt his back. Jan rushed over. "Don't worry—nothing happened to me," Edek whispered. "I'm pretending in order to avoid the hard work."[2]

A ginger-haired German, about Edek's age, approached. "How old are you?"[3]

"Seventeen," said Edek. He was actually twenty-one.

"How long have you been in here?"

"More than two years."

"And you are still alive?" The German took pity and told Edek to grab an empty flour bag and lie down in the corridor.

The plan had been to leave at around 10:00 P.M. Witold was about to signal to the others that it was time to make a move when Jan shot him a worried look. He'd spotted an off-duty SS man and his girlfriend through the window of a storeroom, taking shelter from the rain under the eaves of the roof. They would have to wait for the downpour to ease and the couple to leave.

The hours passed and with them their chances of escape diminished. It was close to midnight when the rain finally stopped and the lovers left. By then, there was only one more batch of bread to fire. It was now or never.

Witold and Jan left for the storage room, and when Edek joined them, Jan was already dressed in his civilian clothes and had retrieved the wrench from where he'd hidden it a few days before. On cue, Witold started to chop wood loudly as Jan slipped out of the room to go to the door, where he started to unscrew the nut that secured the outside latch.

Just then, the ginger-haired guard poked his head into the

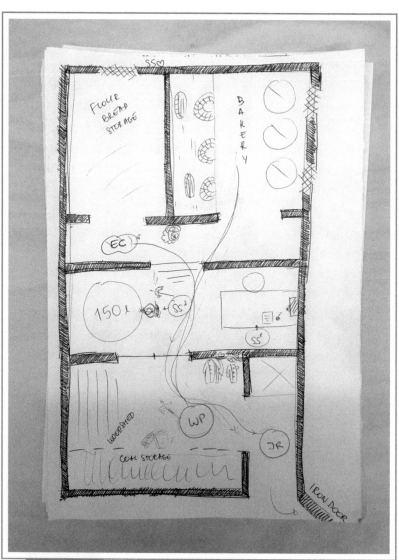

Map of bakery.

storage room. He took a look at Witold and Edek. "Where's the other one?" he asked.[4]

They froze. It seemed certain that Jan would be caught, but he had just enough time to dash into the toilet and drop his pants, which is where the SS man found him. "Oh, there you are," the guard said, still suspicious. He walked over to the door and turned his flashlight on to inspect it. Somehow, he failed to notice that Jan was in civvies or that the bolts were pulled back and the nut for the latch was missing.

As soon as they were able, Edek and Witold grabbed their clothes—there was no time to change—and joined Jan at the door. Jan now had the forged key in the lock. It wouldn't budge. He tried again and again and then threw his body against the door. Witold and Edek did the same. The door seemed to bend, and suddenly it flew open and cold air rushed in. Witold glimpsed the stars and then saw Jan disappearing toward the river. He and Edek tore after him.[5]

Shots rang out, but the three men didn't look back. After they had gone 200 yards, they were shielded by darkness, and they jogged in single file along the riverbank away from the town, pulling on their civilian pants and shirts as they went. Up ahead they heard the rattle of a train and then saw a line of lit carriages crossing the bridge over the river. How many had traveled in the opposite direction never to return? They saw the outline of a sentry box atop the railway embankment and dropped to the wet ground.[6]

Nothing was stirring. After a few minutes, they moved closer and closer until they were certain that the box was

empty. Witold set off across the bridge, the others close behind. To his right was the outline of Oświęcim's castle; an open field and the curving line of the river lay to his left.

They reached the other side of the bridge and dropped down the embankment to the muddy fields. Both the river and the tracks ran east, the direction they wanted. It was slow going along the bank, which was tangled with dead reeds and nettles damp from the rain. The riverbank smelled of wild garlic, and they caught a startling whiff of almonds from flowering stands of hagberries.

On the other side of the tracks, they saw the searchlights play around the chimneys of the vast IG Farben synthetic rubber factory, which was still under construction. Thousands of prisoners had died building it, and it was still not complete.

It took the best part of an hour before they were finally past the immense complex.[7]

By then they were almost ten miles from the camp, and the sky was starting to lighten. The river was broader now, and shrouded in early-morning mist. On the opposite bank, they could see trees that promised cover. "We could use a boat right around now," said Jan.[8]

As luck would have it, they came across a waterlogged vessel chained to a stake beside the bank. The chain was secured with a simple bolt. Jan produced his wrench—which fit!— and they scrambled aboard.

They had to wade through the last few yards of icy water after they hit a sandbar. Witold climbed up the opposite bank to find that a mile of open terrain separated them from the forest. Jan broke into an adrenaline-charged sprint, with Witold and Edek struggling after him. Jan reached the woods first.[9]

Witold and Edek lost sight of him until they were deep in the forest's shadow, when suddenly, Jan stepped out from behind a tree, arms outstretched, a big grin on his face. "Allow me the honor of welcoming you to the open forest!" he declared.[10]

They embraced him and planted kisses on his cheeks. Witold collapsed onto his back on a bed of moss and dried pine needles. The forest was alive with early-morning bird-song, trilling larks, and rude crows, yet what struck him most deeply was the silence, "a silence far from the roar of

Metków forest, where Witold, Jan, and Edek rested.

humanity . . . far from man's scheming . . . a silence in which there was not a living soul . . . what a contrast with the camp in which I felt I had spent a thousand years."[11]

Witold took a jar of honey and a teaspoon from his pocket and offered spoonfuls to Jan and Edek. "We were enchanted by everything," he recalled. "We were in love with the world . . . just not with its people."[12]

They skirted around villages for the next few days, occasionally knocking on doors for food or water, never stopping for long. The line of the Vistula brought them east, to the outskirts of Kraków. Then they left the river behind them and struck out for the Niepołomice forest. On the other side lay their destination, Bochnia, where they hoped to find Edmund's family waiting for them.

It was a warm spring morning, and they followed the curving forest road until it brought them to a forester's whitewashed house. Its green shutters were closed, and there were no signs of life. As they passed the yard, they saw a German soldier walking toward them with a rifle slung over his shoulder. Witold knew their shaved heads made them instantly recognizable as escaped prisoners. They kept moving, trying to keep calm, and had gone a dozen paces when the German shouted, "Halt!"

They walked on.[13]

"Halt!" he shouted again and cocked his rifle. Witold turned back toward him, smiling. "Everything's good," he said. A second soldier came out of the house.

"Boys, run for it!" Witold hissed. He hurdled fallen tree trunks and weaved between bushes, bullets whizzing past. Then he felt a sharp impact on his right shoulder. *Bastard*, he thought, but there was no pain, and he ran on. He could make out Edek sprinting to his left and called over to him once they were deep in the woods. They converged and finally stopped.[14]

Gunshots rang out in the distance. There was no sign of Jan. Edek inspected Witold's wound—the bullet had passed through his shoulder without touching the bone. He dressed it with iodine and bandages from a supply he'd brought from the camp. Three more holes had pierced Witold's trousers and jacket without striking flesh. He'd been unbelievably lucky. There seemed little chance of finding Jan in the forest, so they decided to make for Bochnia in the hope that he would too.[15]

They found Edmund's family home the next morning. His father-in-law, Józef Obora, was working in his garden and gave them a big grin when he saw them. This seemed odd until they ventured inside and found Jan stretched out on a bed in one of the rooms, unharmed and fast asleep, his feet sticking out from under the bedspread. They leaped on the bed to hug him and then spent a few happy hours catching up, eating, and getting to know the Oboras.

The conversation turned to the camp, and Witold grew restless. Despite his injury and his exhausted state, he insisted on meeting someone from the underground straight away.[16]

A couple of days later, an underground operative collected Witold, and they set off to the next town, Nowy Wiśnicz. Edek and Jan stayed behind to recuperate. At one point, as Witold and the operative paused in a forest glade in brilliant sunshine, Witold thought to ask the name of the commander he was going to meet.

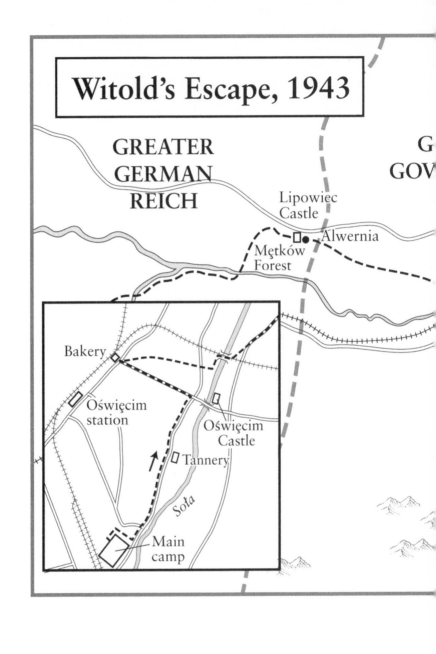

Witold's Escape, 1943

GREATER GERMAN REICH

G
GOV

Lipowiec Castle

Alwernia

Mętków Forest

Bakery

Oświęcim station

Oświęcim Castle

Tannery

Soła

Main camp

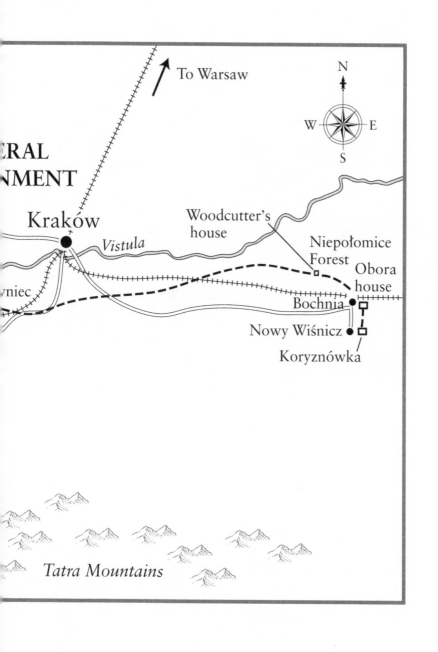

To Warsaw

N

W · E

S

ERAL
NMENT

Kraków

Vistula

Woodcutter's
house

Niepołomice
Forest

Obora
house

Bochnia

Nowy Wiśnicz

Koryznówka

niec

Tatra Mountains

Tomasz Serafiński, c. 1940.

"Tomasz Serafiński" was the reply. Tomasz Serafiński was the alias Witold had been using for the past three years. "Everything okay?" asked his guide on seeing Witold's reaction.[17]

"It's nothing. I'm just a bit tired," Witold replied. "Let's go a little faster."[18]

They crested a ridge and saw the old castle of Nowy Wiśnicz on the wooded hillside opposite and the little town spread out below it. Tomasz's home lay on the other side of the castle, his guide explained. The Gestapo operated out of a monastery nearby, so they would have to be careful.

Witold charged up the hill, convinced that some strange fate had brought him there. The house was a rustic-style

The room where Witold wrote his first report after escaping the camp.

small manor house made of wood, with cedar shingles on the roof and flowers around the porch. The land sloped down to a river, and there was an orchard and a barn beside a pool. Commander Serafiński's wife, Ludmiła, received them on the veranda at the back of the house.

"I'm here to give Tomasz his name back," Witold announced.[19]

Ludmiła played along when Witold introduced himself as Tomasz Serafiński to her slight, bookish husband. "But I'm also Tomasz Serafiński," said the other man, looking puzzled. He listened as Witold reeled off his own biographical details and then his Auschwitz number. "There was no knowing how anyone might react to this," recalled Witold. Tomasz

Jan, Witold, and Edek outside the Serafiński home.

simply opened his arms wide, a slight smile on his open face, and embraced him.[20]

Tomasz was an agricultural engineer and a gentleman farmer like Witold, who felt at home in his company and at his dining table overlooking the orchard. While they ate—fried rye dough was a family staple—Witold told Tomasz about the camp and the planned uprising.

He wouldn't need a large force to attack, he explained, just a modest diversion at the camp gates. Tomasz thought it was a wild proposal, but he agreed to present Witold's case to the local branch of the underground in Kraków. The Gestapo had infiltrated the group, and half its leaders were in jail or on the run. Those Tomasz met didn't believe Witold's story of escaping the camp and feared he was a German agent. They refused to help.[21]

Undeterred, Witold set about writing a new report for the underground in Warsaw. It gave a brief overview of the camp and a description of the underground's structure and organization. His point was clear: Auschwitz contained a force capable of staging an uprising. He demanded immediate action.[22]

Jan and Edek came to visit a week later, and Witold asked them to make a record of the crimes they had witnessed to include with his report. They'd all been shocked to realize how little the public knew of the atrocities the Germans were carrying out in Auschwitz.[23]

Witold decided to travel to Warsaw himself to lobby the underground to take action. Word had likely reached him of arrests among the leadership there also: The Gestapo had captured Rowecki at the end of June.

A few days before his departure in August, he received a letter from Stefan Bielecki. Witold tore it open, but there was no mention of an uprising. Instead, Stefan wrote that the underground headquarters in Warsaw were "very favorably disposed" to giving Witold a medal for his work. Witold threw the letter away in disgust. He didn't want a ribbon. He wanted action.[24]

FOURTEEN

When Witold returned to Warsaw on Monday, August 23, 1943, nearly three years after volunteering to enter Auschwitz, he found the city in the grip of a bloody guerrilla campaign. There was no doubt that the Germans were still in control, but following a devastating loss in Stalingrad at the start of the year and the Allied invasion of Italy in July, perhaps they would not be for much longer.[1]

Over a quiet dinner, Eleonora shared all the news she had of Maria and the children, who were living in Ostrów Mazowiecka. They were safe, but it was too risky for Witold to visit. A German official had commandeered the family home and forced Maria to move to the attic and work as his housekeeper. Maria came to Warsaw every few weeks to collect stationery supplies for a bookshop she helped run, and Eleonora gave Witold the address of the stationery store so he could leave his wife a message.[2]

In the meantime, Witold needed to convince the underground's new leader, General Tadeusz Komorowski, to authorize an attack on Auschwitz. Tightened security and a paranoid atmosphere made it difficult to arrange a meeting. Stefan Bielecki suggested that Witold come to work in the underground's operational wing, which carried out targeted killings and sabotage of German supply lines. That was the group most likely to plan any Auschwitz operation. But even meeting the wing's head, Karol Jabłoński, proved difficult. Witold needed to have his credentials checked and rechecked, with each message passing through a web of safe houses and couriers.

It was a frustrating time. Few seemed to even know there was an underground in Auschwitz capable of staging an uprising. Even fewer talked about the mass murder of Jews. Anti-Semitic articles continued to appear in the right-wing underground press, and gangs of blackmailers roamed the streets looking for any of the estimated 28,000 Jews in hiding. The Nazis offered high rewards for information and shot any Jews they caught, along with those families who sheltered them. At one stage, almost a tenth of the city—more than 90,000 Poles—were actively involved in the rescue effort.[3]

The underground also ran a significant relief operation, known as Żegota, to help Jewish families in hiding, but the leadership generally avoided confronting its own anti-Semitic elements in favor of preserving the sense of unity it felt would be needed to reclaim Poland's independence. There was nothing Witold could do but wait.

In the meantime, he was finally reunited with Maria. Instead of leaving her a message at the stationery store, he decided to surprise her in person. He bought a few presents for her: a navy blue dress patterned with flowers, a nightdress, and a bottle of perfume. For several days, he hung around the street, waiting for her to show up. At last, she came. How often had he imagined that moment? When they were finally in each other's arms, he didn't talk about the camp, or the war. For that moment, he tried to forget.[4]

The next morning, Witold wrote letters to his children, Andrzej and Zofia, for Maria to take home with her. She returned a couple of weeks later bearing Zofia's reply and a flower from her little garden. "It's nice to see you're such a good farmer," Witold wrote back. "And that you love the worm, beetle, pea or bean and everything that lives." He and Maria discussed bringing the children to Warsaw for a visit, but they both knew this was impossible, given the worsening violence.[5]

Witold was finally granted a meeting with Karol Jabłoński, the head of the underground's operational wing, on October 29. Witold made his case for ending the camp's horrors. He stressed that his men were primed for an uprising and that with a diversionary attack on the gates of Auschwitz, a sizable proportion of the prisoners could escape.[6]

Jabłoński assured Witold that he knew all about Auschwitz. "After the war I will show you how thick are the Auschwitz files in our archives," he said. "All yours are there too." Witold responded that the thickness of the files brought no relief to those in the camp.[7]

Jabłoński was definitive: There would be no attack on Auschwitz. The Germans were in retreat from the Soviets, and it seemed inevitable that they would be forced out of Poland. That was the moment for the underground to emerge from

Kochana Zosieńko!

Jestem bardzo rad z pierw-
-szego Twego listu do mnie.
Andrzejek też mógł by - po-
mimo chorej nóżki, list na-
pisać, bo przecie list się pisze
rączką, a nie nóżką - trzeba
tylko być więcej zdecydowa
nym, - no, ale jak przyszram
że on napisze do mnie na-
stępnym razem. Bardzo
się cieszę, że jesteś taką za-

A letter to Zofia from Witold, dated October 18, 1943.

hiding and declare Polish independence before the Russians arrived. They would need to conserve their forces until then.

Witold had no choice but to accept the underground's decision. Around that time, he learned that the majority of the Auschwitz underground leadership had been rounded up and shot. He was devastated by what he saw as his failure to persuade Warsaw to take action. He understood the practical objections to the mission that Jabłoński had raised but remained certain of the moral case for attacking the camp. After all, the imperative to face down such evil was what had kept his men fighting.[8]

Witold wanted people like Jabłoński to feel the righteous anger that he had felt upon arriving in the camp. But even his friends struggled to grasp what he told them, shutting him down or changing the subject, or worse, trying to commiserate with him. He didn't want anyone's pity.[9]

He found it difficult to connect with people now. Their ideas seemed so small to him. "I can no longer relate to my friends or other people," he wrote later. "I didn't want to be different, but I was, after that hell." He sought out former prisoners—"People of Oświęcim," he called them. He didn't have to explain himself to them, and they didn't fuss over the small stuff either.

Sławek, his first mattress mate, had been released from the camp in 1941 and lived in the same building as Eleonora. He made good on his promise and prepared for Witold the dish he had dreamed of that first winter in the camp: potato blinis, fried in butter until they were toasted at the edges, topped with lashings of sour cream.[10]

It was around that time that Witold started work on a new

report about Auschwitz. For the first time, he told the story of his experience through his thoughts and impressions, and documented the moments of individual bravery he had witnessed. His hope was to connect the reader to the moral universe of the camp. "Perhaps some families can then find images of their loved ones in my story," he wrote in his introduction.[11]

He continued to work for the underground through the autumn and winter of 1943 and extracted some funding from headquarters to support former prisoners and their families. Among those he gave money to was Barbara Abramow-Newerley, whose husband, Igor, was in the camp. She needed the money to pay for care packages for Igor and to support several Jewish families that she knew who were in hiding. Barbara was herself Jewish, but she lived under her husband's Catholic name and guarded her secret carefully.[12]

Then one day that autumn, Barbara asked Witold over to her apartment. She was distraught. A week or so before, she explained, there had been a knock on the door—a man who claimed to be a friend of one of the Jews her husband, Igor, had rescued before his arrest. The man said he'd come to collect money on behalf of their mutual acquaintance. Barbara had given him some money, and he had left.

A few days later, he came back and said that Igor's friend was dead but that he still wanted more money. He was a Jew himself, he explained, and needed cash. He threatened to report her to the Gestapo if she didn't cough up. Barbara gave him what little she had, but he still wanted more and promised to come back.[13]

"Barbara, please calm down," Witold told her. "We will

take care of it. You will receive the money and then we will see." The blackmailer got his money, but that was the last time he showed up. His fate is not clear, but it seems that Witold arranged for his execution.[14]

The onset of winter brought a lull in German roundups and shootings, so Maria brought Andrzej and Zofia to Warsaw to visit their father. Witold was waiting for them at Eleonora's apartment. For the occasion, Eleonora had made molded red jellies, which she put in a bathtub filled with cold water to help them set.

It had been more than three years since Witold had last seen his children. Andrzej was eleven years old, tall and awkward. Zofia was one year younger, bright and pretty. They hugged. Andrzej had brought a small pop gun to show Witold and soon dashed outside to play Germans and Poles with Eleonora's son Marek. Zofia lingered. She thought her father looked thinner, older, and at one point she caught him looking pensive and fiddling with something in his pocket. When she asked him what it was, he pulled out a small crust of bread. He explained that he always kept one with him, just in case.[15]

The next morning, Witold took the children out early for a walk—to "teach them a few tricks," he said. He demonstrated how to use the reflection of a shop window to see if they were being followed, or to pretend to tie their shoelaces so they could survey the street. He presented it as a game, and it was, but the children knew he was being serious too.[16]

After the lull, the city swiftly returned to violence. The underground launched 87 attacks in December, forcing the Germans to barricade office buildings and keep off the streets unless armed or walking in groups. A giant puppet of Hitler was hung from the scaffolding of a building site in the center of town, to the delight of residents. The SS reprisals were typically bloody.[17]

Witold continued to work on his report. As his links to the camp frayed, his priorities shifted. In early 1944, he was introduced to Emil Fieldorf, head of the Warsaw underground's sabotage wing. Fieldorf was recruiting a resistance against the Soviets, who seemed likely to occupy Poland after Germany's downfall.

Around March of that year, Fieldorf approached Witold to join an anti-Soviet cell. Witold was reticent at first. He had just been reunited with his family. The Germans were on the verge of defeat, and on some level, he longed for peace. But he also knew his duty. Even had he wanted it, there was no going back to how life had been. He took the oath and swore in the name of God and Poland to fight to the death if need be.[18]

Shortly after, he met up with Maria and Eleonora in the little town of Legionowo, fifteen miles north of Warsaw, where some of Maria's relatives lived. They went for a picnic in the woods, near the Vistula. The sun was out, but it was still cold. Maria wore the navy dress with the floral print that Witold had bought her in Warsaw, and he had on a white shirt buttoned to the neck and a pair of baggy, woolen knickers. He didn't tell Maria about his new oath.

Someone had brought a camera, and Witold agreed for his and Maria's photo to be taken. When she got home to Ostrów Mazowiecka, she found a picture of their picnic in her blazer pocket. Somehow, Witold had developed the film and hidden the photo for her as a memento for when he was gone.[19]

Witold and Maria in Legionowo, c. May 1944.

FIFTEEN

n July 1944, Witold finished his tenth report on Auschwitz in four years, certain that most of his comrades from the camp were dead. The Germans had occupied Hungary that spring and were in the process of deporting half the country's 800,000 Jews to Auschwitz. Up to 5,000 were gassed each day, outstripping the capacity of the crematoria. Once again, the camp authorities were burning bodies in giant pyres.[1]

Finally, the Allies acknowledged the camp's significance. Two Slovak Jews, Rudolf Vrba and Alfred Wetzler, had escaped from Auschwitz in April 1944. Their report about the gas chambers in Birkenau and the impending destruction of Hungary's Jews captured the attention of Western leaders. Witold's reports had helped lay the groundwork for its acceptance.

Even so, the Allies still rejected a proposal to bomb the camp as being too difficult and too costly. Some Jewish groups suggested enlisting the Polish underground to attack the camp—the very strategy Witold had been advocating—but US officials judged that the Poles lacked the strength to mount an offensive.

Instead, the Allied leaders decided to focus on defeating the Germans. In the wake of the Allied landings on the beaches of Normandy in June and the Soviet advance on Poland in July, they believed the collapse of the Third Reich was imminent.[2]

Witold secured a meeting with the underground leadership on July 25 to present his report along with statements from Edek, Jan, and several of his couriers whom he had tracked down in Warsaw. Tadeusz Komorowski, the underground's leader, was too busy to meet and passed Witold off to a deputy, Jan Mazurkiewicz, who told him merely that he would get his chance to fight the Germans in the impending battle for Warsaw.[3]

Witold's report was for the history books now. He buried a copy in a friend's garden and prepared for battle. The Soviets were expected to reach the east bank of the Vistula and surround Warsaw any day. Stalin's intentions toward Poland had become clear to the other Allies. As Stalin saw it, Russia had borne the brunt of the war, and Russia should set the terms of the postwar settlement, which included having Poland as a client state.[4]

Komorowski was faced with the choice of surrendering to the Soviets or trying to seize the city in the hope of gaining the support of the other Allies. Timing was critical. They needed to wait until the Soviets were almost upon them and the Germans were on the point of fleeing. There might be only hours to secure the city before the Soviets entered. If they attacked too soon, they would have to take on a German garrison of 13,000 men with only enough supplies and ammunition for a few days of fighting.[5]

That July, German troops drifted back through Warsaw from the front, a steady flow of dirty and bedraggled men carrying their injured comrades. Crowds of Poles gathered in the heat on Jerozolimskie Avenue to watch. "It was an unforgettable spectacle," recalled one member of the underground, Stefan Korboński. "The July sun shed so much light on this procession of misery that one could see every hole in the uniforms, every stain on the bands, every spot of rust on the rifles."[6]

A few girls waved handkerchiefs and called out in mock sadness, "Goodbye, goodbye, we will never see you again!" Policemen who heard them did nothing to intervene. SS men and off-duty soldiers drank in the street, declaring to one passerby that they were "sick of this war!" German moving vans and trucks piled with furniture clogged the roads heading west. Rumors spread that surrender was imminent.[7]

Hitler declared that Warsaw would be held at all costs and dispatched 8,000 frontline troops and over 200 tanks to launch a counteroffensive against the Soviets. The city vibrated to distant artillery and mortar fire. In the confusion, Komorowski received flawed intelligence that the Soviets had swatted the Germans aside and that their arrival was imminent. He impulsively sent messengers across the city to rally the underground to rise up the next day, August 1. In fact, the Germans weren't fleeing at all and had fought the Red Army to a standstill.[8]

Witold awoke on August 1 to the sound of the fighting on the opposite bank of the Vistula. He had arranged to meet his fellow Auschwitz escaper Jan Redzej near Komorowski's headquarters at around midday. He hid his handgun and spare bullets under a light jacket and set off. The streets were full of would-be insurgents, their guns and supplies hidden under heavy coats or in bags.[9]

Witold and Jan were making their way through the rainy streets when the uprising began, at 5:00 P.M., with an explosion of gunfire. They cut through what remained of the ghetto, destroyed by the Germans the year before to quell an uprising by the remnants of Warsaw's Jewish community. They ducked for cover amid stacks of bricks as German gendarmes fired at them from a nearby police station. Then they made for a restaurant on nearby Twarda Street, ducking between doorways for cover from rooftop snipers. Bodies were strewn across the street.

At the restaurant, they found an officer, Major Leon Nowakowski, surrounded by staff. Witold didn't reveal his name and rank to Nowakowski, and the commander didn't ask too many questions. He told Witold and Jan to form a platoon.[10]

The fighting quieted as darkness fell. Hitler's troops in the city had been taken by surprise, and the center of Warsaw and the Old Town were largely in the hands of the insurgents, along with the districts of Czerniaków and Mokotów. But, contrary to Polish hopes, the Germans had not fled and they retained control of the police headquarters, governor's office, and key rail and road links over the Vistula.[11]

The local German commander didn't consider the uprising serious enough to divert troops from their counteroffensive against the Soviets; he left it to the SS to put down the revolt.

Himmler was informed of the "disturbances" at 5:30 P.M. His first act was to telephone the Sachsenhausen concentration camp, where the underground leader Stefan Rowecki had been held since his capture, and order his execution. Next, he informed Hitler. "The timing is unfortunate," admitted the Reichführer-SS, "but from a historical perspective what the Poles are doing is a blessing. After five or six weeks we shall leave. But by then Warsaw will be liquidated; and this city, which is the intellectual capital of a 16- to 17 million strong nation . . . will cease to exist."

That evening, Himmler announced that the city would be razed and that "every citizen of Warsaw is to be killed, including men, women, and children."[12]

The next morning, August 2, Witold and Jan joined a small group of men in the city center to hunt down snipers. It was slow work, but after several hours of sneaking around the roofs, they had killed them all. The underground radio was reporting, erroneously, that the Soviets were almost in the city, and people flooded ecstatically onto the streets. Polish flags appeared in windows, and the loudspeakers on street corners played the national anthem for the first time in nearly five years. The music soared above the crackle of explosions and gunfire.

Over the next few days, Witold succeeded in carving out a parcel of territory, but he suspected they'd made all the easy gains they were going to. The city's water supply had been shut off; they had little food; and, most worrying of all, they were running low on ammunition. He constructed a makeshift barricade to block the Germans.[13]

Elsewhere in the city, the underground consolidated its hold but at a great cost. A tenth of their force, 2,000 fighters, died without seriously denting the German garrison, which had lost 500 men. And still there was no sign of the Soviets.

Spirits remained high behind the hastily constructed barricades. Soup kitchens opened to feed civilians and off-duty rebels. "Morale is fantastic," Komorowski radioed London that night from the Old Town.[14]

The next day brought German Messerschmitt fighter planes, scouting for Soviet resistance. When they met none, a squadron of stukas roared in and

The Polish flag raised over one of the buildings Witold's men captured.

dropped several tons of incendiary bombs over the Old Town. Witold took the opportunity to attack the Germans holed up in the nearby district office. The skirmish ended with a grenade down the stairwell that killed a sergeant and injured two more men.[15]

They had just enough time to drag their casualties back to their base when they heard the cry of "Tanks!" Eighty panzers attacked Witold's barricade, indiscriminately shelling buildings as they advanced. The front of the building he was in took a direct hit, sending a fireball through the ground-floor rooms that miraculously failed to hurt anyone.[16]

Half a dozen men attacked the district office the next day, only to be repulsed again. Jan set off with some men to try to approach the building from the rear. A short while later, Witold was horrified to see Jan being half carried, half dragged back into the building, bleeding heavily from a gunshot wound and struggling to breathe. He died an hour later, and they buried him in a shallow grave in the courtyard.[17]

An underground sapper unit showed up in the afternoon with enough dynamite to blast the Germans out of the district office. They laid a charge on the ground floor and triggered an explosion that ripped through the building. A dozen or so Germans emerged from the rubble, three SS men among them. The leader of the group had shot himself rather than be captured. Witold's men threw his body out the window onto the street in disgust.[18]

The sappers had brought news of the fighting elsewhere. Rebels had attacked the Gęsiówka concentration camp to the north, freeing 348 Jewish prisoners. But German reprisals had begun, and they were brutal. In the western suburb of Wola, the SS went from apartment to apartment, shooting civilians. Within a few hours they'd killed 2,000 people, and within three days more than 40,000.[19]

Witold's men hunkered down for a week, returning fire only when they had to. Then, at around 4:00 P.M. on August 12, three tracked vehicles suddenly burst through the smoke. The first leveled its cannon toward the barricade and fired. The blast forced Witold back from the window.[20]

By the time he returned, a German force of Russian mercenaries was rushing the building. Witold shot at them, but that only drew the attention of a tank, which fired back at him. The percussive force of the explosion knocked him off his feet. A moment's quiet followed, broken by the sound of the building's door being kicked in.[21]

The best Witold and the others could do was fight a

rearguard action room by room. They managed to hold off the offensive until darkness fell and the assault finally eased, but by then, they were down to their last rounds of ammunition. Witold sent a runner to headquarters with a request for more. At around 2:00 A.M., the answer came back: Headquarters had nothing to spare, and they should abandon their position.[22]

Witold found refuge in the basement of an apartment block across the street, the only place safe from the threat of snipers. He tried to get some sleep even as the ground shook with distant explosions. Half the 40 fighters who'd joined him on the other side of the street were dead. At best, they'd managed to block the passage of tanks down one street for a few days. All around him the other surviving insurgents, mostly kids in outsize police and military outfits, dozed in the low light.

The next morning, Witold watched from the top of a pile of rubble as the Russian mercenaries occupied his old position. The Polish flags were torn down, and a loudspeaker was set up in one of the windows of a hotel. It crackled into life, and a voice in a Russian accent urged them, in Polish, to surrender. "We have food and water," the voice announced. "We won't harm you."[23]

Thousands of residents had taken refuge in the city center to escape the massacres taking place in the suburbs. As the weeks passed, food became ever more scarce, and large crowds gathered at makeshift wells to draw water. By early September, a month into the uprising, no one shouted encouragement to the insurgents anymore; they were more likely to snap at them. "You bandits, leave us alone," declared one woman.[24]

The underground held out for another three weeks, but one Polish-held neighborhood after another fell, and surrender appeared inevitable. There was a brief flurry of excitement in mid-September when Soviet forces finally routed the Germans from the eastern shore of the Vistula. A Soviet-trained force of around 1,600 Polish soldiers crossed the river by boat to link up with the rebels. But without Soviet air or artillery support, they were quickly beaten back. It seemed Stalin was content to let the Germans crush the Poles before he ordered his troops in.

Komorowski made a brief tour of the front line on September 22, the fifty-third day of the battle for Warsaw, and concluded that they couldn't hold out any longer. He finally agreed to a ceasefire.[25]

The uprising against the Germans, for which Witold had first planned in the heady days after the invasion in 1939, then had dreamed of for so long in Auschwitz, had finally ended in defeat. More than 130,000 people died in the fighting, most of them civilians. Of the 28,000 Jews hiding in the city, fewer than 5,000 survived. Warsaw lay in ruins.[26]

Tadeusz Komorowski shakes hands with the German commander Erich von dem Bach-Zelewski after signing the act of surrender, October 1944.

SIXTEEN

A long line of prisoners wound its way out of the shattered city, their destination a temporary transit camp in a former cable factory. Witold, a prisoner once again, was startled to see Eleonora in the crowd gathered at the entrance.

They managed to exchange a few words. Eleonora had been stuck outside the city during the uprising and was desperately searching for her son. Witold asked her to bring him civilian clothes in case he had a chance to escape.[1]

However, that very night he was loaded onto a train bound for a POW camp near Lamsdorf, in Silesia. The prisoners were greeted by a crowd of local Germans who yelled "Bandits!" and threw stones at them as they marched through the rain toward the camp. They were left in the yard overnight, and the next morning, they were robbed of their belongings and locked up in a concrete barracks without windows, mattresses, or bedding.[2]

Witold spent a week in the camp. Then he and the other officers were transferred by train to a facility in Murnau, southern Bavaria. Murnau's proximity to Switzerland meant that the Red Cross visited often, and the Germans treated it as a model camp. The prisoners, who numbered approximately 5,000, were well fed and had no work duties. During the day, they organized talks, lectures, and soccer games in the yard. In the evenings, they put on plays, for which the guards helped organize costumes, wigs, and makeup.[3]

The prisoners followed the final days of the war on several camp radios. In early October 1944, Soviet troops swept into Hungary and Slovakia and reached the borders of the Reich proper in East Prussia. In the West, American forces under General Dwight Eisenhower were briefly held up by a German counterattack in the Ardennes Forest over Christmas, but by January 1945, their progress resumed.

Then came the news the camp had been waiting for—and dreading. On January 17, 1945, Soviet-led forces captured Warsaw, and Stalin moved swiftly to install Polish Communists to head a new administration. The underground leadership realized that their organization was too weak to oppose the Soviet occupation and announced the dissolution of the secret army with the final order that while the struggle would continue, "each of us must be his own commander." The liberation of Auschwitz by Soviet forces on January 27 was scarcely mentioned in the press.

The commander of a Polish contingent in Italy, General Władysław Anders, called on Poles to oppose the Communist takeover and rally to him. The prisoners in Murnau debated whether to carry on the fight for Poland's freedom. Most wanted to put the war behind them and go home as soon as they were liberated.

In March 1945, American and British forces crossed the Rhine at multiple points. Cologne fell, followed by Frankfurt. Then, on April 29, the prisoners awoke to shots directly north of the camp. They assembled in the roll-call square to watch as an American reconnaissance plane circled overhead and tipped its wings. In the early afternoon, the prison's commander, Captain Oswald Pohl, ordered his men to stack their weapons and place white flags in the yard. He informed the prisoners that while he planned to surrender, a die-hard SS unit was on its way to liquidate the camp.[4]

The prisoners heard the crunch of three American tanks approaching from one direction—and the roar of half a dozen SS vehicles from the other. The SS reached the gates first, but the tanks were upon them immediately.

The Nazi officer in the lead car drew his gun and started shooting. The lead tank responded with its cannon, hitting the German and his driver. The prisoners ran to the fence to watch the battle but had to scatter when the bullets started flying. The SS fled, to cheers from the prisoners, who threw open the gate.

A tank pulled in, and the American gunner popped his head up out of his turret. "You guys are free," he said in Polish.[5]

Germany surrendered eight days later, on May 8, to jubilation in the camp. A few days after that, Komorowski, newly released from German custody, visited. He told them to stay where they were and await further instruction. As the days and weeks passed, many slipped away. Witold waited.[6]

It was July before one of General Anders's officers

appeared with orders for Witold and several dozen others to accompany him to Italy. They traveled first to the port of Ancona, where elements of Anders's II Corps, which had fought under British command during the Italian campaign, was stationed.

The British wanted to demobilize the force, which numbered 50,000. Anders angrily informed them that most of his men came from eastern Poland in the territory now incorporated into the Soviet Union and those who did return had been arrested by the new Communist regime.[7]

In Ancona, Witold met with the head of intelligence for II Corps and discussed with him the idea of creating an underground intelligence network in Poland. The intelligence chief told Witold that he would need approval from General Anders and instructed him to wait in Porto San Giorgio, a couple of hours south along the Adriatic coast, which served as an R&R post for the Poles.

Upon arrival in Porto San Giorgio, Witold was directed to a villa on the beach, where he quickly settled in. He joined the other Polish soldiers strolling on the sand and took off his shoes. The water was warm around his toes and the easterly breeze soft on his face.

Witold tried to savor the moment, but he was soon thinking of Auschwitz, the scenes rising unbidden and triggered by the smallest things: a face on the street, a turn of phrase. There was no way to free himself from the feelings that came up with the memories: anger, remorse, and guilt.

Finally, he got a pad of paper and started writing another report. This time, he was ready to give freer rein to his emotions. "So, I am to write down the driest of fact, which is what

The beach at Porto San Giorgio.

my friends want me to do," he wrote in the introduction. "Well, here I go . . . but we were not made of wood, let alone stone . . . though I often envied it; one still had a heart beating, sometimes in one's mouth."

He saw his experiences in a new light. He had judged his mission to be a failure by his original objectives to alert the world about the camp. But with the Soviet takeover of Poland, he felt that the story of resistance in the camp might inspire and instruct the country now. He hoped that those who read his report would take a moment to consider the "falsehood, the lies and self-interest" filling the country when compared to the sacrifice of his men in telling the truth.

He had few other duties that August and usually wrote in the cool, bright mornings. A soldier friend of his from Warsaw, Jan Mierzanowski, came down to visit. He recalled Witold emerging onto the beach in the afternoons with a stack of papers under his arms, each page marked with his looping script. For a few lira, the two men would rent a pedalo (Italian for "paddle boat"), a twin-hulled contraption. Jan took the oars as Witold read aloud from his papers.

Finally, in early September, Witold was summoned by Anders to Rome to discuss his proposals. Witold planned on operating in small circles of acquaintances. He wouldn't recruit anyone or even necessarily reveal his role. That way he could avoid directly implicating his friends while involving them in the cause.[8]

When he returned to Poland, he found a country in tumult. Soviet forces and the police patroled the streets during the day, but at night the last radical fringes of the underground emerged to attack Polish officials of the new Communist regime and burn police stations and cars. There were more than 500 assassinations a month across the country, and in some areas, a full-blown insurgency still raged.

Meanwhile, a public health crisis was brewing, and hunger was widespread. Soviet forces had requisitioned most of the harvest, and they impeded the work of an international relief agency distributing supplies. Desperate hordes ransacked shops and warehouses, looking for food or items to barter. Typhus and dysentery were endemic, and there were more than 250,000 cases of venereal disease, mostly as a result of rape by Soviet soldiers.[9]

Witold reached Warsaw in early December. Even in the winter cold, the stench of unburied bodies and open sewers and latrines was strong. Almost 70 percent of the city was rubble, and it had lost more than half its million residents during the war. A giant picture of Stalin hung near one of the damaged bridges.[10]

Witold tried to locate members of the anti-Soviet organization he'd joined before the uprising, but most were dead, arrested, or displaced. Indeed, the Soviet secret police and their Polish proxies had detained 40,000 former members of the underground since the end of the war and had deported most of them to the gulags of Siberia. Witold eventually tracked down an old recruit, Makary Sieradzki, who agreed to host him in his remarkably undamaged apartment on Pańska Street in the city center.[11]

Over the next few weeks, Witold turned the apartment into his operational headquarters. He acquired a typewriter on the black market to produce reports and found a carpenter to build him a secret compartment in the floor. He started reaching out to friends and acquaintances who'd taken jobs in various government ministries and gently pushed them for useful information. Intermittently, he wrote reports for General Anders that captured the dissonances of living under Soviet rule.[12]

Witold had returned thinking he would find a Soviet republic, but he was surprised to discover how much of Poland endured. Churches still opened their doors to the homeless; women's groups ran soup kitchens; and scout troops

Witold, c. 1946.

helped the soldiers clear away rubble. Witold felt his opposition to the regime softening.[13]

Predictably, his thoughts turned to Auschwitz. He bumped into a former block mate from the camp, Witold Różycki, on a tram that March, and the two men agreed to visit the camp in the hope of finding closure.

After its liberation in January 1945, Auschwitz was used to house German prisoners, but in March 1946, the Polish regime announced the camp would be turned into a permanent memorial. Thousands made the pilgrimage that spring. Some went in search of loved ones or to pay their respects to the dead. Others were former prisoners who wanted to see the place that still consumed their thoughts.

One of the blocks contained items salvaged from around the site. Its basement was divided into small alcoves: a pile of children's slippers in one, human hair in another, prosthetic limbs in a third. The fact that these items belonged to murdered Jews, who comprised the vast majority of the camp's victims, was not hidden, but because most of the visitors were ethnic Poles, the exhibitions foregrounded Polish suffering and were framed in Christian terms. The penal block was also open. Stacks of flowers and candles in jars were arranged at the base of the wall where so many of Witold's friends had been shot.[14]

The Nazis had blown up the gas chambers and crematoria in Birkenau in an attempt to hide their crimes, but the ruined structures were plainly discernible.

Witold observed the camp without comment. He'd come looking for answers but found none.[15]

He moved into a little apartment on Skrzetuskiego Street on the southern outskirts of Warsaw. The place was empty during the days, and he tapped away at his portable type-writer beside the window. Sometimes he headed into the town center to see Andrzej, whose scout troop was being bused from Ostrów Mazowiecka into the city on weekends to clear rubble. Witold didn't approach his son, choosing to watch him from a distance.

That Christmas saw a new level of terror as Stalin enjoined Polish Communists to break the remaining opposition to their rule ahead of elections scheduled for January 1947. Thousands of people were jailed and the officials of rival parties beaten up. The rigged elections saw the Communists and their allies capture 80 percent of the vote, and Poland effectively became a single-party dictatorship.[16]

Witold returned to his reports and the completion of his memoir. He still stuggled to make sense of his experience, and there is implicit in the tortured prose of this time a recognition that perhaps the horrors of the camp would never be comprehensible. Instead, he dwelt on what the camp had taught him on how to live this life as a free man.

"I have listened to many confessions of my friends before their deaths," he wrote toward the end of 1946. "They all

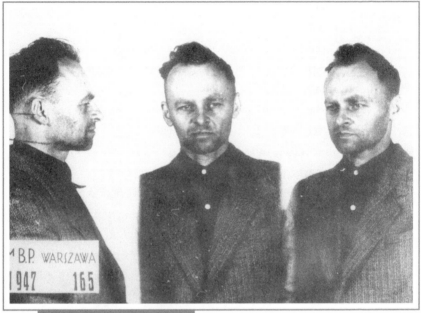

Witold's arrest photo, May 1947.

reacted in the same unexpected manner: they regretted they hadn't given enough to other people, of their hearts, of the truth . . . the only thing that remained after them on Earth, the only thing that was positive and had a lasting value, was what they could give of themselves to others."[17]

In May 1947, Witold was arrested by the Communist authorities after one of his men was betrayed. Between May and November 1947, he was interrogated and tortured more than 150 times. He told them the truth, he told them lies, he told them what he thought they wanted to hear. Then he signed what they told him to sign and was returned to his cell.

Government-run newspapers were filled with headlines declaring Witold to be the ringleader of the "Anders gang" and in the pay of Western imperialists. He was charged with treason and put on a show trial that was to be recorded and broadcast on the radio.[18]

During the subsequent trial, Maria and Eleonora were briefly allowed to approach him. Eleonora asked if they could do anything.[19]

"Auschwitz was just a game compared to this," he told them. "I'm very tired. I want a swift conclusion." On another occasion, Witold handed over a battered copy of Thomas á Kempis's *Imitation of Christ* that he'd been allowed in his cell and asked Maria to read it and share with the children. "No matter what page you open it on, simply read it and it will help you," he told her. His faith had not left him.[20]

On the final day of the trial, Witold was given an opportunity to respond. He rose slowly to his feet. "I tried to live my

Witold at court in 1948.

life in such a fashion," he told the courtroom, "so that in my last hour, I would rather be happy than fearful. I find happiness in knowing that the fight was worth it."[21]

He was sentenced to death. Some of Witold's former Auschwitz friends banded together to sign a petition to the Polish prime minister, Józef Cyrankiewicz, an ex-prisoner himself. They cited Witold's extraordinary work and patriotism. But Cyrankiewicz was unswayed, and the man who organized the petition was promptly fired from his job.[22]

Maria also wrote to the president, Bolesław Bierut, begging him on behalf of her children to spare Witold's life. "We have been living in hope for a peaceful life together with him for a long time," she pleaded. "We not only love him, but we worship him. He loves Poland and this love overshadowed all others."[23]

Bierut too upheld the verdict. Witold was collected from his cell on May 25, an hour after sunset, and brought to a small, single-story building on the prison grounds, where he was ordered to stand against the wall, facing it. Then the executioner raised his pistol and shot Witold Pilecki in the back of the head.[24]

EPILOGUE

The report that Witold wrote in Italy was brought to London by a former underground leader Tadeusz Pełczyński, and there was talk among Polish exiles of finding a publisher. But no one was interested. The public shock that followed the Allied liberation of the concentration and death camps in 1945 had faded, and it was the Cold War that now dominated political discussion.

The Communists also had no desire to turn Witold into a martyr and locked his writing away in the military archives. Witold had effectively been deleted from history.

His story remained hidden on both sides of the Iron Curtain until the 1960s, when Pełczyński agreed to share the report with the Polish historian and fellow exile Józef Garliński, whose 1975 book, *Fighting Auschwitz*, finally attested to Witold's role in the creation of the camp underground. When Communism collapsed in Poland in 1989 and the state archives in Warsaw were opened, academic Adam Cyra and Witold's son, Andrzej Pilecki, now sixty, gained access to a large leather briefcase containing Witold's report from

1943–1944, the memoir of his early life, additional notes, interrogation files, and the crucial key to his coded references. It was the first time the family had had a chance to read about Witold's mission in his own words.[1]

In 2000, Cyra published, in Polish, one of the first biographies of Witold based on the material and on new testimony from Eleonora, Wincenty, and Kon, who had all survived the war and lived to see the collapse of Communism. Cyra's book helped establish Witold's status as a national hero in Poland. But Witold's writings were not fully translated, and his story remained almost unknown in the West, where Auschwitz was better known for its central role in the Holocaust and as the setting for one of humankind's darkest acts.[2]

My hope is that this book will help us all finally hear

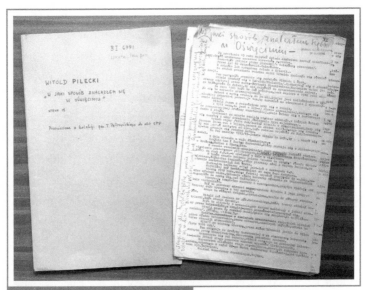

Witold's report written in Italy in 1945.

Witold's message. He became a prisoner in Auschwitz before the Germans understood what the camp would become. He witnessed the Holocaust firsthand as the camp was transformed into a death factory before his eyes. But he refused to look away from what he could not understand. He engaged, and in doing so, he felt compelled to risk his life and to act.

Witold's story demonstrates the courage needed to distinguish new evils from old, to name injustice, and to implicate ourselves in the plight of others. But I think it's important to observe that there were limits to how far Witold's empathy could reach. Witold never came to see the Holocaust as the defining act of World War II. He remained focused on the survival of his men and his country.

Nowadays, strong patriotism can seem outdated or worrisomely like the preserve of the far right. However, Witold was able to distinguish between love of country and nationalist rhetoric. The latter he saw as playing into the Nazis' hands. Patriotism, by contrast, gave him the sense of service and the moral compass necessary for sustaining his mission to the camp.

Ultimately, he couldn't save his comrades, or the Jews. He makes no apologies for that fact. Instead, he suggests in his final writings that we must come to understand our limits, even as he exhorts us to see past them. Above all, he asks us to trust one another.

Witold's defining quality was his ability to place his faith in other people. In the camp, where the SS sought to break the prisoners down and strip them of their humanity and their values, the idea of trust had revolutionary potential. So long as the prisoners could believe in the greater good, they were not defeated. Witold's men perished in many terrible and excruciating ways, but they did so with a dignity that Nazism failed to destroy.

Witold died believing his mission had failed. I've tried to show the opposite to be the case. Against the odds, he succeeded in forging a resistance cell in Auschwitz to report on Nazi crimes. It was the Allies who didn't heed his calls to take action. There are many reasons for this collective failure. But at its heart lies a basic human dilemma we can recognize today: Most people don't instinctively come to the rescue of others, especially when in danger or feeling threatened themselves. Witold reminds us, no matter how gruesome the subject, no matter how difficult our own circumstances, we must never stop trying to understand the plight of others.[3]

ACKNOWLEDGMENTS

This book would not have been possible without the support of Lisa Sandell and her brilliant team at Scholastic. Special thanks to Geoff Shandler at Custom House and Jamie Joseph at Ebury, who commissioned the adult version of the book and shared in my passion for telling Witold's story. The book was first conceived of with the help of my wonderful agents, Larry Weismann and Sascha Alper. I am grateful to Clare Alexander, my agent in the United Kingdom, for her support throughout my career.

Jacob Levenson edited (and reedited) each draft of the manuscript, never gave up correcting my prose, and helped me discover Witold's humanity. Liz Hudson did a marvelous job paring the story to its essence.

Marta Goljan led my research team and joined me in following Witold's footsteps from Krupa to the camp and beyond. She and Katarzyna Chiżyńska spent two years in Oświęcim tracking down and translating hundreds of prisoner accounts and memoirs. Along with Luiza Walczuk in Warsaw, they helped locate and interview dozens of camp survivors and their families, and in the process introduced me to the joys of Polish culture. I'm especially grateful to Katarzyna for her amazing work pulling this book together. Ingrid Pufahl was my fantastic researcher in Washington, DC, who invariably found answers to my many obscure requests. Many thanks also to the rest of the team: Hannah Wadle, Irina Radu, Alexandra Harrington, Karianne Hansen, Iga Bunalska, and Anna Łozińska and Paulina Wiśniewska and other members of the staff of the Pilecki Institute. Filip Wojciechowski offered his insights and many fine runs through Warsaw.

I am hugely grateful to Piotr Cywiński and Andrzej Kacorzyk for opening the doors to my research at the Auschwitz-Birkenau State Museum. Piotr Setkiewicz at the research department fielded my endless queries with good humor and offered his insights on each stage of the manuscript. Adam Cyra was my first guide to Witold's story and generously shared his own research and findings. Wojciech Płosa and Szymon Kowalski ensured I never got lost in the archives. Thanks also to Jerzy Dębski, Jacek Lachendro, Agnieszka Sieradzka, Anna Walczyk, Agnieszka Kita, Sylwia Wysińska, Halina Zdziebko, and Roman Zbrzeski. Mirosław Obstarczyk helped me see the camp through Witold's eyes. Special thanks to Krystyna Zatylna at the Polish Underground Study Trust in London for fielding many requests, and Jarek Garliński for first encouraging me to write the book. On behalf of my research team, I'd also like to thank Klaudia Kieperka from the Polish Institute and Sikorski Museum in London; Ron Coleman, Megan Lewis, and Rebecca Erbelding at the United States Holocaust Memorial Museum; Alla Kucherenko at Yad

Vashem; Dovid Reidel of the Kleinman Holocaust Education Center; Jacek Syngarski of Archivo Polonicum, Freiburg; Fabrizio Bensi of the International Committee of the Red Cross, Geneva; Gerhard Keiper of the Political Archive, German Federal Foreign Office; Carina Schmidt and Peter Haberkorn at Hessian State Archive; and Johannes Beermann of the Fritz-Bauer Institut in Frankfurt.

Over the course of my research, I have had the great privilege of getting to know Witold's family. The great warmth, generosity, and frankness of Andrzej Pilecki and Zofia Pilecka-Optułowicz gave me an early insight into their father's character. Andrzej joined me on several stages of the research, most memorably overnight in Alwernia's seventeenth-century Bernardine monastery, where Witold, Jan, and Edek had been well fed after their escape. When Andrzej couldn't be with us, he made sure we were properly taken care of. Marek Ostrowski has also become a dear friend and mentor. Special thanks also to Dorota Optułowicz-McQuaid, Beata Pilecka-Różycka for many fine cakes, Elżbieta Ostrowska, Tomasz Ostrowski, Edward Radwański, Lidia Parwa, Stanisław Tumielewicz, and Krysztof Kosior. David McQuaid helped me piece together some of the gaps in Witold's story and understand his connections to our own time.

I was also honored to interview those who knew Witold or shared in the struggle of those times: Kazimierz Piechowski, Bohdan Walasek, Jerzy Zakrzewski, Jerzy Bogusz, Janusz Walendzik, Mieczysław Gałuszka, Zofia Zużałek, Jacek and Ryszard Stupka, Józefa Handzlik, Anna Czernicka, Stefan Hahn, Mieczysław Mastalerz, Kazimierz Albin, and Zofia

Posmysz. I am indebted to the families of those connected to Witold's story for sharing their time, memories, and private papers: Maria and Szymon Świętorzecki, Marek and Barbara Popiel, Yaninka Salski, Jarosław Abramow-Newerly, Daniel Piechowski, Jan Tereszczenko, Piotr Woyna-Orlewicz, Ewa Biały, Adam Wojtasiak, Zofia Wiśniewska, Maria Serafińska-Domańska, Stanisław Domański, Jan Dembinski, Jan Jekiełek, Krystyna Klęczar, Wiesław Klęczar, Kazimierz Klęczar, Andrzej Molin, the Stupka family, the Kożusznik family, Krystyna Rybak, Robert Płotnicki, Jacek Dubois, Bożena Sławińska, Henryk Bleja, the Harat family, Beata Ciesielska-Mroziewicz, Felicjan Świerczyna, Piotr Wielopolski, the Mikusz family, Krzysztof Nahlik, Jan Chciuk-Celt, Stefan Pągowski, Tadeusz M. Płużański, Marta Orłowska, Wanda Janta, Ryszard Stagenalski, and Stanisław Mróz.

Thank you to the following for looking over various stages of the manuscript: Anthony Polonsky, Robert Jan van Pelt, Nikolaus Wachsmann, Dariusz Stola, David Engel, Bernard Wasserstein, Yehuda Bauer, Wojciech Kozłowski, Hanna Radziejowska, Rafał Brodacki, Jeffrey Bines, Staffan Thorsell, Wojciech Markert, Kate Brown, Magdalena Gawin, Anna Bikont, Francis Harris, Rufus and Cherry Fairweather, Adam Fairweather, and Suzannah Lipscomb.

I'd also like to thank the following for their insights and assistance: Mikołaj Kunicki, Krzysztof Szwagrzyk, Andrzej Kunert, Wojciech Frazik, Wiesław Jan Wysocki, Zygmunt Stanclik, Mieczysław Wójcik, Anna Początek, Jadwiga Kopeć, Olga Ivanova, Aliaksandr Paskievic, Leon Lauresh, Francois Guesnet, Wojciech Hałka, Małgorzata Zalewska,

Elżbieta Przybysz, Marek Księżarczyk, Piotr Cuber, Mirosław Ganobis, Artur Szyndler of the Auschwitz Jewish Center, Bolesław Opaliński, Krzysztof Kredens, Alfred Wolfsteiner, Annett Bresan of the Sorbian Cultural Archive in Bautzen, Melaney Moisan, Martin Lohman, Bob Body, Hedi Rosskamp, Rolph Walker, Joan and Tom Fitzgibbon, and Michal Teital.

I was assisted in re-creating Witold's escape route by Bogdan Wasztyl, Mirosław Krzyszkowski, Zbigniew Klima, and Marcin Dziubek of Auschwitz Memento, Piotr Grzegorzek on the banks of the Soła, Bolesław Opaliński in Alwernia, Zbigniew Kumala in the Niepołomice Forest, and Stanisław Kobiela in Bochnia. Special thanks to Ales Hitrun and Piotr Kubel for showing me Witold's home in Krupa; Łukasz Politański, the battle scene in Wolbórz; Jacek Szczepański and Jacek Iwaszkiewicz, the family holiday home in Legionowo; and George Dernowski and Maria Radożycka Paoletti, the glorious beach of Porto San Giorgio. Thanks also to Jacek Zięba-Jasiński, who introduced my brother Adam and me to the Tatra courier routes, for which we are grateful.

None of this would have been possible without my wife, Chrissy. She and my three wonderful daughters, Amelie, Marianna, and Tess, are a constant reminder of what Witold was fighting for.

CHARACTERS

Abramow-Newerly, Barbara (1908–1973)   Music teacher in Warsaw whom Witold saved from a blackmailer on account of her Jewish ancestry. Her husband, the writer Igor Abramow-Newerly, was imprisoned in Auschwitz, and Witold supplied funds to Barbara for his support.

Bischoff, Karl (1897–1950)   SS officer and architect who ran the camp's construction office, which was responsible for the building of Birkenau and its gas chambers. He escaped punishment after the war.

Ciesielski, Edward "Edek" (1922–1962)   Arrested as a high school student and sent to Auschwitz on April 1, 1941, Edek was recruited by Witold to the underground in the summer of 1941 and later escaped the camp with him. He was severely wounded in the Warsaw Uprising but survived, and later he wrote the first account of the underground. He died of a stroke before its publication in 1966.

Dering, Władysław (1903–1965)   Polish gynecologist whose arrest for underground activity in Warsaw and his dispatch to Auschwitz in June 1940 was a spur to Witold's mission. He was Witold's first recruit in the camp, and he used his position in the hospital to save prisoners. In May 1943, Dering, as well as other prisoner doctors, participated as a surgeon in the Nazis' experiments in sterilization using X-rays and chemical injections. He also participated as a surgeon in 115 castrations and hysterectomies of mostly Jewish victims. In 1944, Dering was transferred from the camp to work for one of the SS doctors responsible for the program, Carl Clauberg, in his private clinic in Königshütte, Silesia. In 1947, the Polish government opened an investigation against him as a potential war criminal, prompting Dering to flee to London. At a subsequent war crimes trial in 1948, he was cleared of the charge, which he had denied. Dering's case was the subject of further legal action in 1964, when he sued the author Leon Uris and his publisher William Kimber over a book that referred to a "Dr. Dehring" who had performed over 16,000 "sex operations in the camp." The judge subsequently ordered the publisher to pay Dering a halfpenny in damages, the smallest coin of the realm. Dering was also required to pay legal costs for the defense of £25,000.

Dubois, Stanisław "Stasiek" (1901–1942)   Polish politician and writer who entered the camp in September 1940 and worked alongside Witold gathering evidence of Nazi crimes in the camp. His reports on prisoner mortality in the camp in June and July 1942 contained the first data on the Holocaust in Auschwitz to reach Warsaw and London.

Entress, Friedrich (1914–1947)   SS doctor in the camp hospital from December 1941 who played a key role in selecting patients for phenol injections. He was arrested by US forces in 1945, convicted of war crimes, and executed in 1947.

Frank, Hans (1900–1946)   Governor of part of German-occupied Poland following the 1939 invasion. He was executed after standing trial for war crimes at Nuremberg.

Fritzsch, Karl (1903–1945)   Deputy commandant of Auschwitz who pioneered the use of the Zyklon B pesticide to gas inmates. He is believed to have died in Berlin.

Gawron, Wincenty (1908–1991)   Polish artist and wood engraver whom Witold recruited in the camp and engaged to pass on early warnings about the start of the Holocaust in Auschwitz. He later fought in the Warsaw Uprising before immigrating to the United States, where he worked as a carpenter and an engraver in Chicago.

Grabner, Maximilian (1905–1948)   The head of the camp's Gestapo unit tasked with eliminating underground members. He directed some of the first gassings of Jewish families in Auschwitz. In 1943, he was arrested as part of an SS investigation into corruption in the camp and subsequently sentenced to twelve years in prison for carrying out extrajudicial killings in the penal block (a bizarre charge, given the official mass murder of Jews in the camp). After the war, he was arrested by US forces and handed over to the Polish authorities to stand trial in 1947. He was executed in 1948.

Himmler, Heinrich (1900–1945)   German police chief and head of the SS who oversaw the concentration camp system. He visited Auschwitz in March 1941 to authorize its rapid expansion ahead of the invasion of the Soviet Union, and again in July 1942 to observe the selection and gassing of a transport of Dutch Jews. Committed suicide.

Höss, Rudolf (1900–1947)   Commandant of Auschwitz during Witold's time in the camp. Tried by Polish authorities in 1947 and hanged in Auschwitz in April of that year.

Jabłoński, Karol (1903–1953)   Polish officer and head of sabotage operations in Warsaw to whom Witold pitched the idea of attacking Auschwitz.

Jaster, Stanisław (1921–1943)   High school graduate who entered the camp in November 1940. He escaped the camp in an SS car in June 1942 and delivered to Warsaw a report from Witold about the mass murder of Jews in Birkenau. He was later executed by the underground for allegedly being an informer. He was exonerated after the war.

Karcz, Jan (1892–1943)   A cavalry officer who created an underground cell in Birkenau that reported on the mass murder of Jews in Birkenau.

Klehr, Josef (1904–1988)   Austrian cabinetmaker who served as a noncommissioned officer in the camp's hospital. He helped pioneer the use of phenol injections to kill patients. He was also employed in the so-called disinfection unit that worked in the gas chambers of Birkenau. Klehr initially escaped prosecution at the end of the war, but eventually stood trial in Frankfurt in 1963. The court convicted him of murder in 475 cases, assistance in the joint murder of at least 2,730 cases, and sentenced him to life imprisonment plus an additional fifteen years.

Komorowski, Tadeusz (1895–1966)   Polish officer who assumed military control of the underground following the arrest of Stefan Rowecki in

1943. Komorowski made the decision to launch the Warsaw Uprising.

Kożusznikowa, Władysława (1905–1976)   Housewife from the village of Przecieszyn, near the camp, who worked with Helena Płotnicka to deliver supplies to prisoners.

Krankemann, Ernst (1895–1941)   German barber sentenced to indefinite detention over spousal abuse claims in 1935. He was among the first kapos to arrive in Auschwitz, where he ran the penal company of Jews and priests. He was likely murdered by prisoners on a transport bound for gassing at a facility outside Dresden.

Küsel, Otto (1909–1984)   A German kapo in Auschwitz in charge of labor assignments. He saved Witold's life by offering him a stove-fitting job. He helped the underground switch between squads and tried to spare sick prisoners the worst jobs. He later joined one of the escapes in 1942 that smuggled Holocaust material out of the camp. Originally a drifter from Berlin, Otto was arrested by the German police for stealing and ended up in the concentration camp system. He was among the first kapos to arrive in the camp in May 1940. After the war, he was honored with Polish citizenship.

Obojski, Eugeniusz "Gienek" (1920–1943)   An apprentice cook in Warsaw before the war, he arrived in the first transport to Auschwitz in June 1940 and was put in charge of the hospital's morgue. He was one of Witold's first recruits and an important smuggler of medicine and supplies into the camp, including the underground's short-lived radio transmitter.

Obora, Józef (1888–1974?)   Polish businessman from Bochnia who sheltered Witold, Edek, and Jan after their escape from the camp.

Ostrowska, Eleonora (1909–2008)   Sister-in-law of Maria, Witold's wife, and Witold's point of contact in Warsaw during his time in Auschwitz. She hosted the inaugural meeting of the underground cell Tajna Armia Polska (the Secret Polish Army) in her apartment and was an active member of the underground throughout the war.

Palitzsch, Gerhard (1913–1944)   SS officer and the camp's executioner. His wife died of typhus in 1942. He raped at least one Jewish female prisoner and was transferred from the camp in 1943. He is thought to have died outside Budapest in 1944.

Piechowski, Kazimierz "Kazik" (1919–2017)   Polish student who entered Auschwitz as one of its first prisoners in June 1940. He escaped the camp dressed as an SS soldier in a German staff car in June 1942 with Eugeniusz Bendera, Józef Lempart, and Stanisław Jaster, who carried a report about the mass murder of Jews in Birkenau.

Piekarski, Konstanty "Kon" or "Kot" (1913–1990)   Polish engineering student and officer who arrived in Auschwitz on the same transport as Witold and was recruited by him into the underground in 1940. He helped Witold steal a radio transmitter from the SS construction office.

Pietrzykowski, Tadeusz "Teddy" (1917–1991)   Polish professional boxer and early recruit of Witold's in the camp. He defeated the German kapo Walter Dunning in a boxing match. He later witnessed one of the first gassings of Jews in Auschwitz and used lice infected with typhus to attack SS officers and kapos.

Pilecki, Andrzej (born 1932)   Witold's son.

Pilecka, Maria (1906–2002)   Witold's wife.

Pilecka, Zofia (born 1933)   Witold's daughter.

Płotnicka, Helena (1902–1944)   Housewife from the village of Przecieszyn, near the camp, who worked with Władysława Kożusznikowa to deliver supplies to prisoners. She was later arrested and brought to Auschwitz, where she died of typhus.

Porębski, Henryk (1911–?)   Polish prisoner who worked in the camp as an electrician. He entered the camp in October 1940 and established the first links between the underground in the main camp and the Jewish squad that worked in the gas chambers of Birkenau.

Rawicz, Kazimierz (1896–1969)   Polish officer who entered the camp in January 1941 and united the underground's factions at Witold's request. In 1942, he devised a plan to stage an uprising to destroy the camp and enable a mass breakout.

Redzej, Jan (1904–1944)   Polish primary school teacher who entered the camp on the same transport as Witold and later conceived of the idea of escaping from the camp from an outside bakery. He died fighting alongside Witold in the Warsaw Uprising.

Romanowicz, Michał (?–1940)   A cavalry officer and an early recruit of Witold's who helped him switch work details and arranged the transmission of Witold's first report from the camp via Aleksander Wielopolski.

Rowecki, Stefan (1895–1944)   Polish officer and leader of the underground in Warsaw until his arrest in 1943. He conceived of Witold's original mission to Auschwitz.

Różycki, Witold (1906–?)   A Polish officer who entered the camp on the same transport as Witold. After the war, he accompanied him on a visit to Auschwitz.

Ruszczyński, Zbigniew (1914–1943)   Polish architect who entered the camp in 1941 and hatched the plan to steal a radio transmitter from the SS construction office.

Schwela, Siegfried (1905–1942)   SS doctor who worked in the camp's hospital from 1941. He was a pioneer of injecting patients with phenol and took part in early gas experiments. He was likely killed by prisoners using typhus-infected lice in 1942.

Serafiński, Tomasz (1902–1966)   Polish lawyer, agricultural engineer, and gentleman farmer whose identity card Witold used upon registering in the camp. After his escape from the camp, Witold stayed at Tomasz's home in Nowy Wiśnicz. Tomasz presented Witold's plan to attack the camp to the underground in Kraków but was rejected. Later, he was expelled from the organization for his support of Witold. He was arrested and interrogated by the SS in December 1943 in connection with Witold's escape but did not reveal what he knew.

Sieradzki, Makary (1900–1992)   Polish civil servant and underground member who sheltered Witold upon his return to Poland in 1945. He was later tried alongside Witold and sentenced to fifteen years in prison.

Sikorski, Władysław (1881–1943)   Polish general and former prime minister who became the leader of Poland's exile government in 1940.

Staller, Alois (1905–?)   A German kapo in Auschwitz who ran Witold's first block and selected him as a room supervisor. Staller was a former factory worker and Communist from the Rhineland. He had been arrested for putting up anti-Nazi posters in 1935 and detained indefinitely in the Sachsenhausen concentration camp a year later. He was indicted as a war criminal in 1963, but the case was dropped for lack of evidence.

Stupka, Helena (1898–1975)   Oświęcim resident who established the first links between inmates and the outside world.

Surmacki, Władysław (1888–1942)   A Polish officer and engineer whose arrest in Warsaw for underground work and his dispatch to Auschwitz in August 1940 prompted Witold's mission. In the camp, Surmacki worked as an inmate surveyor in the construction office and established the underground's first links with the outside world via Helena Stupka.

Świętorzecki, Karol (1908–1991)   Karol was an early recruit of Witold's in the camp. They arrived on the same transport and worked in the same block as room supervisors. Witold used Karol to distribute news around the camp that was gleaned from the underground's illegal radio monitoring. Karol served as a messenger for Witold upon his release from the camp in May 1941.

Szelągowska, Maria (1905–1989)   Polish chemist and underground worker. She helped Witold type up and edit his 1945 report. She later worked with him in Warsaw gathering intelligence and preparing reports for sending to the exile leader Władysław Anders. She was tried at the same time as Witold in 1948 and sentenced to death, later commuted to life imprisonment. She was released from prison in 1955.

Szpakowski, Sławomir "Sławek" (1908–?)   A postcard painter from Kielce who was arrested at the same time as Witold. The two men shared a mattress for their first few weeks in the camp and worked together on a demolition crew. He was released from the camp in 1941.

Trojnicki, Ferdynand (1895–?)   A Polish officer before the war and a member of Tajna Armia Polska, Ferdynand was an early recruit of Witold's who helped arrange a job for him in the carpentry unit. He was subsequently released from the camp in November 1941 and likely brought news of Soviet gas experiments and creation of the Birkenau camp to Warsaw.

Westrych, Wilhelm (1894–1943)   Ethnic German from Poland who worked as the kapo of the carpentry workshop in Auschwitz. He gave Witold a job on this squad and shielded him from other kapos.

Wielopolski, Aleksander (1910–1980)   Polish engineer and member of the so-called Musketeers underground cell. He was arrested during the same roundup as Witold and sent to the camp. He was released in October 1940 and carried Witold's first report about the camp.

Włodarkiewicz, Jan (1900–c. 1942)   Polish officer who fought as a partisan with Witold in the weeks after the German invasion. In November 1939, he and Witold formed the underground cell in Warsaw known as Tajna Armia Polska. He suggested Witold's name to the underground leadership for the mission to Auschwitz. He died in unknown circumstances in 1942 while running a sabotage and intelligence unit based in eastern Poland.

Zabawski, Edmund (1910–?)   Teacher from outside the town of Bochnia in southern Poland. He introduced Witold to his fellow escaper Jan Redzej and contacted his family on Witold's behalf to shelter them upon leaving the camp. He later passed on to the underground leadership Witold's plans to attack the camp.

SELECT BIBLIOGRAPHY

LIST OF ABBREVIATIONS

AAN—Archiwum Akt Nowych

AN—Archiwum Narodowe w Krakowie

APMA–B—Archiwum Państwowego Muzeum Auschwitz–Birkenau

ASS MON—Archiwum Służby Sprawiedliwości Ministerstwa Obrony Narodowej

AZHRL—Archiwum Zakładu Historii Ruchu Ludowego

BA—Bundesarchiv

CAW—Centralne Archiwum Wojskowe

DGFP—Deutsche Gesellschaft für Personalführung

FBI—Fritz Bauer Institut

HHStAW—Hessisches Staatsarchiv Wiesbaden

HIA—Hoover Institution Archives

IP—Instytut Pileckiego

IPN—Instytut Pamięci Narodowej

LHCMA—Liddell Hart Centre for Military Archives, King's College London

NA—The National Archives in London

NARS—National Archives and Records Service

NRW—Archive in Nordrhein-Westfalen

PAN—Polska Akademia Nauk

PISM—The Polish Institute and Sikorski Museum

PMA-B—Państwowe Muzeum Auschwitz–Birkenau

PUMST—The Polish Underground Movement Study Trust / SPP— Studium Polski Podziemnej

TOnO—Towarzystwo Opieki nad Oświęcimiem

UOP—Urząd Ochrony Państwa

USHMM—United States Holocaust Memorial Museum

WFD—Wytwórnia Filmów Dokumentalnych

WIH—Wojskowy Instytut Historyczny

YVA—Yad Vashem Archives

ŻIH—Żydowski Instytut Historyczny

Abramow-Newerly, Jarosław. Interview, October 2, 2017.

———. *Lwy mojego podwórka*. Warszawa: Rosner & Wspólnicy, 2002.

Albin, Kazimierz. Interview, May 21, 2016.

———. *List gończy. Historia mojej ucieczki z Oświęcimia i działalności w konspiracji*. Warszawa: PMA-B. Książka i Wiedza, 1996.

Allen, Arthur. *The Fantastic Laboratory of Dr. Weigl: How Two Brave Scientists Battled Typhus and Sabotaged the Nazis*. New York: W. W. Norton & Company, 2014.

Applebaum, Anne. *Iron Curtain: The Crushing of Eastern Europe, 1944– 1956*. London: Penguin Books, 2012.

Banach, Ludwik. [Testimony], Proces załogi esesmańskiej, vol. 55, PMA-B, pp. 102–103.

Bartosiewicz, Henryk. [Interview] September 14, 1970, Stagenhoe. Ossolineum. 87/00, archive of Józef Garliński.

Bartosiewicz, Henryk. Oświadczenia, vol. 84, APMA-B, pp. 117–138.

Bartosik, Igor; Martyniak, Łukasz; Setkiewicz, Piotr. *Wstęp*, in: idem. *Początki obozu Birkenau w świetle materiałów źródłowych*. Oświęcim, PMA-B, 2017.

Bartoszewski, Władysław. *Mój Auschwitz: rozmowę przeprowadzili Piotra M. A. Cywiński i Marek Zając*. Kraków: Znak, 2010.

————. *1859 dni Warszawy*. Kraków: Znak, 2008.

Bartoszewski, Władysław; Komar, Michał. *Wywiad rzeka*. Warszawa: Świat Książki, 2006.

Bartys, Czesław. Oświadczenia, vol. 63, APMA-B, pp. 132–138.

Bednorz, Róża. *Lamsdorf Łambinowice. Zbrodnie cierpienia pamięć*. Katowice: Muzeum Martyrologii i Walki Jeńców Wojennych w Łambinowicach, 1981.

Bernacka, Monika. "Otto Küsel. Green Triangle. On the 100th Anniversary of his Birth." *Oś*, 2009/5, pp. 8–9.

Białas, Stanisław. Oświadczenia, APMA-B, vol. 94, pp. 23–26.

Bielecki, Jerzy. *Kto ratuje jedno życie . . . Opowieść o miłości i ucieczce z Obozu Zagłady*. Oświęcim: Chrześcijańskie Stowarzyszenie Rodzin Oświęcimskich, 1999.

Bidakowski, Kazimierz; Wójcik, Tadeusz (eds.), *Pamiętniki lekarzy*. Warszawa: Czytelnik, 1964.

Biernacki, Edward. [List], Materiały Ruchu Oporu, vols. 1–2, APMA-B, p. 10.

Bikont, Anna. *The Crime and the Silence: Confronting the Massacre of Jews in Wartime Jedwabne*. Translated by Alissa Valles. New York: Farrar, Straus and Giroux, 2015.

Blum, Aleksander *O broń i orły narodowe*. Pruszków: Ajaks, 1997.

Bogusz, Jerzy. Interview, December 19, 2015.

Breitman, Richard. *Official Secrets: What the Nazis Planned, What the British and Americans Knew*. London: Allen Lane, 1998.

Breitman, Richard; Laqueur, Walter. *Breaking the Silence*. New York: Simon & Schuster, 1987.

Breitman, Richard; Lichtman, Allan J. *FDR and the Jews*. Cambridge: Harvard University Press, 2014.

Brochwicz-Lewiński, Zbigniew. [Raport], CAW, I.302.4. 466.

Brown, Kate. *A Biography of No Place: From Ethnic Borderland to Soviet Heartland*. Cambridge: Harvard University Press, 2009.

Bryan, Julien. *Warsaw: 1939 Siege*. New York: International Film Foundation, 1959.

Brzoza, Czesław; Sowa, Andrzej Leon. *Historia Polski 1918–1845*. Kraków: Wydawnictwo Literackie, 2009.

Butterly, John R.; Shepherd, Jack. *Hunger: The Biology and Politics of Starvation*. Hanover: Dartmouth College Press, 2010.

Carter, John Franklin. [Report on Poland and Lithuania], NARS, RG 59, 800.20211/924.

Chrościcki, Tadeusz Lucjan. Oświadczenia, vol. 11, APMA-B, pp. 1–11.

Ciesielski, Edward. [Raport 1943], AAN, 202/ XVIII/1, pp. 1–91.

Ciesielski, Edward. *Wspomnienia oświęcimskie*. Kraków: Wydawnictwo Literackie, 1968.

Collingham, Lizzie. *The Taste of Empire. How Britain's Quest for Food Shaped the Modern World*. Rochester: Vintage Digital, 2017.

Cyra Adam. "Jeszcze raz o prof. Marianie Batce": http://cyra.wblogu .pl/tag/batko. May 16, 2011.

Cyra, Adam. "Dr Władysław Dering—pobyt w Auschwitz i więzieniu brytyjskim." *Biuletyn informacyjny AK*. 2015/2, pp. 73–79.

Cyra, Adam. *Rotmistrz Pilecki: Ochotnik do Auschwitz*. Warszawa: RM, 2014.

Czarnocka, Halina, and Andrzej Suchcitz (eds.). *Armia Krajowa w dokumentach 1939–1945*, vol. I, part 1–2. Warszawa: IPN, SPP, PISM, 2015.

Czech, Danuta. *Auschwitz Chronicle, 1939–1945*. New York: Henry Holt, 1997.

————. *Kalendarz wydarzeń w KL Auschwitz*. Oświęcim: PMA-B, 1992.

Davies, Norman. *Powstanie '44*. Kraków: Znak, 2004.

Dekel, Mikhal. [Browar Near Skater's Pond.] Courtesy of the author.

Dembiński, Stanisław. [Raport], December 28, 1940. Dokumentacja Oddziału VI Sztabu Naczelnego Wodza, 1940. PUMST, A. 680.

Dering, [Wspomnienia.] Material courtesy of Adam Cyra, pp. 1–200.

Dębski, Jerzy. *Oficerowie Wojska Polskiego w obozie koncentracyjnym Auschwitz 1940–1945. Słownik biograficzny*. Oświęcim: PMA-B, 2016.

Diem, Rudolf, "Ś.P. Kazimierz Jarzębowski." *Przegląd geodezyjny*. 1947/2, pp. 45–47.

Diem, Rudolf. Wspomnienia, vol. 172, APMA-B. pp. 1–235.

Dobrowolska, Anna. *The Auschwitz Photographer*. Warsaw: Anna Dobrowolska, 2015.

Drzazga, Alojzy. Oświadczenia, vol. 33, APMA-B, pp. 45–56.

Dwork, Debórah; van Pelt, Robert Jan. *Auschwitz*. New York: W. W. Norton & Company, 2002.

Engel, David. *In the Shadow of Auschwitz: The Polish Government-in-Exile and the Jews, 1939–1942*. Ann Arbor, MI: UMI Books on Demand, 2005.

Faliński, Sławomir. "Ideologia Konfederacji Narodu." *Przegląd Historyczny*, 1985/76 (1), pp. 57–76.

Favez, Jean-Claude. *The Red Cross and the Holocaust*. Translated by John Fletcher and Beryl Fletcher. Cambridge: Cambridge University Press, 1999.

Fejkiel, Władysław. *Więźniarski szpital w KL Auschwitz*. Oświęcim: PMA-B, 1994.

Fieldorf, Maria; Zachuta, Leszek. *Generał Fieldorf "Nil." Fakty, dokumenty, relacje*. Warszawa: Oficyna Wydawnicza RYTM, 1993.

Filip, Lucyna. *Żydzi w Oświęcimiu*. Oświęcim: Scientia, 2003.

JACK FAIRWEATHER

Fleming, Michael. *Auschwitz, the Allies and Censorship of the Holocaust.* Cambridge: Cambridge University Press, 2014.

Foot, M. R. D. *Six Faces of Courage: Secret Agents against Nazi Tyranny.* Barnsley: Leo Cooper, 2003.

Frank, Hans. *Extracts from Hans Frank's Diary.* "Thomas J. Dodd Papers." University of Connecticut, Storrs, November 10, 1939.

Frączek, Seweryn. Wspomnienia, vol. 66, APMA-B, pp. 162–165.

Garliński, Józef. *Fighting Auschwitz: The Resistance Movement in the Concentration Camp.* London: Orbis Books, 1994.

Gawron, Wincenty. *Ochotnik do Oświęcimia.* Oświęcim: Wydawnictwo Calvarianum, 1992.

———. Wspomnienia, vol. 48, APMA-B, pp. 1–331.

Gilbert, Martin. *Auschwitz and the Allies.* London: Vintage UK, 2001.

Gistedt, Elna. *Od operetki do tragedii. Ze wspomnień szwedzkiej gwiazdy operetki warszawskiej.* Translated by M. Olszańska. Warszawa: Czytelnik, 1982.

Gliński, Bogdan. Oświadczenia, vol. 95, APMA-B, pp. 63–90.

Głowa, Stanisław. Oświadczenia, vol. 108, APMA-B, pp. 1–103.

———. Wspomnienia, vol. 94, APMA-B, pp. 138–139.

Goebbels, Joseph. *The Goebbels Diaries, 1942–1943.* Translated by Louis P. Lochner. London: Penguin Books, 1984.

Gombrowicz, Witold. *Polish Memories.* New Haven: Yale University Press, 2011.

Gorzkowski, Kazimierz. *Kroniki Andrzeja. Zapiski z podziemia 1939–1941.* Warszawa: Wydawnictwo Naukowe PWN, 1989.

Gross, Jan T. *Polish Society Under German Occupation: the Generalgouvernement 1939–1944.* Princeton; Guilford: Princeton University Press, 1979.

Gutheil, Jorn-Erik. *Einer, muß überleben: Gespräche mit Auschwitzhäftlingen 40 Jahre danach.* Düsseldorf: Der Kleine Verlag, 1984.

Gutman, Israel; Krakowski, Shmuel. *Unequal Victims: Poles and Jews During World War Two*. New York: Holocaust Library, 1986.

Hackmann, Rüdiger; Süß, Winfried eds. *Hitler's Kommissare. Sondergewalten in der nationalsozialistischen Diktatur*. Göttingen: Wallstein Verlag, 2006.

Hahn, Stefan L. Interview, April 24, 2018; May 5, 2018.

Hałgas, Kazimierz. Oświadczenia, vol. 95, PMA-B, pp. 231–247.

Hałgas, Kazimierz. "Oddział chirurgiczny szpitala obozowego w Oświęcimiu w latach 1940–1941." *Przegląd Lekarski* 1971/1, pp. 48–54.

Hałko, Lech. *Kotwica herbem wybranym*. Warszawa: Askon, 1999.

Harat, Andrzej. *Działalność Armii Krajowej w Okręgu Śląskim we wspomnieniach porucznika Andrzeja Harata: działalność AK na terenie Libiąża*. Ewa Dęsoł-Gut and Ewa Kowalska (eds.). Libiąż: Urząd Miejski, 2016.

Hastings, Max. *Bomber Command*. London: Zenith Press, 2013.

Herbert, Ulrich. *Hitler's Foreign Workers: Enforced Foreign Labor in Germany Under the Third Reich*. Cambridge: Cambridge University Press, 1997.

Heuener, Jonathan. *Auschwitz, Poland, and the Politics of Commemoration, 1945–1979*. Athens: Ohio University Press, 2003.

Heydecker, Joe J. *Moja wojna. Zapiski i zdjęcia z sześciu lat w hitlerowskim Wehrmachcie*. Translated by Barbara Ostrowska. Warszawa: Świat Książki, 2009.

Hilberg, Raul. *The Destruction of the European Jews*. New Haven: Yale University Press, 1961.

Hill, Mavis Millicent; Williams, Leon Norman. *Auschwitz in England*. London: Panther, 1966.

Hodubski, Franciszek. Protokół przesłuchania świadka, Ostrów Mazowiecka. August 5, 1947, IPN Bl 407/63. K. 296/47, GK 264/63, SOŁ 63, pp. 0343–0344.

Hoess, (Höss) Rudolf. *Commandant of Auschwitz: The Autobiography of Rudolf Höss*. Translated by Constantine FitzGibbon. London: Phoenix, 2000.

————. *Death Dealer: The Memoirs of the SS Kommandant at Auschwitz.* Translated by Andrew Pollinger. Cambridge: Da Capo Press, 1996.

Iranek-Osmecki, Kazimierz. *Powołanie i przeznaczenie: wspomnienia oficera Komendy Głównej AK 1940–1944.* Warszawa: Państwowy Instytut Wydawniczy, 1998.

Iranek-Osmecki, Kazimierz; Zawadzki-Żenczykowski, Tadeusz et al. (ed.). *Armia Krajowa w dokumentach 1939–1945*, vols. I–VI. Wrocław-Warszawa-Kraków: Ossolineum, 1991–2015.

Iwaszko, Tadeusz; Kubica, Helena; Piper, Franciszek; Strzelecka, Irena; Strzelecki, Andrzej (eds.) *Auschwitz 1940–1945. Central Issues in the History of the Camp*, vol. I-V. Translated by William Brandt. Oświęcim: PMA-B, 2000.

Jagoda, Zenon, Stanisław Kłodziński, and Jan Masłowski. *Oświęcim nieznany.* Kraków: Wydawnictwo Literackie, 1981.

Jaworski, Czesław Wincenty. *Wspomnienia oświęcimskie.* Warszawa: Instytut Wydawniczy PAX, 1962.

Jekiełek, Wojciech. *W pobliżu Oświęcimia.* Warszawa: Ludowa Spółdzielnia Wydawnicza, 1966.

Jezierski, Alfons Sylwester. [Wspomnienia], CAW, I.302.4.466.

Kajtoch, Janina. Wspomnienia, vol. 27, APMA-B, pp. 1–149.

Kantyka, Jan; Kantyka, Sławomir. *Oddani sprawie. Szkice biograficzne więźniów politycznych KL Auschwitz-Birkenau*, vols. I–II. Katowice: Fundacja dla Wspierania Śląskiej Humanistyki. Zarząd Wojewódzki Towarzystwa Opieki nad Oświęcimiem, 1999.

Kielar, Wiesław. *Anus Mundi: Five Years in Auschwitz.* Translated by Susanne Flatauer. Harmondsworth: Penguin, 1982.

Kisielewicz, Danuta. *Oflag VIIA Murnau.* Opole: Centralne Muzeum Jeńców Wojennych w Łambinowicach-Opolu, 1990.

Klukowski, Zygmunt. *Diary from the Years of Occupation 1939–44.* Champaign: University of Illinois Press, 1993.

Kłodziński, Stanisław. "Dur wysypkowy w obozie Oświęcim I," *Przegląd Lekarski.* 1965/ 1, pp. 46–76.

————. "Pierwsza oświęcimska selekcja do gazu. Transport do 'sanatorium Dresden.'" *Przegląd Lekarski*, 1970/1, pp. 39–50.

————. "Pierwsze zagazowanie więźniów i jeńców radzieckich w obozie oświęcimskim." *Przegląd Lekarski*, 1972/1. pp. 80–94.

————. "Rola kryminalistów niemieckich w początkach obozu oświęcimskiego." *Przegląd Lekarski*, 1974/1, pp. 113–126.

Kobrzyński, Stefan. Wspomnienia, vol. 129, APMA-B, pp. 1–49.

Kochanski, Halik. *The Eagle Unbowed: Poland and the Poles in the Second World War*. Cambridge: Harvard University Press, 2014.

Komisja Historyczna. *Polskie siły zbrojne w drugiej wojnie światowej*, vol. 1, Instytut Historyczny im. gen. Sikorskiego, London, 1952.

Komski, Jan. Oświadczenia, vol. 71, APMA-B, pp. 57–78.

Korboński, Stefan, *Fighting Warsaw: The Story of the Polish Underground State, 1939–1945*. New York: Hippocrene Books, 2004.

Kowalczyk, August. *A Barbed Wire Refrain: An Adventure in the Shadow of the World*. Translated by Witold Zbirohowski-Kościa. Oświęcim: PMA-B, 2011.

Kowalski, Edward. Wspomnienia, vol. 96, APMA-B, pp. 158–265.

Kowalski, Stanisław. *Niezapomniana przeszłość: Haftling 4410 opowiada*. Oświęcim: PMA-B, 2001.

Kozłowiecki, Adam. *Ucisk i strapienie*, vol. I–II. Kraków: WAM, 1995.

Król, Henryk. Oświadczenia, vol. 76, PMA-B, pp. 191–210.

Kuciński, Dominik. *August Fieldorf "Nil."* Warszawa: Bollinari Publishing House, 2016.

Kuczbara, Janusz. [Grypsy], Materiały Ruchu Oporu, vol. X, PMA-B. p. 6, p. 9, p. 11.

Lacki, Stanisław. "Burza nad Nowogródczyzną. (Kronika)." *Ziemia Lidzka—Miesięcznik krajoznawczo-regionalny*, 1939/IV (7–8), pp. 229–30: http://pawet.net/files/zl_1939_7_8.pdf. September, 9, 2019.

Landau, Ludwik. *Kronika lat wojny i okupacji*, vols. I–III. Warszawa: PWN, 1962–1963.

Langbein, Herman. *People in Auschwitz*. Translated by Harry Zohn. Chapel Hill and London: University of North Carolina Press, 2004.

Laqueur, Walter. *The Terrible Secret: Suppression of the Truth about Hitler's Final Solution*. London: Penguin Books, 1982.

Lasik, Aleksander, Wacław Długoborski, Franciszek Piper, William Brand, et al. *Auschwitz 1940–1945: Central Issues in the History of the Camp*, vols. 1–5. Oświęcim: PMA-B, 2000.

Levi, Primo. *The Drowned and the Saved*. Translated by Raymond Rosenthal. New York: Simon & Schuster, 2017.

Lifton, Robert Jay. *The Nazi Doctors: Medical Killing and the Psychology of Genocide*. New York: Basic Books, 1988.

Lipstadt, Deborah E. *Beyond Belief: The American Press and the Coming of the Holocaust, 1933–1945*. New York: Touchstone, 1993.

Lukas, Richard C. *The Forgotten Holocaust: The Poles under German Occupation, 1939–1944*. New York: Hippocrene Books, 2013.

Łapian family. Interview, May, 15, 2017.

Ławski, Zenon. Wspomnienia, vol. 154/154a, APMA-B. pp. 1–393.

Machnowski, Jan. "Sprawa ppłk. Gilewicza." *Kultura*. Paryż, 1963/ 4, pp.125–130.

Malinowski, Kazimierz. *Tajna Armia Polska, Znak, Konfederacja Zbrojna: Zarys genezy, organizacji i działalności*. Warszawa: Instytut Wydawniczy Pax, 1986.

Manor, Alexander; Ganusovitch, Itzchak; Lando, Aba (eds.) *Book of Lida*, Irgun yotse Lida be–Yiśra'el u–V.a'ad ha–'ezrah li–Yehude Lida ba–Artsot ha–Berit, Tel Aviv: 1970.

Marczewska, Krystyna; Ważniewski, Władysław (eds.). *Zeszyty Oświęcimskie: numer specjalny (I) opracowany przez ZakładWe Historii Partii przy KC PZPR przy współpracy Państwowego Muzuem w Oświęcimiu*. Oświęcim: PMA-B, 1968.

Margolis, Arye (ed.) *Memorial Book of the Community of Ostrów Mazowiecka*. Tel Aviv: Association of Former Residents of Ostrów Mazowiecka, 1960.

Markert, Wojciech. *77. Pułk Strzelców Kowieńskich w latach 1918–1939.* Pruszków: Ajaks, 2003.

Marrus, Michael (ed.) *The Nazi Holocaust. Part 5: Public Opinion and Relations to Jews.* Berlin: De Gruyter, 1989.

Moczarski, Kazimierz. *Conversations with an Executioner: An Incredible 255-Day-Long Interview with the Man Who Destroyed the Warsaw Ghetto.* Englewood Cliffs, NJ: Prentice-Hall, 1981.

Molenda, Antoni; Władysław Plaskura (1905–1987). Biuletyn. *Towarzystwo Opieki nad Oświęcimiem,* Katowice 1995.

Motz, Eugeniusz. [Testimony.] August 28, 1971, Warszawa.

Müller, Filip. *Eyewitness Auschwitz: Three Years in the Gas Chambers.* Chicago: Ivan R. Dee, 1999.

Münch, Hans. *Analyse von Nahrungsmittelproben (1947).* Opracowania, vol. 19, PMA-B, pp. 5–47.

Nosal, Eugeniusz. Oświadczenia, vol. 106, APMA-B, pp. 29–30.

———. Oświadczenia, vol. 132, APMA-B, pp. 164–191.

Nowacki, Zygmunt. Wspomnienia, vol. 151, APMA-B, pp. 65–163.

Nowak, Jan. *Courier from Warsaw.* Detroit: Wayne State University Press, 1983.

O'Connor, Gary. *The Butcher of Poland: Hitler's Lawyer Hans Frank.* Staplehurst: Spellmount Publishers, 2014.

Ollier, Michael. E-mail. August 16, 2001.

Olson, Lynne; Cloud, Stanley. *For Your Freedom and Ours: The Kosciuszko Squadron—Forgotten Heroes of World War II.* Estbourne: Gardners Books, 2004.

Olson, Lynne. *Last Hope Island.* New York: Random House, 2017.

Olszowski, Jan. "Więźniarska kancelaria w obozie oświęcimskim." *Przegląd Lekarski.* 1982/1–2, pp. 182–187.

Orłowska, Marta. Interview. November 13, 2018.

Osęka, Piotr. "Zabawa pod barykadą." *Przekrój,* 2004/8 [no pages given].

Ostańkowicz, Czesław. *Ziemia parująca cyklonem*. Łódź: Wydawnictwo Łódzkie, 1967.

Ostrowska, Eleonora. [Wspomnienia 1], Warszawa 1981/1982. Material courtesy of Andrzej Ostrowski.

———. [Wspomnienia 2: Upadek powstania na Starym Mieście i okres popowstaniowy], Warszawa 1993, pp. 1–12. Material courtesy of Andrzej Ostrowski.

———. Wspomnienia, vol. 179, PMA-B, pp. 143–158.

Ostrowska, Joanna; Zaremba, Marcin. "Kobieca gehenna." *Polityka*, 2009/10, pp. 64–66.

Ostrowski, Marek. Interviews, March 9, 2016; May 1, 2016; October 10, 2017.

Paczuła, Tadeusz. Oświadczenia, vol. 108, APMA-B, p. 70–72.

Paczyńska, Irena, ed. *Grypsy z Konzentrationslager Auschwitz Józefa Cyrankiewicza i Stanisława Kłodzińskiego*. Kraków: Wydawnictwo UJ, 2013.

Paczyński, Józef. Oświadczenia, vol. 100, APMA-B, pp. 92–122.

Patricelli, Marco. *Ochotnik: O rotmistrzu Witoldzie Pileckim*. Translated by K. Żaboklicki. Kraków: Wydawnictwo Literackie, 2013.

Paulsson, Gunnar S. *Secret City: The Hidden Jews of Warsaw, 1940–1945*. New Haven: Yale University Press, 2013.

Pawlicki, Tadeusz (dir.) *Witold*. Studio A. Munka, 1990.

Pawłowski, Marek T.; Walczak, Małgorzata (dirs.) *Jaster. Tajemnica Hela*, Polski Instytut Sztuki Filmowej, 2014.

Piechowski, Kazimierz. *Byłem numerem . . . : historie z Auschwitz*. Warszawa: Wydawnictwo Sióstr Loretanek, 2003.

Piechowski, Kazimierz. Interview, October 14, 2016.

Piekarski, Konstanty. *Escaping Hell: The Story of a Polish Underground Officer in Auschwitz and Buchenwald*. Toronto: Dundum Press, 2009.

Pieńkowska, Janina. [Wspomnienia 1]. AAN, 2/2505/0/-/194,

Fundacja Archiwum Polski Podziemnej 1939–1945. Foundation of the Polish Undergroud Archives, 1939–1945.

Pietrzykowski, Tadeusz. Oświadczenia, vol. 88, APMA-B, pp. 1–38.

Pilecka, Maria. [Dzieje rodu Pileckich. Saga], Materiały, vol. 223c, APMA-B, pp. 1–116.

―――. [List do Bolesława Bieruta], date unknown, ASS MON, vol. 5, p. 194. In: Cyra, *Rotmistrz*.

Pilecka-Optułowicz, Zofia. Interviews, February 1, 2016; May 17, 2016; July 14, 2016.

Pilecki, Andrzej. Interviews, February 1, 2016; February 2, 2016; February 5, 2016; March 11, 2016; May 16, 2016; May 17, 2016; May 19, 2016; May 21, 2016; July 11, 2016. October 10, 2017; July 20, 2018.

Pilecki, Witold. Akta sprawy przeciwko Witoldowi Pileckiemu i innym. "Meldunek Nr 2", Materiały, vol. 223b, APMA-B. p. 555.

Pilecki, Witold. Akta sprawy przeciwko Witoldowi Pileckiemu i innym. Protokół przesłuchania Makarego Sieradzkiego, Materiały, vol. 223a, APMA-B, pp. 361–367.

Pilecki, Witold. Akta sprawy przeciwko Witoldowi Pileckiemu i innym. Protokół przesłuchania Marii Szelągowskiej, Materiały, vol. 223, APMA-B, pp. 154–191.

Pilecki, Witold. [Klucz do raportu W z 1943 roku], Wspomnienia, vol. 183, PMA-B, p. 79.

Pilecki, Witold. [List do córki], October 18, 1943, IPN: https://biogramy .ipn.gov.pl/bio/wszystkie-biogramy/rotmistrz-witold-pileck /pilecki-nieznany/listy/108383,List-do-corki-z-1943-r.html November 20, 2019.

Pilecki, Witold. [Pod Lidą], Materiały, vol. 223c, PMA-B, pp. 26–54.

Pilecki, Witold. [Raport—Nowy Wiśnicz], Wspomnienia, vol. 130, PMA-B, pp. 110–120.

Pilecki, Witold. [Raport 1945], PUMST, BI.874, pp. 1–104.

Pilecki, Witold. [Raport teren S], AAN, 202/XVIII/1, p. 8.

Pilecki, Witold. [Raport W]. AAN, 202/XVIII/1, pp. 64–87.

Pilecki, Witold. [Raport—Nowy Wiśnicz]. Wspomnienia, vol. 130, APMA-B, pp. 110–120.

Pilecki Witold. [W jaki sposób znalazłem się w Oświęcimiu], PUMST, BI 6991.

Pilecki, Witold. [Zamiast wstępu—słów kilka do przyjaciół moich tych, którzy byli stale na ziemi]. Materiały, vol. 223c, PMA-B, pp. 1–5.

Pilecki, Witold. [Życiorys], Materiały, vol. 223c, PMA-B. [no pages given.]

Pilecki, Witold. Akta sprawy przeciwko Witoldowi Pileckiemu i innym. [Tragedia kielecka], Materiały, vol. 223a, PMA-B, pp. 542–543.

Pilecki, Witold. Akta sprawy Witolda Pileckiego. Protokół rozprawy głównej, vol. 5, ASS MON, pp. 25–26. In: Cyra, *Rotmistrz*.

Pilecki, Witold. Akta sprawy Witolda Pileckiego, vol. 5, ASS MON, pp. 107–117. In: Cyra, *Rotmistrz*.

Pilecki, Witold. Akta sprawy Witolda Pileckiego. Zeznanie w śledztwie Witolda Pileckiego, ASS MON, vol. 1, p. 74. In: Cyra, *Rotmistrz*.

Pilecki, Witold. *Report W KL Auschwitz 1940–1943 by Captain Witold Pilecki.* Translated by Adam J. Koch. Melbourne: Andrzej Nowak with the Polish Association of Political Prisoners in Australia, 2013.

Pilecki, Witold. Wspomnienia, vol. 179, PMA-B, pp. 299–313.

Pilecki, Witold. Akta sprawy przeciwko Witoldowi Pileckiemu i innym. Protokół przesłuchania Tadeusza Sztrum de Sztrema, Materiały, vol. 223a, APMA-B, pp. 397–402.

Pilecki, Witold. Akta sprawy przeciwko Witoldowi Pileckiemu i innym. Protokół przesłuchania Witolda Pileckiego, Materiały, vol. 223, APMA-B, pp. 10–317.

Pilecki, Witold. Akta sprawy przeciwko Witoldowi Pileckiemu i innym. Protokół rozprawy głównej, Materiały, vol. 223b, APMA-B, pp. 659–692.

Pilecki, Witold. Akta sprawy przeciwko Witoldowi Pileckiemu i innym. Protokół rozprawy głównej. Spis adresów, Materiały, vol. 223b, APMA-B, pp. 639–642.

Pilecki, Witold. Akta sprawy przeciwko Witoldowi Pileckiemu i innym Tragedia Kielecka, Materiały, vol. 223a, APMA–B, pp. 542–543.

Pilecki, Andrzej; Krzyszkowski, Mirosław; Wasztyl, Bogdan. *Pilecki. Śladami mojego taty.* Kraków: Znak, 2015.

Pilecki, Witold. *The Auschwitz Volunteer: Beyond Bravery.* Translated by Jarek Garliński. Los Angeles: Aquila Polonica, 2014.

Piper, Franciszek, Teresa Świebocka, and Danuta Czech (eds.). *Auschwitz: Nazi Death Camp.* Oświęcim: PMA-B, 2009.

Płużański, Tadeusz M. *Obława na wyklętych. Polowanie bezpieki na Żołnierzy Wyklętych,* Zakrzewo: Replika, 2017.

Pogozhev, Andrey. *Escape from Auschwitz.* Barnsley: Pen & Sword Military, 2007.

Porębski, Henryk. Oświadczenia, vol. 102, APMA-B, pp. 27–28.

———. Oświadczenia, vol. 21, APMA-B, pp. 11–31.

———. Oświadczenia, vol. 22, APMA-B, pp. 59–60.

Ptakowski, Jerzy. *Oświęcim bez cenzury i bez legend.* London: Myśl Polska, 1985.

Puławski, Adam. *W obliczu zagłady. Rząd RP na uchodźstwie, Delegatura Rządy RP na Kraj, ZWZ-AK wobec deportacji Żydów do obozów zagłady (1941–1942).* Lublin: IPN, 2009.

Rablin, Andrzej. Oświadczenia, vol. 29, APMA-B, pp. 78–85.

Radlicki, Ignacy. *Kapo odpowiedział - Auschwitz. Wspomnienia adwokata z obozu koncentracyjnego.* Warszawa: Redakcja "Palestry," 2008.

Rawicz, Barbara. Interview, March 5, 2017.

Rawicz, Kazimierz. [List], August 8, 1956; [List], 1957; [List], August 8, 1957; [List], August 22, 1957; August 31, 1957; [List], September 23, 1957; [List], September 25, 1957; [List]. date unknown, 1957. [Manuscript in the private archives of Marek Popiel.]

Rawicz-Heliman, Kazimierz. [Pobyt w obozie w Oświęcimiu], pp. 1–64. [Manuscript in possession of Marek Popiel.]

———. [List do L. Serafińskiej], August 4, 1958. Materiały, vol. 220, PMA-B, pp. 167–168.

———. Oświaczenia, vol. 27, APMA-B, pp. 33–41.

———. Oświaczenia, vol. 27, APMA-B, pp. 41a–41h.

Redzej, Jan. [Raport 1943], AAN, 202/XVIII/1, pp. 33–47a.

Rees, Laurence. *Auschwitz: A New History.* New York, PublicAffairs, 2015.

Remlein, Janusz. [Wspomnienia]: https://www.1944.pl/archiwum -historii-mowionej/janusz-remlein,1137.html. November 11, 2018.

Richie, Alexandra. *Warsaw 1944: Hitler, Himmler, and the Warsaw Uprising.* New York: Farrar, Straus and Giroux, 2013.

Ringelblum, Emmanuel. *Notes from the Warsaw Ghetto.* San Franciso: Pickle Partners Publishing, 2015.

———. *Polish–Jewish Relations During the Second World War.* Evanston: Northwestern University Press, 1992.

Rostkowski, Jerzy. *Świat Muszkieterów. Zapomnij albo zgiń.* Warszawa Rebis, 2016.

Russell, Sharman. *Apt. Hunger: An Unnatural History.* New York: Basic Books, 2008.

Segieda, Napoleon. HIA. Stanislaw Mikolajczyk Papers. Box 28, Folder 7.

Serafiński, Tomasz. [Ucieczka skazanych], Nowy Wiśnicz 1965. Material courtesy of Maria Serafińska-Domańska.

Setkiewicz, Piotr. *Voices of Memory 6: The Auschwitz Crematoria and Gas Chambers.* Oświęcim: PMA-B, 2011.

————. "Pierwsi Żydzi w KL Auschwitz." *Zeszyty Oświęcimskie*, 2016/29, pp. 7–46.

————. "Zapomniany czyn Mariana Batko." *Pro Memoria*, 06.2002–01.2003/17–18, pp. 61–64.

————. *Z dziejów obozów IG Farben Werk Auschwitz 1941–1945.* Oświęcim: PMA-B, 2006.

————. *Zaopatrzenie materiałowe krematoriów i komór gazowych Auschwitz: koks, drewno, cyklon.* In: Setkiewicz, Piotr (ed.). *Studia nad dziejami obozów koncentracyjnych w okupowanej Polsce.* Oświęcim: PMA-B, 2011, pp. 46–74.

Siciński, Antoni. "Z psychopatologii więźniów funkcyjnych. Ernst Krankemann." *Przegląd Lekarski*, 1974/1, pp. 126–130.

Siedlecki, Janusz Nel. *Beyond Lost Dreams.* Lancaster: Carnegie Publishing, 1994.

Sierchuła, Rafał; Utracka, Katarzyna. "Historia oddziału WIG— rtm. Witolda Pileckiego." *Grot. Zeszyty Historyczne poświęcone historii wojska i walk o niepodległość*, 2015/39–40, pp. 213–223.

Słuchoński, Artur. [Wspomnienia], *Kroniki terroru*, IP, 019 Sluchonski_Artur_2_skan_AK: www.chroniclesofterror.pl. November 26, 2018.

Smoczyński, Juliusz. "Ostatnie dni Stanisława Dubois." *Kurier Polski* 25. February 3, 1980. [no pages given].

Smoleń, Kazimierz. "'Czarna giełda' w obozie." *Wolni ludzie*, 1948/3, p. 4.

Smoleń, Kazimierz, Danuta Czech, Tadeusz Iwaszko, Barbara Jarosz, Franciszek Piper, Irena Strzelecka, and Teresa Świebocka, eds. *KL Auschwitz Seen by SS.* Translated by Constantine FitzGibbon and Krystyna Michalik. Oświęcim: PMA–B, 2005.

Snyder, Timothy. *Black Earth: The Holocaust as History and Warning.* New York: Tim Duggan Books, 2016.

Sobański, Tomasz. *Ucieczki oświęcimskie.* Warszawa: Wydawnictwo MON, 1987.

Sobolewicz, Tadeusz. *But I Survived*. Oświęcim: PMA-B, 1998.

Stapf, Adam. Oświadczenia, vol. 29, APMA-B, pp. 86–94.

———. Oświadczenia, vol. 148, APMA-B, pp. 96–138.

———. Wspomnienia, vol. 110, APMA-B, pp. 75–105.

Stargardt, Nicholas. *The German War: A Nation under Arms, 1939–1945. Citizens and Soldiers*. New York: Basic Books, 2015.

Steinbacher, Sybille. *Auschwitz: A History*. Translated by Shaun Whiteside. London: Harper Perennial, 2006.

Stępień, Jan. Wspomnienia, vol. 179, APMA-B, pp. 176–177.

Stoves, Rolf O. G. *Die 1. Panzer—Division 1935–1945*. Dornheim: Podzun–Verlag, 1976.

Stranský, Karl. Oświadczenia, vol. 84, APMA-B, pp. 44–58.

Strzelecka, Irena. *Voices of Memory 3: Medical Crimes. The Hospitals in Auschwitz*. Oświęcim: PMA-B, 2008.

Stupka, Helena. Oświadczenia, vol. 68, APMA-B, pp. 124–132.

Stykowski, Jacek. Interview, September 12; September 24, 2018.

Syzdek, Włodzimierz. "W 45 rocznicę śmierci Stanisława Dubois. Był człowiekiem działania." *Za wolność i lud*, 22.08.1987/34, p. 5.

Szarbel, Dawid. [Zeznanie], IPN, BU_2188_14, pp. 110–113.

Szczepański, Marian. Video recollection, July 14, 1995. PMA-B, V—246.

Szmaglewska, Seweryna. *Smoke over Birkenau*. Translated by Jadwiga Rynas. Warszawa: Książka i Wiedza; Oświęcim: PMA-B, 2008.

Szpakowski, Ludomir. Interview, January 31, 2017.

Szpilman, Władysław. *The Pianist: The Extraordinary True Story of One Man's Survival in Warsaw, 1939–1945*. Translated by Anthea Bell. New York: Picador, 2000.

Szwajkowski, Kazimierz, [Zeznania], IPN, Oddziałowa Komisja Ścigania Zbrodni Przeciwko Narodowi Polskiemu, S/139/12/Zn, pp. 137–142.

Świebocki, Henryk, ed. *London Has Been Informed . . . : Reports by Auschwitz Escapees.* Oświęcim: PMA-B, 2002.

Świętorzecki, Karol. Interviews, February 14, 1970; February 14, 1972.

————. Oświadczenia, vol. 76, APMA-B, pp. 88–110.

————. Wspomnienia, vol. 86, APMA-B, pp. 232–237.

Tabeau, Jerzy. [Sprawozdanie]. In: *Zeszyty oświęcimskie, Raporty uciekinieerów z KL Auschwitz.* Oświęcim: PMA-B, 1991, pp. 77–130.

Taul, Roman. Oświadczenia, vol. 9, APMA-B, pp. 1264-1271.

————. Oświadczenia, vol. 9, APMA-B, pp. 1273-1285.

Tereszczenko, Jan B. Interview, November 1, 2016.

————. *Wspomnienia warszawiaka egocentrysty. "JA."* Warszawa: Muzeum Historyczne m. st. Warszawy, 2012.

Tomaszewski, Aleksander. Wspomnienia, vol. 66, PMA-B, pp. 107–114.

Tooze, Adam. *The Wages of Destruction: The Making and Breaking of the Nazi Economy.* London: Penguin, 2008.

Tracki, Krzysztof. *Młodość Witolda Pileckiego.* Warszawa: Wydawnictwo Sic!, 2014.

Tumielewicz, Józef. [Kronika.] Material courtesy of Stanisław Tumielewicz.

Unknown author. [Zasady konspiracji.] AAN, 2/2505/0/—/194— Fundacja Archiwum Polski Podziemnej 1939–1945. Foundation of the Polish Underground Archives, 1939–1945.

Urbanek, Jerzy. Oświadczenia, vol. 44, APMA-B, pp. 1–13.

Urbańczyk, Zygmunt. [Wspomnienia], vol. 54, APMA-B, p. 11–50.

Vrba, Rudolf. *I Cannot Forgive.* Vancouver: Regent College Publishing, 1997.

Wachsmann, Nikolas. *KL: A History of the Nazi Concentration Camps.* New York: Farrar, Straus and Giroux, 2016.

Walasek, Bohdan. Interview, May 19, 2016.

Walendzik, Janusz. Interview, October 12, 2016.

Westermann, Edward B. "The Royal Air Force and the Bombing of Auschwitz: First Deliberations, January 1941." *Holocaust and Genocide Studies*, 2001/15, pp. 70–85.

Wielopolski, Piotr. Interview, May 18, 2017.

Wierusz, Witold. Oświadczenia, vol. 77, APMA-B, pp. 13–37.

Wilkinson, Peter. *Foreign Fields: The Story of an SOE Operative.* Staplehurst: Spellmount Publishers, 2013.

Wilmot, Chester. [Notes on Interrogation of General Franz Halder]. Liddell Hart Papers. LHCMA, LH 15/15/150/2.

Wolny, Edward. Oświadczenia, vol. 33, APMA-B, pp. 25–26.

Wołosiuk, Bruno. *"Znałem rotmistrza Pileckiego."* Słowo Powszechne, 1980/49, pp. 19–26.

Wood, E. Tomas. *Karski: How One Man Tried to Stop the Holocaust.* Lubbock: Gihon River Press and Texas Tech University Press, 2014.

Wysocki, Wiesław Jan. *Rotmistrz Witold Pilecki 1901–1948.* Warszawa: Rytm, 2009.

Zabawski, Edmund. Wspomnienia, vol. 98, APMA-B, p. 83–103.

Zagórski, Wacław. *Seventy Days.* Translated by John Welsh. London: Panther Books, 1959.

Zakrzewski, Jerzy. Interview, October 17, 2016.

Zalc, Claire; Bruttman, Tal (eds.) *Microhistories of the Holocaust.* New York: Berghahn Books, 2016.

Zaremba, Marcin. *Wielka trwoga. Polska 1944–1947.* Kraków: Znak, 2012.

Zawadzki, Antoni. [Zeznania], IPN, Oddziałowa Komisja Ścigania Zbrodni Przeciwko Narodowi Polskiemu, S/139/12/Zn, pp. 124–128.

Zimmerman, Joshua D. *The Polish Underground and the Jews, 1939–1945.* Cambridge: Cambridge University Press, 2015.

Ziółkowski, Michał. *Byłem od początku w Auschwitz*. Gdańsk: Marpress, 2007.

Znak, [Deklaracja ideowa grupy "ZNAK"], AAN, 2/2505/0/-/194, pp. 2–3.

Znak, 1940/27, AN, 1925.

Лаўрэш, Леанід Лявонцьевіч. "Лідчына ў 1936–1939 гг. у люстэрку прэсы." *Лідскі летапісец*, 2014/66 (2), pp. 25–93.

Лаўрэш, Леанід Лявонцьевіч. "Яўрэі Ліды." *Маладосць*, 2016/4, pp. 141–154.

Лаўрэш, Леанід Лявонцьевіч. "13 траўня 1901 г. нарадзіўся Вітольд Пілецкі." *Лідскі Летапісец*, 2016/2 (74), pp. 15–19.

END NOTES

INTRODUCTION

1 Ostrowski, Interview, March 9, 2016; Ostrowska, [Wspomnienia 1], p. 5.

2 Ostrowski, Interview, March 9, 2016.

CHAPTER ONE

1 Pilecki, [Pod Lidą], Materiały, vol. 223c, APMA-B, p. 36; Dmytruk, "Z Novogo," cited in Brown, *A Biography*, loc. 954; Tumielewicz, [Kronika], p. 229; Lacki, "Burza," pp. 229–30; Pilecka, [Dzieje], vol. 223c, APMA-B, p. 104; Pilecki, [W jaki], PUMST, p. 8.

2 Kochanski, *The Eagle*, p. 57; Wilmot, [Notes], LHCMA, LH 15/15/150/2.

3 Kochanski, *The Eagle*, p. 57; Pilecki, [W jaki], PUMST, BI 6991, p. 8; Лаўрэш, "13 траўня," pp. 15–19; Лаўрэш, "Лідчына," p. 76; Brochowicz-Lewiński, [Raport], CAW, I.302.4. 466.

4 Pilecki, Interview, May 21, 2016.

5 Tracki, *Młodość*, p. 112; Pilecka, [Dzieje], Materiały, vol. 223c, APMA-B, pp. 94–96; Pilecki, [Życiorys], Materiały, vol. 223c, APMA-B, no pages given; Tracki, *Młodość*, pp. 178–79, p. 185; Cyra, *Rotmistrz*, p. 22.

6 AAN, 2/213/0/9/8498, and AAN, 2/213/0/9/8499; Pilecka-Optułowicz, Interview, July 14, 2016; Pilecki, Krzyszkowski, Wasztyl, *Pilecki*, p. 30; Pilecki, Interview, February 1, 2016; Pilecki, Krzyszkowski, Wasztyl, *Pilecki*, p. 30; Tracki, *Młodość*, p. 187, pp. 188–91.

7 Kochanski, *The Eagle*, pp. 30–32; Bikont, *The Crime*, pp. 11–26, Ringelblum, *Polish*, p. 11; Brzoza, Sowa, *Historia*, p. 135; Brown, *A Biography*, loc. 534; Лаўрэш, "Яўрэі," pp. 141–54; Лаўрэш, "Лідчына," p. 64; Gelman, *Jewish*, cited in Manor, Ganusovitch, Lando, *Book of Lida*, p. 83; Ярмонт, *В тени*, pp. 93–94, cited in Лаўрэш, "Лідчына," p. 76.

8 Pilecki, [W jaki], PUMST, BI 6991, p. 7; Pilecki, Interview, February 2, 2016; Gombrowicz, *Polish*, p. 32. Witold evicted a Jewish tenant who'd leased the estate's land in 1922. There is no evidence to suggest racial animus behind the incident. Pilecka, [Dzieje], Materiały, vol. 223c, APMA-B, pp. 15–18. Cooperatives in Poland had a role in boosting the economic interests of their communities, which often had an ethnic dimension.

9 Markert, *77*, p. 53; Pilecki, Interview, October 10, 2017; Pilecka-Optułowicz, Interview, May 17, 2016.

10 Pilecki, Interview, February 1, 2016, and October 10, 2017.

11 Pilecki, Interview, October 10, 2017.

12 Pilecki, Interview, May 21, 2017; Pilecki, [Pod Lidą], Materiały, vol. 223c, AP-MA-B, p. 26.

13 Pilecki, Interview, February 1, 2016. Komisja, *Polskie*, vol. 1, part 1, p. 191, p. 247; Kochanski, *The Eagle*, p. 46, pp. 55–57; Thomas, *German*, p. 8; Blum, *O broń*, pp. 20–41; Jezierski, [Wspomnienia], CAW, I.302.4.466; Stoves, *Die 1.*, p. 57.

14 Stoves, *Die 1.*, p. 57; Pilecki, [W jaki], PUMST, BI 6991, p. 8; Blum, *O broń*, pp. 20–41; Jezierski, [Wspomnienia], CAW, I.302.4.466.

15 Pilecki, [W jaki], PUMST, BI 6991, p. 9; Kochanski, *The Eagle*, p. 69; Wilkinson, *Foreign*, p. 72.

16 Kochanski, *The Eagle*, pp. 48–49; Pilecki, [W jaki], PUMST, BI 6991, p. 9.

17 Pilecki, [W jaki], PUMST, BI 6991, p. 11.

18 Ibid.

19 Kochanski, *The Eagle*, pp. 76–79.

20 Ibid, pp. 89–90.

21 Pilecki, [W jaki], PUMST, BI 6991, p. 11; Pilecki, Interview, March 11, 2016.

22 Pilecki, [W jaki], PUMST, BI 6991, p. 13.

23 Ibid.

24 Ibid.

25 Widelec, *Diary*, cited in Margolis, *Memorial*, p. 422; Lewitt, *When*, cited in Margolis, *Memorial*, p. 442; Nejmark, *The Destruction*, cited in Margolis, *Memorial*, p. 445; Dekel, [Browar], p. 15, p. 101; Hodubski, Protokół, Ostrów Mazowiecka, August 5, 1947, IPN, Bl 407/63, K 296/47, GK 264/63, SOŁ 63, pp. 0343–44; Słuchoński, [Wspomnienia], IP, 019 Sluchonski_Artur_2_skan_AK; Pilecki, Interview, March 11, 2016.

26 Pilecki, Interview, March 11, 2016.

27 Pilecki, [W jaki], PUMST, BI 6991, p. 14.

28 Nowak, *Courier*, p. 58; Richie, *Warsaw*, p. 147; Goebbels, *Diaries*, p. 37; Landau, *Kronika*, vol. I, p. 48; Korboński, *Fighting*, p. 7; Bryan, *Warsaw*, p. 19, p. 25; Goebbels, *Diaries*, p. 37; Bryan, *Warsaw*, p. 24; Goebbels, *Diaries*, p. 37.

29 Snyder, *Black*, loc. 423; Lukas, *Forgotten*, loc. 72. Herbert, *Hitler's*, pp. 61–94. Tooze, *Wages*, loc. 6701. Frank, *Extracts*, p. 110, cited in Kochanski, *The Eagle*, p. 98.

30 Frank, *Extracts*, p. 368, cited in O'Connor, *Butcher*, loc. 2008; Olson, *For Your*, p. 203.

31 Snyder, *Black*, loc. 196; Hilberg, *The Destruction*, pp. 64–74; Winstone, *Dark*, loc. 1693.

32 Pilecki, [W jaki], PUMST, BI 6991, p. 14; Bartoszewski, *1859*, p. 91; Sobolewicz, *But I*, p. 70; Lukas, *Forgotten*, loc. 942. See Rowecki,

[Meldunek], August 13, 1941, in Iranek-Osmecki et al., *Armia*, vol. II, p. 36; Ostrowska, [Wspomnienia 1], p. 2; Malinowski, *Tajna*, p. 27; Nowak, *Courier*, p. 59; Frank, *Extracts*, p. 5896; Bartoszewski, *1859*, p. 99.

CHAPTER TWO

1 Pilecki, [W jaki], PUMST, BI 6991, p. 14; Bartoszewski, *1859*, p. 91; Sobolewicz, *But I*, p. 70; Lukas, *Forgotten*, loc. 942. See Rowecki, [Meldunek], August 13, 1941, in Iranek-Osmecki et al., *Armia*, vol. II, p. 36; Ostrowska, [Wspomnienia 1], p. 2; Malinowski, *Tajna*, p. 27; Nowak, *Courier*, p. 59; Frank, *Extracts*, p. 5896; Bartoszewski, *1859*, p. 99.

2 Ostrowska, [Wspomnienia 1], p. 2; Ostrowski, Interview, May 1, 2016; Ostrowski, Interview, October 10, 2017.

3 Ostrowski, Interview, May 1, 2016; Tereszczenko, *Wspomnienia*, p. 83.

4 *Znak*, [Deklaracja], AAN, 2/2505/0/-/194, p. 3; Tereszczenko, Interview, November 1, 2016; Ostrowska, [Wspomnienia 1], p. 3.

5 Pilecki, [W jaki], PUMST, BI 6991, p. 14–15; Malinowski, *Tajna*, p. 29.

6 Pilecki, [W jaki], PUMST, BI 6991, p. 14; Unknown author, [Zasady konspiracji], AAN, 2/2505/0/-/194.

7 Pilecki, [W jaki], PUMST, BI 6991, p. 14; Unknown author, [Zasady konspiracji], AAN, 2/2505/0/-/194; Rablin, Oświadczenia, vol. 29, APMA-B, p. 82.

8 Rablin, Oświadczenia, vol. 29, APMA-B, p. 82.

9 Ostrowska, [Wspomnienia 1], pp. 3–4; Pilecki, [W jaki], PUMST, BI 6991, 14.

10 Malinowski, *Tajna*, p. 100.

11 Szpilman, *The Pianist*, p. 54; Dwork, van Pelt, *Auschwitz*, p. 144.

12 Pilecki, interview, May 17, 2016; Pilecka-Optułowicz, Interview, May 17, 2016; Łapian, Interview, May, 15, 2017.

13   Pilecki, Interview, May 16, 2016.

14   Szwajkowski, [Zeznania], IPN, S/139/12/Zn, pp. 137–142; Zawadzki, [Zeznania], IPN, S/139/12/Zn, pp. 124–28; Roth, *Murder*, cited in Zalc, Bruttman, *Micro-histories*, p. 227; Gutman, Krakowski, *Unequal*, p. 48; Zimmerman, *The Polish*, p. 74, p. 83.

15   Gross, *Polish*, p. 254; Tereszczenko, *Wspomnienia*, p. 85; Tereszczenko, Interview, November 1, 2016; *Znak*, 06.05.1940/6–7, cited in Malinowski, *Tajna*, pp. 12–15. A later edition of *Znak* rejected the Nazis' brutal treatment of Jews, which the writers felt was alien to the Polish culture. Nonetheless, "nothing changes the fact, that Jews are in Poland an element unwanted and even harmful, and the elimination of their influences from our national life will still be our main purpose." *Znak*, 1940/27, AN, 1925, pp. 3–4.

16   Pilecki, [W jaki], PUMST, BI 6991, p. 15; Tereszczenko, Interview, November 1, 2016; Nowak, *Courier*, p. 39; *Znak*, May 1940/6–7, cited in Malinowski, *Tajna*, pp. 12–15; Faliński, "Ideologia," pp. 57–76; Kochanski, *The Eagle*, p. 97; Pilecki, [W jaki], PUMST, BI 6991, p. 15; Pilecki, Wspomnienia, vol. 179, APMA-B, p. 312; Pilecki, [W jaki], PUMST, BI 6991, p. 14; Bartoszewski, *1859*, p. 70. Jan Włodarkiewicz's own views on Jews are not recorded, but it's likely they aligned closely with those espoused in *Znak*.

17   Zimmerman, *The Polish*, p. 67.

18   Favez, *The Red*, pp. 136–37; Zimmerman, *The Polish*, p. 67; Fleming, *Auschwitz*, p. 32; Wood, *Karski*, loc. 1109; Winstone, *Dark*, loc. 1244.

19   Pilecki, [W jaki], PUMST, BI 6991, p. 15; Pilecki, Wspomnienia, vol. 179, APMA-B, p. 313; Pilecki, [W jaki], PUMST, BI 6991, p. 15; *Znak*, 15.07.1940/14, cited in Malinowski, *Tajna*, pp. 173–75; Znak, [Deklaracja], AAN, 2/2505/0/-/194, pp. 2–3. Jan's declaration made no specific reference to Jews, but its language is typical of nationalists of the time—he sought to define Polishness along religious and sectarian lines. Pilecki, [W jaki], PUMST, BI 6991, p. 15; Pilecki, Wspomnienia, vol. 179, APMA-B, p. 313.

20   Malinowski, *Tajna*, p. 70.

21 Winstone, *The Dark*, loc. 1329; Lasik et al., *Auschwitz*, vol. I, pp. 49–50; Bartoszewski, *1859*, p. 157; Cyra, *Rotmistrz*; Pieńkowska, [Wspomnienia 1], AAN, 2/2505/0/-/194, p. 2.

22 Malinowski, *Tajna*, p. 88; Cyra, "Dr Władysław," p. 74; Kantyka, Kantyka, *Władysław*, in Kantyka, *Oddani*, p. 266.

23 Malinowski, *Tajna*, p. 54, p. 88; Ostrowska, [Wspomnienia 1], p. 4; Wachsmann, *KL*, pp. 7–9; Tabeau, [Sprawozdanie], in *Zeszyty* (1991), p. 105; Wachsmann, *KL*, p. 191; Malinowski, *Tajna*, p. 54, p. 88; Ostrowska, [Wspomnienia 1], p. 4. It's not clear exactly how many prisoners had died in Auschwitz by the end of August. Records are incomplete, and only the name of one murdered inmate has been preserved.

24 Pilecki, [W jaki], PUMST, BI 6991, p. 15; Malinowski, *Tajna*, p. 100. Malinowski says the meeting took place at the end of August, but this contradicts the timeline.

25 Pilecki, [W jaki], PUMST, BI 6991, p. 15; Pilecki, [W jaki], PUMST, BI 6991, p. 15; Ostrowska, [Wspomnienia 1], p. 4; Gawron, *Ochotnik*, p. 114; Pilecki, Akta sprawy, Zeznanie w śledztwie Witolda Pileckiego, ASS MON, vol. 1, p. 74.

26 Pilecki, [W jaki], PUMST, BI 6991, p. 15.

27 Malinowski, *Tajna*, p. 54; Gawron, *Ochotnik*, p. 114.

28 Pilecki, [W jaki], PUMST, BI 6991, p. 15; Pilecki, Interview, February 1, 2016.

29 Pilecki, [W jaki], PUMST, BI 6991, p. 15; Pilecki, Wspomnienia, vol. 179, APMA-B, p. 313; Dering, [Wspomnienia], p. 11; Malinowski, *Tajna*, p. 33.

30 Pilecki, [W jaki], PUMST, BI 6991, p. 15; Pilecki, Interview, February 1, 2016.

31 Pilecki, Interview, February 1, 2016; Ostrowski, Interview, March 9, 2016.

32 Cyra, *Rotmistrz*, p. 45; Ostrowska, [Wspomnienia 1], p. 5.

33 Ostrowski, Interview, March 9, 2016; Ostrowska, [Wspomnienia 1], p. 5.

34   Ostrowska, [Wspomnienia 1], p. 5.

35   Ostrowska, Wspomnienia, vol. 179, APMA-B, p. 148; Gorzkowski, *Kroniki*, p. 51.

36   Pilecki, [Raport 1945], PUMST, BI 874, p. 1; Bartoszewski, *Mój*, pp. 12–14.

37   Czech, *Auschwitz*, p. 29; Bartoszewski, *Mój*, pp. 14–16; Korboński, *Fighting*, p. 49; Pilecki, [Raport 1945], PUMST, BI 874, p. 1; Bartoszewski, *Mój*, pp. 16–17; Kowalski, *Niezapomniana*, pp. 154–58; Ptakowski, *Oświęcim*, pp. 12–13; Redzej, [Raport 1943], AAN, 202/ XVIII/1, p. 34.

38   Pilecki, [Raport 1945], PUMST, BI 874, p. 1.

39   Pilecki, [Raport 1945], PUMST, BI 874, pp. 1–2; Piekarski, *Escaping*, pp. 8–12; Redzej, [Raport 1943], AAN, 202/XVIII/1, p. 34; Bartoszewski, *Mój*, p. 18; Nowacki, Wspomnienia, vol. 151, APMA-B, p. 133.

40   Pilecki, [Raport 1945], PUMST, BI 874, p. 2; Kowalski, *Niezapomniana*, p. 161; Bogusz, Interview, December 19, 2015; Pilecki, [Raport 1945], PUMST, BI 874, 4.

41   Pilecki, [Raport 1945], PUMST, BI 874, p. 3.

42   Pilecki, [Raport 1945], PUMST, BI 874, p. 3; Kowalski, *Niezapomniana*, p. 163; Stapf, Wspomnienia, vol. 110, APMA-B, p. 75–81.

43   Pilecki, [Raport 1945], PUMST, BI 874, p. 3.

44   Pilecki, [Raport 1945], PUMST, BI 874, p. 4; Stapf, Oświadczenia, vol. 29, AP-MA-B, p. 89; Albin, Interview, May 21, 2016; D-Au-I-2, *Häftlings-Personal-Karte*, 7, APMA-B, p. 234; Pilecki, [Raport 1945], PUMST, BI 874, p. 4.

45   Pilecki, [Raport 1945], PUMST, BI 874, p. 4; Bartoszewski, *Wywiad*, p. 46; Kowalski, *Niezapomniana*, pp. 164–65; Pilecki, [Raport 1945], PUMST, BI 874, p. 4; Piekarski, *Escaping*, p. 16.

46   Lasik et al., *Auschwitz*, vol. I, pp. 66–68; Nowacki, Wspomnienia, vol. 151, APMA-B, p. 133.

47 Siedlecki, *Beyond*, p. 149; Pilecki, [Raport 1945], PUMST, BI 874, p. 4; Redzej, [Raport 1943], AAN, 202/XVIII/1, p. 36a; Ciesielski [Raport 1943], AAN, 202/XVIII/1, p. 55; Bartoszewski, *Mój*, p. 20; Świętorzecki, Oświadczenia, vol. 76, APMA-B, p. 95; Nowacki, Wspomnienia, vol. 151, APMA-B, p. 65.

CHAPTER THREE

1 Kowalski, *Niezapomniana*, p. 166; Fejkiel, *Medycyna*, in Bidakowski, Wójcik, *Pamiętniki*, p. 412; Pilecki, [Raport 1945], PUMST, BI 874, p. 4.

2 Dering, [Wspomnienia], p. 9; Piekarski, *Escaping*, p. 23; Kowalski, *Niezapomniana*, p. 166.

3 Gawron, *Ochotnik*, p. 17; Paczyński, Oświadczenia, vol. 100, APMA-B, p. 95; Piekarski, *Escaping*, p. 22; Głowa, Wspomnienia, vol. 94, APMA-B, p. 117.

4 FBI, FAP 1, HA 29, Bl. 4908–14; NRW, W, GSTA Hamm 3369,3367 Q 211 a; Fejkiel, *Medycyna*, in Bidakowski, Wójcik, *Pamiętniki*, p. 413; Świętorzecki, Oświadczenia, vol. 76, APMA-B, p. 95.

5 Wachsmann, *KL*, pp. 60–63.

6 Iwaszko et al., *Auschwitz*, vol. II, p. 66; Szczepański, video recollection, July 14, 1995, APMA-B, V-246.

7 Pilecki, [Raport 1945], PUMST, BI 874, p. 4.

8 Pilecki, [Raport 1945], PUMST, BI 874, p. 19; Redzej, [Raport 1943], AAN, 202/XVIII/1, p. 45a; Piekarski, *Escaping*, loc. 325; Piekarski, *Escaping*, p. 25; Siedlecki, *Beyond*, p. 155.

9 Fejkiel, *Medycyna*, in Bidakowski, Wójcik, *Pamiętniki*, p. 419; Bartoszewski, *Mój*, p. 20; Fejkiel, *Medycyna*, in Bidakowski, Wójcik, *Pamiętniki*, p. 419.

10 Szczepański, video recollection, July 14, 1995, APMA-B, V-246; Iwaszko et al., *Auschwitz*, vol. II, p. 70; Kowalski, *Niezapomniana*, p. 223; Siedlecki, *Beyond*, 155; Ciesielski, [Raport 1943], AAN, 202/XVIII/1, p. 7; Redzej, [Raport 1943], AAN, 202/XVIII/1, p. 34, p. 34a; Piekarski, *Escaping*, p. 27.

11 Siedlecki, *Beyond*, p. 155; Kowalski, *Niezapomniana*, p. 233; Langbein, *People*, p. 133, p. 65; Siedlecki, *Beyond*, p. 155; Pilecki, *The Auschwitz*, loc. 563; Pilecki, [Raport 1945], PUMST, BI 874, p. 3.

12 Langbein, *People*, p. 70; Wachsmann, *KL*, p. 501. See Gawron, Wspomnienia, vol. 48, APMA-B, pp. 9–13 and p. 38 for description of Jewish prisoners being denounced by fellow Poles.

13 D-Aul–2, 1–5, APMA-B, cited in Czech, *Auschwitz*, p. 373; Iwaszko et al., *Auschwitz*, vol. II, p. 372, p. 374.

14 Iwaszko et al., *Auschwitz*, vol. II, pp. 371–80; Kowalski, *Niezapomniana*, p. 188, p. 191; Siedlecki, *Beyond*, p. 152.

15 Wachsmann, *KL*, p. 497; Bielecki, *Kto ratuje*, p. 130; Smoleń, "Czarna," p. 4; Kowalski, *Niezapomniana*, p. 175.

16 Müller, *Eyewitness*, p. 5; Langbein, *People*, p. 70.

17 Piekarski, *Escaping*, p. 85; Świętorzecki, Interview, February 14, 1972.

18 Piekarski, *Escaping*, p. 33; Ziółkowski, *Byłem*, p. 31; Kowalski, *Niezapomniana*, 234; Kowalski, *Niezapomniana*, p. 233; Szpakowski, Interview, January 31, 2017; Wachsmann, *KL*, p. 501.

19 Lasik et al., *Auschwitz*, vol. I, pp. 66–68; Nosal, Oświadczenia, vol. 132, APMA-B, p. 165; Bartys, Oświadczenia, vol. 63, APMA-B, p. 135; Iwaszko et al., *Auschwitz*, vol. II, pp. 294–96; Favez, *The Red*, p. 27, pp. 137–41.

20 Piekarski, *Escaping*, p. 21.

21 Ibid.

22 Ibid, pp. 30–32.

23 Ibid, p. 30.

24 Iwaszko et al., *Auschwitz*, vol. II, p. 311; Diem, Wspomnienia, vol. 172, APMA-B, 11, p. 14, p. 30.

25 Iwaszko et al., *Auschwitz*, vol. II, p. 61; Bartoszewski, *Mój*, pp. 36–38; Fejkiel, *Medycyna*, in Bidakowski, Wójcik, *Pamiętniki*, p. 461; Kowalski, *Niezapomniana*, pp. 172–73.

26 Szczepański, video recollection, July 14, 1995, APMA-B, V-246.

27 Urbanek, Oświadczenia, vol. 44, APMA-B, p. 8; Ciesielski, Wspomnienia, 40; Pilecki, [Raport 1945], PUMST, BI 874, pp. 5–6; Dering, [Wspomnienia], p. 70; Dembiński, [Raport], PUMST, A. 680, p. 593.

CHAPTER FOUR

1 Iwaszko et al., *Auschwitz*, vol. II, pp. 312–15; Fejkiel, *Więźniarski*, pp. 46–49; Piekarski, *Escaping*, p. 36; Strzelecka, *Voices*, vol. 3, p. 10; Dering, [Wspomnienia], p. 24; Diem, Wspomnienia, vol. 172, APMA-B, p. 45, p. 77, p. 122.

2 Iwaszko et al., *Auschwitz*, vol. II, p. 216; Langbein, *People*, pp. 50–84; Fejkiel, *Więźniarski*, p. 216; Dering, [Wspomnienia], p. 11, p. 14, p. 41.

3 Pilecki, [Raport 1945], PUMST, BI 874, p. 20; Czech, *Kalendarz*, p. 19. This nutrition formula is from an SS study carried out by Dr. Hans Münch between 1943 and 1944, although he wrote up the results only in 1947 while awaiting trial in Poland for war crimes. Münch, *Analyzis*, Opracowania, vol. 19, APMA-B, pp. 5–47; Collingham, *The Taste*, loc. 293.

4 Lasik et al., *Auschwitz*, vol. I, p. 171; Piekarski, *Escaping*, p. 23, p. 28; Świętorzecki, Interview, February 14, 1970.

5 Pilecki, [Raport 1945], PUMST, BI 874, p. 6; Dering, [Wspomnienia], p. 70.

6 Piekarski, *Escaping*, p. 35.

7 Iwaszko et al., *Auschwitz*, vol. II, pp. 378–80; Świętorzecki, Oświadczenia, vol. 76, APMA-B, p. 96; Piekarski, *Escaping*, p. 35; Kowalski, *Niezapomniana*, p. 177; Ciesielski, [Raport 1943], AAN, 202/XVIII/1, p. 6; Radlicki, *Kapo*, pp. 64–65; Siciński, "Z psychopatologii," pp. 126–30; [Krankemann], HHStAW Fonds 430/1, no. 9402.

8 Pilecki, [Raport 1945], PUMST, BI 874, p. 6; Ciesielski, [Raport 1943], AAN, 202/XVIII/1, p. 7.

9 Pilecki, [Raport 1945], PUMST, BI 874, p. 6.

10 Pilecki, [Raport 1945], PUMST, BI 874, p. 7; Piekarski, *Escaping*, p. 143; Dwork, van Pelt, *Auschwitz*, pp. 177–81.

11 Dwork, van Pelt, *Auschwitz*, pp. 177–81.

12 Pilecki, *The Auschwitz*, loc. 814; Pilecki, [Raport 1945], PUMST, BI 874, p. 7; Pilecki, [Raport 1945], PUMST, BI 874, pp. 7–8; Pilecki, *The Auschwitz*, loc. 833; Pilecki, [Raport 1945], PUMST, BI 874, p. 8.

13 Pilecki, [Raport 1945], PUMST, BI 874, p. 8.

14 Pilecki, [Raport 1945], PUMST, BI 874, p. 6, p. 27; Kielar, *Anus Mundi*, p. 34; Kłodziński, "Rola," pp. 113–26; Ciesielski, [Raport 1943], AAN, 202/XVIII/1, p. 3; Pilecki, [Zamiast], Materiały, vol. 223c, APMA-B, p. 1.

15 Pilecki, [Zamiast], Materiały, vol. 223c, APMA-B, p. 2–3.

16 Pilecki, [Raport 1945], PUMST, BI 874, p. 9; Ciesielski, [Raport 1943], AAN, 202/XVIII/1, p. 5; Redzej, [Raport 1943], AAN, 202/XVIII/1, p. 36; Radlicki, *Kapo*, p. 87; Dobrowolska, *The Auschwitz*, loc. 1687; Albin, *List*, p. 53; Urbanek, Oświadczenia, vol. 44, APMA-B, p. 3; Wolny, Oświadczenia, vol. 33, APMA-B, p. 17; Białas, Oświadczenia, vol. 94, APMA-B, p. 24; Kowalski, *Niezapomniana*, pp. 245–47.

17 Gutheil, *Einer*, pp. 79–92; Albin, *List*, p. 49; Bernacka, "Otto," pp. 8–9; Pilecki, [Raport 1945], PUMST, BI 874, p. 10.

18 Pilecki, *The Auschwitz*, loc. 929; Pilecki, [Raport 1945], PUMST, BI 874, p. 10.

19 Ibid.

20 Pilecki, [Raport 1945], PUMST, BI 874, p. 10.

21 Lasik et al., *Auschwitz*, vol. I, pp. 70–71.

22 Filip, *Żydzi*, p. 51, pp. 139–43; Steinbacher, *Auschwitz*, p. 9; Dwork, van Pelt, *Auschwitz*, p. 205.

23 Pilecki, [Raport 1945], PUMST, BI 874, pp. 10–11.

24 Ibid, p. 11.

25 Ibid, pp. 10–11.

CHAPTER FIVE

1 Pilecki, [Raport 1945], PUMST, BI 874, p. 11.

2 Hoess, *Commandant*, loc. 200; Pilecki, [Raport 1945], PUMST, BI 874, p. 12; Dwork, van Pelt, *Auschwitz*, p. 188; Pilecki, [Raport 1945], PUMST, BI 874, p. 11.

3 Pilecki, [Raport 1945], PUMST, BI 874, p. 13.

4 Ibid.

5 Siedlecki, *Beyond*, p. 151.

6 Pilecki, *The Auschwitz*, loc. 2418; Pilecki, [Raport 1945], PUMST, BI 874, p. 12.

7 Świętorzecki, Interview, February 14, 1970; Pilecki, [Raport 1945], PUMST, BI 874, p. 6; Radlicki, *Kapo*, pp. 68–71, p. 87.

8 Świętorzecki, Interview, February 14, 1970; Pilecki, [Raport 1945], PUMST, BI 874, p. 6.

9 Pilecki, [Raport 1945], PUMST, BI 874, p. 8; Kielar, *Anus Mundi*, p. 44; Kowalski, Wspomnienia, vol. 96, APMA-B, p. 242; Pilecki, [Klucz], Wspomnienia, vol. 183, APMA-B, p. 79; Cyra, *Rotmistrz*, p. 50.

10 Iwaszko et al., *Auschwitz*, vol. II, p. 69; Fejkiel, *Medycyna*, in Bidakowski, Wójcik, *Pamiętniki*, p. 472; Iwaszko et al., *Auschwitz*, vol. II, p. 61; Dobrowolska, *The Auschwitz*, loc. 3310, loc. 3356, loc. 3363; Ziółkowski, *Byłem*, pp. 45–46; Smoleń, "Czarna," p. 4.

11 Nowacki, Wspomnienia, vol. 151, APMA-B, p. 139; Piekarski, *Escaping*, p. 46.

12 Piekarski, *Escaping*, p. 45.

13 Ibid.

14 Piekarski claimed that Witold told him Auschwitz was to become "a very large extermination camp to house Polish freedom fighters," but it's likely he was applying the camp's later function to his memory of his conversation with Witold. Piekarski, *Escaping*, p. 44.

15 Czech, *Auschwitz*, pp. 29–39; Kowalczyk, *Barbed*, p. 35; Langbein, *People*, p. 70.

16 Fejkiel, *Więźniarski*, p. 120; Pilecki, Interview, May 17 and 19, 2016; Pilecka–Optułowicz, Interview, February 1, 2016; Szpakowski, Interview, January 31, 2017.

17 Iwaszko et al., *Auschwitz*, vol. II, pp. 419–26; Ostrowska, [Wspomnienia 1], p. 5; Pilecki, [Raport 1945], PUMST, BI 874, p. 29; Wysocki, *Rotmistrz*, p. 47.

18 Iwaszko et al., *Auschwitz*, vol. II, pp. 429–33; Pilecki, [Raport 1945], PUMST, BI 874, p. 36; Iwaszko et al., *Auschwitz*, vol. II, p. 430; Wielopolski, Interview, May 18, 2017; Rostkowski, *Świat*, p. 57; Rowecki, [Wytyczne do działań sabotażowo-dywersyjnych], March 19, 1940, in Czarnocka et al., *Armia*, vol. I, p. 313; Sosnkowski, [List], November 28, 1940, no. 162 [no. 94], in Iranek-Osmecki et al., *Armia*, vol. II, p. 649; Wachsmann, *KL*, p. 483. Although the SS had ordered that prisoners should not normally be released during wartime, Auschwitz had a looser policy in its early months. Cyra, *Rotmistrz*, p. 42; Garliński, *Fighting*, p. 276; Dębski, *Oficerowie*, s.v. Aleksander Wielopolski.

19 Pilecki, [Raport 1945], PUMST, BI 874, p. 19; Dębski, *Oficerowie*, s.v. Aleksander Wielopolski; Pilecki, [Raport 1945], PUMST, BI 874, p. 35; Setkiewicz, "Pierwsi," p. 16; Carter, [Report], NARS, 800.20211/924, RG 59.

20 Dembiński, [Raport], PUMST, A. 680, p. 593; Hastings, *Bomber*, loc. 1543; Westermann, "The Royal," p. 197; Lasik et al., *Auschwitz*, vol. I, p. 266; Dembiński, [Raport], PUMST, A. 680, 593.

21 Pilecki, [Raport 1945], PUMST, BI 874, p. 36; Czech, *Auschwitz*, p. 32.

22 Nowacki, Wspomnienia, vol. 151, APMA-B, p. 145; Kozłowiecki, *Ucisk*, p. 205.

23 Dering, cited in Garliński, *Fighting*, p. 25.

24   Kielar, *Anus Mundi*, p. 40.

25   Garliński, *Fighting*, p. 25; Kielar, *Anus Mundi*, p. 40; Czech, *Auschwitz*, p. 32; Setkiewicz, *Zaopatrzenie*, p. 57.

26   Pilecki, [Raport 1945], PUMST, BI 874, p. 14.

27   Ibid.

28   Pilecki, *The Auschwitz*, loc. 1028; Pilecki, [Raport 1945], PUMST, BI 874, p. 14; Paczuła, Oświadczenia, vol. 108, APMA-B, p. 72; Setkiewicz, *Voices*, vol. 6, p. 6.

29   Pilecki, [Raport 1945], PUMST, BI 874, p. 13; Ciesielski, [Raport 1943], AAN, 202/XVIII/1, p. 4.

30   Piekarski, *Escaping*, p. 54; Iwaszko et al., *Auschwitz*, vol. II, pp. 81–82; Fejkiel, *Więźniarski*, p. 23; Collingham, *The Taste*, loc. 235; Russell, *Hunger*, loc. 234, loc. 1245, loc. 1374; Butterly, Shepherd, *Hunger*, p. 158.

31   Dering, [Wspomnienia], p. 17; Iwaszko et al., *Auschwitz*, vol. II, p. 300.

32   Pilecki, *The Auschwitz*, loc. 1174; Piekarski, *Escaping*, p. 75.

33   Pilecki, [Raport 1945], PUMST, BI 874, p. 16.

34   Ibid.

35   Kowalski, *Niezapomniana*, p. 201; Ringelblum, *Notes*, loc. 1777.

CHAPTER SIX

1   Czech, *Auschwitz*, p. 40; Świętorzecki, Oświadczenia, vol. 76, APMA-B, pp. 101–2; Dobrowolska, *The Auschwitz*, loc. 3017; Bartoszewski, *Mój*, pp. 53–54.

2   Świętorzecki, Wspomnienia, vol. 86, APMA-B, p. 233; Dobrowolska, *The Auschwitz*, loc. 3017.

3   Strzelecka, *Voices*, vol. 3, p. 8, p. 21; Redzej, [Raport 1943], AAN, 202/XVIII/1, 38; Tomaszewski, Wspomnienia, vol. 66, APMA-B, p. 108; Ławski, Wspomnienia, vol. 154/154a, APMA-B, p. 69.

4   Pilecki, [Raport 1945], PUMST, BI 874, p. 23.

5   Rablin, Oświadczenia, vol. 29, APMA-B, p. 80; Piper, Świebocka,

Czech, *Auschwitz*, vol. III, 198; Dwork, van Pelt, *Auschwitz*, pp. 219–22. The almond smell was added by Zyklon B's manufacturers to allow the gas to be detected.

6 Strzelecka, *Voices*, vol. 3, p. 29; Pilecki, [Raport 1945], PUMST, BI 874, pp. 23–24; Redzej, [Raport 1943], AAN, 202/XVIII/1, p. 37a; Pilecki, [Raport 1945], PUMST, BI 874, p. 25.

7 Pilecki, [Raport 1945], PUMST, BI 874, p. 25.

8 Pilecki, [Raport 1945], PUMST, BI 874, pp. 24–25; Król, Oświadczenia, vol. 76, APMA-B, p. 204; Pilecki, [Raport 1945], PUMST, BI 874, p. 26; Lifton, *The Nazi*, pp. 30–35, pp. 129–33.

9 Langbein, *People*, p. 393; Lifton, *The Nazi*, p. 266; Dering, [Wspomnienia], pp. 193–94.

10 Dering, [Wspomnienia], p. 83.

11 Hahn, Interview, April 24, 2018; Fleming, *Auschwitz*, p. 59; Stargardt, *The German*, p. 66, p. 119; Breitman, *Official*, p. 156.

12 Olson, *Last*, loc. 2335.

13 Wielopolski, Interview, May 18, 2017; Dembiński, [Raport], PUMST, A. 680, p. 593, pp. 591–92; Westermann, "The Royal," p. 197. Rowecki included Wielopolski's report in his later "Report on the internal situation until January 30th 1941," which reached London in March 1941 via Stockholm; "Part III. The camp in Oświęcim" described the camp's conditions and suffering of prisoners (PUMST, A. 441, p. 10).

14 Świętorzecki, Interview, February 14, 1972; Taul, Wspomnienia, vol. 62, APMA-B, p. 36.

15 Gutheil, *Einer*, pp. 79–92; Ptakowski, *Oświęcim*, p. 97; Gliński, Oświadczenia, vol. 95, APMA-B, p. 6; Drzazga, Oświadczenia, vol. 33, APMA-B, p. 51; Pilecki, [Raport 1945], PUMST, BI 874, p. 35; Pilecki, [Raport 1945], PUMST, BI 874, p. 26.

16 Świętorzecki, Oświadczenia, vol. 76, APMA-B, p. 97; Pilecki, [Raport 1945], PUMST, BI 874, p. 32.

17 Świętorzecki, Interview, February 14, 1972; Wachsmann, *KL*, p. 207; Setkiewicz, *Z dziejów*, p. 55; Dwork, van Pelt, *Auschwitz*, p. 207.

18   Frączek, Wspomnienia, vol. 66, APMA-B, p. 162.

19   Pilecki, [Raport 1945], PUMST, BI 874, p. 30; Kowalski, *Niezapomniana*, 240–65; Kowalczyk, *Barbed*, vol. II, p. 10.

20   Piekarski, *Escaping*, p. 83; Hoess, *Commandant*, p. 121.

21   Piekarski, *Escaping*, p. 83; Pilecki, [Raport W], AAN, 202/XVIII/1, p. 74.

22   Pilecki, *Report W*, pp. 40–41; Pilecki, [Raport W], AAN, 202/XVIII/1, p. 74.

23   Pilecki, *The Auschwitz*, loc. 1725; Pilecki, [Raport 1945], PUMST, BI 874, 28.

24   Pilecki, [Raport 1945], PUMST, BI 874, p. 29.

25   Ibid, p. 28.

26   Ibis, pp. 28–29.

27   Pietrzykowski, Oświadczenia, vol. 88, APMA-B, p. 10.

28   Pietrzykowski, Oświadczenia, vol. 88, APMA-B, pp. 9–10; Rablin, Oświadczenia, vol. 29, APMA-B, p. 97.

29   Pietrzykowski, Oświadczenia, vol. 88, APMA-B, p. 10; Albin, *List*, pp. 89–90; Pilecki, [Raport 1945], PUMST, BI 874, p. 6, p. 27.

30   Pietrzykowski, Oświadczenia, vol. 88, APMA-B, p. 11.

31   Ibid.

32   Ibid.

33   Piekarski, *Escaping*, p. 99; Lasik et al., *Auschwitz*, vol. I, p. 19; Gawron, *Ochotnik*, pp. 23–26.

34   Świętorzecki, Oświadczenia, vol. 76, APMA-B, pp. 104–5; 202/III-8, p. 21, in Marczewska, Ważniewski et al., *Zeszyty* (1968), p. 6. Świętorzecki, Oświadczenia, vol. 76, APMA-B, p. 101; Gawron, *Ochotnik*, pp. 26–28; Kowalczyk, *Barbed*, vol. II, p. 14, p. 36; Kowalski, *Niezapomniana*, p. 218, p. 223; Setkiewicz, *Zapomniany*, pp. 61–65; Cyra, *Jeszcze raz*, no pages given; Kowalski, *Niezapomniana*, p. 228; Pilecki, [Raport 1945], PUMST, BI 874, p. 37; Redzej, [Raport 1943], AAN, 202/XVIII/1, p. 40a.

35 Cywiński, Lachendro, Setkiewicz, *Auschwitz*, p. 196; Pilecki, [Raport 1945], PUMST, BI 874, p. 6. No record of Warsaw's response to Karol's report has been preserved.

36 Świętorzecki, Oświadczenia, vol. 76, APMA-B, p. 106; Gawron, *Ochotnik*, p.203; Świętorzecki, Oświadczenia, vol. 76, APMA-B, p. 105.

37 Pietrzykowski, Oświadczenia, vol. 88, APMA-B, pp. 19–20.

CHAPTER SEVEN

1 Garliński, *Fighting*, p. 71; Stargardt, *The German*, p. 158; Snyder, *Black*, loc. 475; Wachsmann, *KL*, pp. 259–60; Dwork, van Pelt, *Auschwitz*, pp. 258–62. On June 23, Höss ordered the Jews in the penal company to be beaten to death, likely as a symbolic contribution to the war effort. Hałgas, Oświadczenia, vol. 89, APMA-B, p. 165; Setkiewicz, "Pierwsi," p. 26; Kobrzyński, Wspomnienia, vol. 129, APMA-B, p. 28.

2 Rawicz, [Pobyt], p. 21.

3 Dwork, van Pelt, *Auschwitz*, p. 262; Wachsmann, *KL*, pp. 259–60, p. 279; Czech, *Auschwitz*, p. 74.

4 Ciesielski, [Raport 1943], AAN, 202/XVIII/1, p. 8; Pilecki, [Raport 1945], PUMST, BI 874, p. 39; Redzej, [Raport 1943], AAN, 202/XVIII/1, p. 41a; Porębski, Oświadczenia, vol. 22, APMA-B, p. 59; Wolny, Oświadczenia, vol. 33, APMA-B, p. 19; Redzej, [Raport 1943], AAN, 202/XVIII/1, p. 41a; Lasik et al., *Auschwitz*, vol. I, p. 67.

5 Ciesielski, *Wspomnienia*, p. 69.

6 Ibid.

7 Gawron, *Ochotnik*, pp. 72–99; Ciesielski, *Wspomnienia*, pp. 45–47; Hoess, *Commandant*, p. 157.

8 Redzej, [Raport 1943], AAN, 202/XVIII/1, p. 39; Kłodziński, "Dur," p. 47.

9 Iwaszko et al., *Auschwitz*, vol. II, p. 296, p. 322; Diem, Wspomnienia, vol. 172, APMA-B, p. 120; Pilecki, [Raport 1945], PUMST, BI 874, p. 54.

10 Wachsmann, *KL*, p. 246; Allen, *The Fantastic*, loc. 319; Diem, Wspomnienias, vol. 172, APMA-B, p. 9.

11 Hill, Williams, *Auschwitz*, p. 63; Jaworski, *Wspomnienia*, p. 183.

12 In 1947, the Polish government charged Dering with war crimes relating to his role as a surgeon during Nazi experiments on the sex organs of mostly Jewish male and female prisoners. Dering, who was in London at the time, was arrested and investigated by British authorities. Dering insisted that he was one of several prisoners ordered by the Germans to perform the operations and that as a prisoner he had no choice but to obey. After a nineteen-month investigation, he was released and allowed to remain in the United Kingdom. IPN, GK_174_183_ pda, BU_2188_14, BU_2188_15, GK_164_27_tl.

13 Kowalski, *Niezapomniana*, p. 231.

14 Kłodziński, "Pierwsza," p. 43; Cyra, "Dr Władysław," p. 75.

15 Czech, *Auschwitz*, p. 75; Strzelecka, *Voices*, vol. 3, p. 12; Ławski, Wspomnienia, vol. 154/154a, APMA-B, p. 21; Hałgas, "Oddział," p. 53.

16 Kłodziński, "Pierwsza," p. 43; Czech, *Kalendarz*, p. 75.

17 Dering, [Wspomnienia], p. 81; Wachsmann, *KL*, pp. 243–52. The T4 program was named after its headquarters' address at Tiergartenstrasse 4 in Berlin.

18 Dering, [Wspomnienia], p. 81; Kłodziński, "Pierwsza," pp. 39–40; Rawicz, [Pobyt], p. 20; Lasik et al., *Auschwitz*, vol. I, p. 86; Czech, *Kalendarz*, p. 75; Stapf, Oświadczenia, vol. 148, APMA-B, p. 101; Dobrowolska, *The Auschwitz*, loc. 3922; Gawron, Wspomnienia, vol. 48, APMA-B, p. 77. According to some accounts, Krankemann was hanged by prisoners during the journey. Pilecki, [Raport 1945], PUMST, BI 874, p. 50.

19 Dering, [Wspomnienia], p. 81; Dering, [Wspomnienia], p. 28; Kowalski, Wspomnienia, vol. 96, APMA-B, p. 203.

20 Kłodziński, "Pierwsze," pp. 83–84.

21 Kielar, *Anus Mundi*, p. 61; Pilecki, [Raport 1945], PUMST, BI 874, p. 50; Wachsmann, *KL*, p. 267.

22   Wachsmann, *KL*, p. 267; Dering, [Wspomnienia], p. 80.

23   Czech, *Auschwitz*, p. 85; Kłodziński, "Pierwsze," p. 84.

24   Kielar, *Anus Mundi*, p. 60; Kłodziński, "Pierwsze," p. 87; Czech, *Auschwitz*, p. 86; Piper, Świebocka, Czech, *Auschwitz*, vol. III, p. 57, p. 117.

25   Kłodziński, "Pierwsze," p. 88.

26   Czech, *Auschwitz*, pp. 86–87; Diem, Wspomnienia, vol. 172, APMA-B, p. 131. "[I saw] for the first time a whole pile of gassed dead bodies," Höss recalled for the Polish magistrate later. "I felt uncomfortable and shuddered, though I had imagined death by gassing as worse." Langbein, *People*, p. 303.

27   Pilecki, [Raport 1945], PUMST, BI 874, p. 39.

28   Diem, Wspomnienia, vol. 172, APMA-B, p. 131; Kielar, *Anus Mundi*, p. 64.

29   Pilecki, [Raport 1945], PUMST, BI 874, p. 39.

30   Pilecki, [Raport 1945], PUMST, BI 874, p. 40. Pilecki, *Report W*, p. 6.

31   Pilecki, *Report W*, p. 6.; Pilecki, [Raport 1945], PUMST, BI 874, p. 40.

32   Pilecki, [Raport 1945], PUMST, BI 874, p. 39; Rablin, Oświadczenia, vol. 29, p. 81; Wachsmann, *KL*, pp. 268–69; Hoess, *Commandant*, p. 147.

33   Czech, *Auschwitz*, pp. 93–102; Gawron, *Ochotnik*, p. 145; Wachsmann, *KL*, p. 280; Nowacki, Wspomnienia, vol. 151, APMA-B, pp. 107–9.

34   Gawron, *Ochotnik*, p. 148.

35   Ibid.

36   Rawicz, [List], September 25, 1957. Rawicz letters courtesy of Andrzej Kunert unless stated otherwise.

37   Dwork, van Pelt, *Auschwitz*, pp. 263–68. The new crematorium was initially to be built at the main camp, but the location was subsequently moved to Birkenau.

38 Setkiewicz, *Zaopatrzenie*, p. 58.

39 Schulte, *London*, in Hackmann, Süß, *Hitler's*, p. 211; Olszowski, "Więźniarska," 182–87; Hoess, *Commandant*, p. 137; for example of memorizing reports, see Rawicz, [Raport], date unknown.

40 Rawicz, [List], 1957.

41 Rawicz, Interview, March 5, 2017; Rawicz, Oświadczenia, vol. 27, APMA-B, p. 38; Pilecki, [Raport 1945], PUMST, BI 874, p. 55.

42 Gawron, *Ochotnik*, p. 103, p. 131.

43 Piekarski, *Escaping*, p. 149; Pilecki, *The Auschwitz*, loc. 2294; Pilecki, [Raport 1945], PUMST, BI 874, p. 42; Czech, *Auschwitz*, p. 105; Banach, Proces Załogi Esesmańskiej, vol. 55, APMA-B, pp. 102–3; Taul, Oświadczenia, vol. 9, APMA-B, p. 1267; Pilecki, [Raport 1945], PUMST, BI 874, p. 37.

44 Rawicz, Oświadczenia, vol. 27, APMA-B, p. 39; Rawicz, [List], 1957; Gawron, *Ochotnik*, pp. 173–174.

45 Gawron, *Ochotnik*, pp. 173–174.

CHAPTER EIGHT

1 Puławski, *W obliczu*, p. 180. The section on Auschwitz in the *Black Book* drew upon "Report on the internal situation until January 30th 1941," which reached London in March 1941 via Stockholm and was partly based on Witold's report (PUMST, A. 441, p. 10).

2 Pilecki, [Raport 1945], PUMST, BI 874, p. 71, p. 47; Syzdek, "W 45," p. 5; Kobrzyński, Wspomnienia, vol. 129, APMA-B, p. 6; Świebocki, *Auschwitz*, vol. IV, pp. 74–77; Syzdek, "W 45," p. 5; Pilecki, [Raport 1945], PUMST, BI 874, p. 45; Stranský, Oświadczenia, vol. 84, AMPA-B, p. 46; Rawicz, [List], August 22, 1957.

3 Rawicz, Oświadczenia, vol. 27, APMA-B, p. 37; Gawron, Wspomnienia, vol. 48, APMA-B, p. 96, p. 98, p. 100; Pilecki, [Raport 1945], PUMST, BI 874, p. 45; Pilecki, *The Auschwitz*, loc. 2262; Pilecki, [Raport 1945], PUMST, BI 874, p. 41; Rawicz, Oświadczenia, vol. 27, APMA-B, p. 37; Gawron, Wspomnienia, vol. 48, APMA-B, p. 96,

p. 98, p. 100; Pilecki, [Raport 1945], PUMST, BI 874, p. 45; Pilecki, *The Auschwitz*, loc. 2262; Pilecki, [Raport 1945], PUMST, BI 874, p. 41.

4 Lasik et al., *Auschwitz*, vol. I, p. 181; Rawicz, Oświadczenia, vol. 27, APMA-B, 37; Rawicz, [List], August 31, 1957.

5 202/I-32, p. 71, in Marczewska, Ważniewski et al., *Zeszyty* (1968), p. 54. In fact, the number of surviving Soviet POWs that spring was around 150. Schulte, *London*, in Hackmann, Süß, *Hitler's*, pp. 222–23.

6 Urbańczyk, Wspomnienia, vol. 54, APMA-B, p. 35; Diem, "Ś. P. Kazimierz," pp. 45–47; Stupka, Oświadczenia, vol. 68, APMA-B, p. 124.

7 Stupka, Interview, September 24, 2016.

8 Lasik et al., *Auschwitz*, vol. I, pp. 166–67; Breitman, *Official*, pp. 112–14; Pilecki, [Raport 1945], PUMST, BI 874, p. 51; Piekarski, *Escaping*, p. 108.

9 Hahn, Interview, May 5, 2018; Pilecki, [Raport 1945], PUMST, BI 874, p. 51.

10 Pilecki, [Raport 1945], PUMST, BI 874, p. 51; Piekarski, *Escaping*, p. 122.

11 Piekarski, *Escaping*, p. 109.

12 Wachsmann, *KL*, p. 294.

13 Dwork, van Pelt, *Auschwitz*, pp. 263–65, pp. 295–301; Lasik et al., *Auschwitz*, vol. I, pp. 80–81; Wachsmann, *KL*, pp. 294–96; Hilberg, *The Destruction*, p. 138.

14 Dwork, van Pelt, *Auschwitz*, p. 126, p. 294.

15 Molenda, "Władysław," p. 53; Nosal, Oświadczenia, vol. 106, APMA-B, p. 51.

16 Piekarski, *Escaping*, p. 109.

17 Ibid, p. 114.

18 Ibid.

19 Ibid, p. 115.

20 Ibid.

21   Ibid, p. 116.

22   Ibid.

23   Piekarski, *Escaping*, p. 116; Pilecki, [Raport 1945], PUMST, BI 874, p. 51.

CHAPTER NINE

1   Pilecki, [Raport 1945], PUMST, BI 874, p. 35; Redzej, [Raport 1943], AAN, 202/XVIII/1, p. 42. The new camp was at one stage intended for an area near the village of Rajsko. *Raj* in Polish means "paradise," which may have been another reason for the new camp's nickname; Gawron, *Ochotnik*, p. 224. Czech, *Auschwitz*, p. 145; Gawron, Wspomnienia, vol. 48, APMA-B, p. 13.

2   Gawron, *Ochotnik*, p. 227; Gawron, Wspomnienia, vol. 48, APMA-B, p. 13.

3   Gawron, Wspomnienia, vol. 48, APMA-B, p. 13; Pilecki, [Raport 1945], PUMST, BI 874, p. 53.

4   Gawron, *Ochotnik*, p. 227.

5   Ibid.

6   Czech, *Auschwitz*, p. 148; Gawron, *Ochotnik*, p. 247; Pilecki, [Raport 1945], PUMST, BI 874, p. 53.

7   Wolny, Oświadczenia, vol. 33, APMA-B, p. 19; Porębski, Oświadczenia, vol. 22, APMA-B, pp. 59–60; Dwork, van Pelt, *Auschwitz*, p. 301; Czech, *Auschwitz*, p. 151.

8   Czech, *Auschwitz*, p. 151; Pilecki, [Raport 1945], PUMST, BI 874, p. 47, p. 57; Redzej, [Raport 1943], AAN, 202/XVIII/1, p. 41; Pilecki, [Raport 1945], PUMST, BI 874, p. 57. In later describing the scene, Witold used the derogatory term *Żydek* or "little Jew" to describe the victims. Witold used both *Żydzi* and the pejorative diminutive *Żydki* in his 1945 report. He used the latter seven times (out of a total of thirty-seven specific references to Jews). In prewar Polish, *Żydki* could be used in an anti-Semitic context. Witold appears to deploy the term to emphasize the helplessness and weakness of Jews, as in this scene, where he contrasts the plight of the victim with the murderous Jewish kapo.

9 Pilecki, [Raport 1945], PUMST, BI 874, p. 48. No such SS document has come to light.

10 Lasik et al., *Auschwitz*, vol. I, p. 233.

11 Lasik et al., *Auschwitz*, vol. I, pp. 104–6; Pilecki, [Raport 1945], PUMST, BI 874, p. 50.

12 Rawicz, [List], September 23, 1957; Pilecki, [Raport 1945], PUMST, BI 874, p. 50.

13 Ostańkowicz, *Ziemia*, p. 180. Twelve hundred Soviet POWs and patients from the main camp died in the rudimentary hospital known as the Isolation Station in March when the SS restricted their rations to a single cup of soup a day. Czech, *Auschwitz*, p. 157; Rawicz, Oświadczenia, vol. 27, APMA-B, p. 40; Rawicz, [List], September 23, 1957; Piekarski, *Escaping*, p. 132.

14 Wachsmann, *KL*, p. 301; Pietrzykowski, Oświadczenia, vol. 88, APMA-B, p. 18. Müller, *Eyewitness*, p. 19.

15 Broad, [Testimony], cited in Smoleń et al., *KL Auschwitz*, p. 129; Langbein, *People*, p. 69.

16 Paczyński, Oświadczenia, vol. 100, APMA-B, p. 102.

17 Müller, *Eyewitness*, pp. 13–15.

18 Wachsmann, *KL*, pp. 291–94; Gawron, *Ochotnik*, p. 248.

19 Czech, *Auschwitz*, pp. 167–68; Müller, *Eyewitness*, p. 18.

20 Czech, *Auschwitz*, pp. 167–68; Wachsmann, *KL*, pp. 301–2; Pilecki, [Raport 1945], PUMST, BI 874, p. 52; Wolny, Oświadczenia, vol. 33, APMA-B, p. 19; Porębski, Oświadczenia, vol. 22, APMA-B, p. 59. Henryk says he began actively collaborating with the Sonderkommando in June, but he appears to have understood what was happening to the Jews from the start of the gassings. His likely source was a member of the Sonderkommando. The unit was transferred to Birkenau from the main camp on May 9, 1942. Czech, *Auschwitz*, p. 164; Bartosik, Martyniak, Setkiewicz, *Wstęp*, in Bartosik, Martyniak, Setkiewicz, idem, *Początki*, p. 15.

21   Piper, Świebocka, Czech, *Auschwitz*, vol. III, pp. 181–82; Wolny, Oświadczenia, vol. 33, APMA-B, p. 19; Porębski, Oświadczenia, vol. 21, APMA-B, pp. 11–31. For an example of the type of information Sonderkommando members shared, see Pogozhev, *Escape*, loc. 1950; Wachsmann, *KL*, pp. 307–14; Rees, *Auschwitz*, loc. 2153.

22   Gawron, *Ochotnik*, p. 223, p. 234.

23   Gawron, *Ochotnik*, p. 248; Gawron, in Pawlicki (dir.), *Witold*. The extent of Witold's knowledge about the mass murder of Jews in Birkenau is unclear. By his own account, he sent at least one report about the "mass gassing" prior to November 1942. Pilecki, *Report W*, p. 25. Wincenty Gawron attests to his role in carrying one oral report from the camp in May 1942 just as the "little red house" in Birkenau was becoming operational. Wincenty's memoir contains some factual errors but is accurate in many key features and offers an explanation of why the Jews were being targeted, which echoes Witold's own in his subsequent writings. A second report was carried by Stanisław Jaster, a written record of which is preserved from July 1942. It clearly describes the actions of the Sonderkommando, although references to their Jewish identity have been removed. This almost certainly happened as a result of editing in Warsaw. According to Witold, he sent at least one report about the "mass gassing" prior to November 1942. Pilecki, *Report W*, p. 25. The SS looting of Jews arriving in the camp was meticulously planned, but the total wealth extracted is unlikely to have been more than several hundred million Reichsmarks. Wachsmann, *KL*, p. 379.

24   Gawron, *Ochotnik*, p. 250.

25   Ibid, p. 254.

26   Ibid, p. 255, p. 247.

27   Ibid, p. 255.

28   Ibid, p. 257.

29   Ibid, p. 258.

30   Ibid, p. 259.

31   Ibid.

32 Ibid.

33 Ibid, p. 260.

34 Ibid.

35 Ibid, 272.

CHAPTER TEN

1 Hoess, *Commandant*, p. 120; Pilecki, [Raport 1945], PUMST, BI 874, p. 48; Taul, Wspomnienia, vol. 62, APMA-B, p. 27.

2 Piekarski, *Escaping*, p. 85.

3 Pilecki, [Raport 1945], PUMST, BI 874, p. 56; Langbein, *People*, p. 29; Redzej, [Raport 1943], AAN, 202/XVIII/1, p. 45; Ciesielski, [Raport 1943], AAN, 202/ XVIII, 1, p. 58; Piekarski, *Escaping*, p. 85.

4 Czech, *Auschwitz*, p. 165, p. 167.

5 Rawicz, [List], August 8, 1956; Rawicz, Oświadczenia, vol. 27, APMA-B; Rawicz, [Raport], date unknown.

6 Rawicz, [List], August 8, 1956; Rawicz, Oświadczenia, vol. 27, APMA-B; Rawicz, [Raport], date unknown.

7 Pilecki, [Raport 1945], PUMST, BI 874, p. 69, p. 71, p. 111; Rawicz, [List], August 8, 1956; Lasik et al., *Auschwitz*, vol. I, p. 299. It's worth noting that the uprising plan was formulated before the start of the Holocaust in the camp.

8 Pilecki, [Raport 1945], PUMST, BI 874, p. 54; Langbein, *People*, p. 29; Redzej, [Raport 1943], AAN, 202/XVIII/1, p. 45; Ciesielski, [Raport 1943], AAN, 202/ XVIII/1, p. 58.

9 Dering, [Wspomnienia], p. 89; Allen, *The Fantastic*, loc. 550; Gawron, *Ochotnik*, p. 222; Pilecki, [Raport 1945], PUMST, BI 874, p. 48; Motz, [Testimony], August 28, 1971; Allen, *The Fantastic*, loc. 550. See Siedlecki, *Beyond*, p. 167. Allen, *The Fantastic*, loc. 1633; Piekarski, *Escaping*, p. 126; Pietrzykowski, Wspomnienia, vol. 161, APMA-B, p. 141; Langbein, *People*, 240.

10 Dering, [Wspomnienia], p. 86, p. 141; Langbein, *People*, p. 240.

11 Czech, *Auschwitz*, p. 165; Kielar, *Anus Mundi*, p. 128; Dering, [Wspomnienia], p. 90.

12 Pilecki, *Report W*, p. 31; Czech, *Auschwitz*, p. 171; Piekarski, *Escaping*, 138.

13 Pilecki, [Raport 1945], PUMST, BI 874, p. 69; Pilecki, [Raport W], AAN, 202/ XVIII/1, p. 31; Rawicz, [List], September 23, 1957; Bartosiewicz, [Wywiad], Ossolineum, 87/00; Bartosiewicz, Oświadczenia, vol. 84, APMA-B, p. 127; Rawicz, [List], September 23, 1957.

14 Chrościcki, Oświadczenia, vol. 11, APMA-B, pp. 4–5; Czech, *Auschwitz*, p. 174; Pilecki, *The Auschwitz*, loc. 3083; Pilecki, [Raport 1945], PUMST, BI 874, p. 62.

15 Rawicz, [List], August 31, 1957; Szmaglewska, *Dymy*, p. 14.

16 Kowalczyk, *Barbed*, vol. II, p. 155. August was not part of decision-making, but he recalled the order to proceed with the escape. Chrościcki, Oświadczenia, vol. 11, APMA-B, pp. 4–5.

17 Kowalczyk, *Barbed*, vol. I, pp. 159–64.

18 Ostańkowicz, *Ziemia*, p. 187; Czech, *Auschwitz*, p. 178; Dering, [Wspomnienia], 77.

19 Czech, *Auschwitz*, pp. 180–81; Sobolewicz, *But I*, p. 131; Chrościcki, Oświadczenia, vol. 11, APMA-B, pp. 5–6; Langbein, *People*, p. 67.

20 Sobański, *Ucieczki*, pp. 47–48; Piechowski, Interview, October 14, 2016.

21 [Raport], no. 6/42, PISM, A.9. III.2a.55.2a.55. In the version of Witold's message that made it to London, references to the Holocaust in the report were edited out.

22 Piechowski, *Byłem*, p. 70.

23 Ibid, pp. 74–75.

24 Ibid, p. 79.

25 Piechowski, *Byłem*, p. 79; Sobański, *Ucieczki*, pp. 44–50; Pilecki, [Raport 1945], PUMST, BI 874, p. 59; Pawłowski, Walczek (dir.), *Jaster*.

26 Pilecki, *The Auschwitz*, loc. 2976; Pilecki, [Raport 1945], PUMST, BI 874, 59.

CHAPTER ELEVEN

1 Pilecki, [Raport—Nowy Wiśnicz], Wspomnienia, vol. 130, APMA-B, p. 111.

2 Zimmerman, *Polish*, p. 146; Ringelblum, *Notes*, loc. 4337; Wood, *Karski*, loc. 2341.

3 Dwork, van Pelt, *Auschwitz*, pp. 300–302; Wachsmann, *KL*, pp. 302–3.

4 Wachsmann, *KL*, p. 304; Dwork, van Pelt, *Auschwitz*, pp. 302–5; Redzej, [Raport 1943], AAN, 202/XVIII/1, p. 43.

5 Dwork, van Pelt, *Auschwitz*, pp. 302–5; Czech, *Auschwitz*, p. 179; Sobolewicz, *But I*, pp. 134–38; 202/I-31, pp. 95–97, in Marczewska, Ważniewski et al., *Zeszyty* (1968), p. 47; Pilecki, *The Auschwitz*, loc. 2890; Pilecki, [Raport 1945], PUMST, BI 874, p. 57.

6 Pilecki, *The Auschwitz*, loc. 1870; Pilecki, [Raport 1945], PUMST, BI 874, p. 57.

7 Paczyńska, *Grypsy*, p. XXXIII; 202/I-31, pp. 214–29, in Marczewska, Ważniewski et al., *Zeszyty* (1968), p. 70.

8 202/I-31, pp. 95–97, in Marczewska, Ważniewski et al., *Zeszyty* (1968), 47.

9 Vrba, *I Cannot*, p. 9; Höss, *Death*, p. 33.

10 Höss, *Death*, p. 33.

11 For Witold's reporting of the Holocaust, see Pilecki, *Report W*, p. 25; Gawron, *Ochotnik*, p. 248; Gawron, in Pawlicki (dir.), *Witold*; 202/I-31, pp. 214–29, in Marczewska, Ważniewski et al., *Zeszyty* (1968), p. 70; Paczyńska, *Grypsy*, p. XXXIII; Sobański, *Ucieczki*, pp. 47–48; Piechowski, Interview, October 14, 2016; [Raport], no. 6/42, PISM, A.9.III.2a.55.2a.55. In the version of Witold's message that made it to London, references to the Holocaust in the report were edited out. Segieda, [Raport], HIA, box 28, folder 7; Breitman, Laqueur, *Breaking*, p. 124; Laqueur, *The Terrible*, p. 100; Breitman,

Lichtman, *FDR*, loc. 3440; Lipstadt, *Beyond*, p. 321; Gilbert, *Auschwitz*, pp. 88–92; Fleming, *Auschwitz*, pp. 157–62.

12 Czech, *Auschwitz*, pp. 208–11; Wachsmann, *KL*, p. 304.

13 Pilecki, [Raport 1945], PUMST, BI 874, p. 68; Pilecki, [Raport 1943], AAN, 202/XVIII/1, p. 73; Iwaszko et al., *Auschwitz*, vol. II, p. 164.

14 Pilecki, [Raport 1945], PUMST, BI 874, p. 58, p. 68; Piekarski, *Escaping*, p. 148.

15 Langbein, *People*, p. 298; Pilecki, *The Auschwitz*, loc. 4098; Pilecki, [Raport 1945], PUMST, BI 874, pp. 87–88.

16 Pilecki, *The Auschwitz*, loc. 3346, loc. 3748; Pilecki, [Raport 1945], PUMST, BI 874, p. 68, p. 79.

17 Pilecki, [Raport—Nowy Wiśnicz], Wspomnienia, vol. 130, APMA-B, p. 111.

18 Kobrzyński, Wspomnienia, vol. 129, APMA-B, p. 45; Smoczyński, "Ostatnie," no pages given.

19 Olszowski, "Więźniarska," p. 186; Smoczyński, "Ostatnie," no pages given; Kobrzyński, Wspomnienia, vol. 129, APMA-B, p. 46.

20 Pilecki, [Raport 1945], PUMST, BI 874, p. 51; Piekarski, *Escaping*, p. 117; Ciesielski, *Wspomnienia*, p. 68. The existence of a camp radio is based on testimonies of Witold, Edek, and Kon. Taul, Oświadczenia, vol. 9, APMA-B, pp. 1264–71. Rawicz, [List do L. Serafińskiej], August 4, 1958; Materiały, vol. 220, APMA-B, p. 25. Rawicz, however, left the camp before the radio was operational.

21 Biernacki, [List], Materiały Ruchu Oporu, vols. 1–2, APMA-B, p. 10; Kłodziński, [List do W. Jekiełka i T. Lasockiej], November 24, 1942, cited in Paczyńska, *Grypsy*, p. 676; Pilecki, [Raport 1945], PUMST, BI 874, p. 63.

22 Dering, [Wspomnienia], p. 29, p. 103, pp. 139–42.

23 Dering, [Wspomnienia], p. 139; Wierusz, Oświadczenia, vol. 77, APMA-B, p. 21.

24 Czech, *Auschwitz*, p. 229; Pilecki, *Report W*, p. 22.

CHAPTER TWELVE

1 Pilecki, [Raport 1945], PUMST, BI 874, pp. 63–64; Strzelecka, *Voices,* vol. 3, 18.

2 Pilecki, [Raport 1945], PUMST, BI 874, pp. 63–64.

3 Ibid, p. 64.

4 Pilecki, [Raport 1945], PUMST, BI 874, p. 66. Witold describes a bombing raid on the night he entered the hospital suffering from typhus. There is no evidence that such a raid took place, but it might well have formed part of Witold's fevered dreams during his illness.

5 Pilecki, [Raport 1945], PUMST, BI 874, p. 66.

6 Ibid, p. 67.

7 Setkiewicz, *Zaopatrzenie,* p. 60; Redzej, [Raport 1943], AAN, 202/ XVIII/1, 46.

8 Pilecki, *Report W,* p. 19; Iwaszko et al., *Auschwitz,* vol. II, p. 409; Pilecki, *Report W,* p. 19.

9 Pilecki, [Raport 1945], PUMST, BI 874, p. 3; Pilecki, [Raport W], AAN, 202/ XVIII/1, p. 69.

10 Ibid.

11 Frączek, Wspomnienia, vol. 66, APMA-B, pp. 163–64; Pilecki, *Report W,* p. 27; Piekarski, *Escaping,* pp. 144–45; Komski, Oświadczenia, vol. 71, APMA-B, p. 64; Ławski, Wspomnienia, vol. 154/154a, APMA-B, p. 147, p. 148; Harat, [Działalność], no pages given; Kajtoch, Wspomnienia, vol. 27, APMA-B, pp. 1–149; Kuczbara, [Grypsy], Materiały Ruchu Oporu, vol. X, APMA-B, p. 6, p. 9, p. 11; Dwork, van Pelt, *Auschwitz,* pp. 324–25. The escape was conceived of by the camp dentist, Bolesław Kuczbara.

12 Pilecki, [Raport 1945], PUMST, BI 874, p. 74; Ostańkowicz, *Ziemia,* p. 266; Czech, *Auschwitz,* p. 313.

13 Pilecki, [Raport 1945], PUMST, BI 874, p. 75.

14 Pilecki, [Raport 1945], PUMST, BI 874, p. 75; Pilecki, *Report W*, p. 35; Pilecki, [Raport W], AAN, 202/XVIII/1, p. 72; Pilecki, [Raport 1945], PUMST, BI 874, p. 86. By 1943, a third of the prisoners were employed servicing the camp. Iwaszko et al., *Auschwitz*, vol. II, p. 89. Selections in the hospital were also curtailed, and Polish inmates were no longer sent to be gassed as some had prior to December 1942. Wachsmann, *KL*, p. 347.

15 Pilecki, [Raport 1945], PUMST, BI 874, pp. 79–80.

16 Pilecki, [Raport 1945], PUMST, BI 874, p. 69; Ciesielski, [Raport 1943], AAN, 202/XVIII/1, p. 12; Redzej, [Raport 1943], AAN, 202/XVIII/1, p. 45a; Głowa, Wspomnienia, vol. 94, APMA-B, pp. 138–39.

17 Głowa, Oświadczenia, vol. 36, APMA-B, p. 6; Dering, [Wspomnienia], p. 50; Głowa, Oświadczenia, vol. 94, APMA-B, p. 140; Pilecki, *Report W*, p. 115. Witold says two hundred children were murdered, but the total figure was less than one hundred.

18 Iwaszko et al., *Auschwitz*, vol. II, p. 156; Pilecki, *Report W*, p. 44; Pilecki, [Raport W], AAN, 202/XVIII/1, pp. 75–6; Ciesielski, [Raport 1943], AAN, 202/XVIII/1, p. 7.

19 Pilecki, [Raport 1945], PUMST, BI 874, p. 85.

20 Ibid.

21 Pilecki, [Raport 1945], PUMST, BI 874, p. 85; Pilecki, *The Auschwitz*, loc. 4049; Pilecki, [Raport 1945], PUMST, BI 874, p. 86.

22 Zabawski, Wspomnienia, vol. 98, APMA-B, p. 90; Ostrowska, [Wspomnienia 1], p. 5.

23 Pilecki, [Raport 1945], PUMST, BI 874, p. 85.

24 Ibid, p. 91.

25 Pilecki, *The Auschwitz*, loc. 3969; Pilecki, [Raport 1945], PUMST, BI 874, p. 84.

26 Pilecki, [Raport 1945], PUMST, BI 874, p. 88; Langbein, *People*, p. 75; Dering, [Wspomnienia], p. 23; Szarbel, [Zeznanie], IPN, BU_2188_14, pp. 110–13; Garliński, *Fighting*, p. 175; Langbein, *People*, p. 75; Pilecki, [Raport 1945], PUMST, BI 874, p. 88.

27 Pilecki, *The Auschwitz*, loc. 4140; Pilecki, [Raport 1945], PUMST, BI 874, p. 89.

28 Pilecki, *Report W*, p. 61; Pilecki, [Raport 1945], PUMST, BI 874, p. 89; Pilecki, [Raport W], AAN, 202/XVIII/1, p. 81.

29 Zabawski, Wspomnienia, vol. 98, APMA-B, p. 83.

30 Pilecki, [Raport 1945], PUMST, BI 874, p. 91; Pilecki, *The Auschwitz*, loc. 4241; Pilecki, [Raport 1945], PUMST, BI 874, p. 92.

CHAPTER THIRTEEN

1 Pilecki, *The Auschwitz*, loc. 4241; Pilecki, [Raport 1945], PUMST, BI 874, p. 92.

2 Pilecki, [Raport 1945], PUMST, BI 874, p. 93.

3 Ciesielski, *Wspomnienia*, pp. 115–16.

4 Ibid.

5 Ciesielski, *Wspomnienia*, p. 118; Ciesielski, *Wspomnienia*, pp. 121–22.

6 Pilecki, *The Auschwitz*, loc. 4344; Pilecki, [Raport 1945], PUMST, BI 874, p. 94; Pilecki, *The Auschwitz*, loc. 4364; Pilecki, [Raport 1945], PUMST, BI 874, p. 94.

7 Pilecki, [Raport 1945], PUMST, BI 874, p. 95.

8 Ibid.

9 Pilecki, [Raport 1945], PUMST, BI 874, p. 95; Ciesielski, *Wspomnienia*, p. 128; Pilecki, [Raport 1945], PUMST, BI 874, p. 95; Ciesielski, *Wspomnienia*, p. 128; Pilecki, [Raport 1945], PUMST, BI 874, p. 95.

10 Pilecki, [Raport 1945], PUMST, BI 874, p. 96; Ciesielski, *Wspomnienia*, p. 128.

11 Pilecki, [Raport 1945], PUMST, BI 874, p. 96.

12 Ibid.

13 Pilecki, *The Auschwitz*, loc. 4565; Pilecki, [Raport 1945], PUMST, BI 874, 100.

14 Pilecki, *The Auschwitz*, loc. 4565; Pilecki, [Raport 1945], PUMST, BI 874, p. 100; Pilecki, *The Auschwitz*, loc. 4575; Pilecki, [Raport 1945], PUMST, BI 874, p. 100.

15 Pilecki, [Raport 1945], PUMST, BI 874, p. 100.

16 Ibid.

17 Pilecki, [Raport 1945], PUMST, BI 874, p. 101; Pilecki, *The Auschwitz*, loc. 4622; Pilecki, [Raport 1945], PUMST, BI 874, p. 101.

18 Pilecki, *The Auschwitz*, loc. 4622; Pilecki, [Raport 1945], PUMST, BI 874, p. 101.

19 Serafiński, [Ucieczka], p. 2.

20 Pilecki, *The Auschwitz*, loc. 4630; Pilecki, [Raport 1945], PUMST, BI 874, p. 102; Pilecki, *The Auschwitz*, loc. 4637; Pilecki, [Raport 1945], PUMST, BI 874, p. 102.

21 Serafiński, [Ucieczka], p. 3.

22 Pilecki, [Raport—Nowy Wiśnicz], Wspomnienia, vol. 130, APMA-B, pp. 110–13.

23 Pilecki, [Raport 1945], PUMST, BI 874, p. 102.

24 Ibid.

CHAPTER FOURTEEN

1 Gistedt, *Od operetki*, p. 108.

2 Ostrowski, Interview, March 9, 2016; Pilecki, Akta sprawy, Protokół przesłuchania Witolda Pileckiego, Materiały, vol. 223, APMA-B, p. 85.

3 Czarnecka, *Największa*, pp. 109–201; Pawłowski, Walczak (dirs.), *Jaster*; Paulsson, *Secret*, p. 5, p. 21.

4 Paulsson, *Secret*, p. 21; 202/II-35, p. 84, in Marczewska, Ważniewski et al., *Zeszyty* (1968), pp. 79–80; Pilecka-Optułowicz, Interview, May 17, 2016; Ostrowski, Interview, March 9, 2016; Pilecki, Akta sprawy, Protokół przesłuchania Witolda Pileckiego, Materiały, vol. 223, APMA-B, p. 85.

5 Pilecki, [List], October 18, 1943, IPN.

6 Pilecki, [Raport 1945], PUMST, BI 874, p. 103.

7 Pilecki, *The Auschwitz*, loc. 4698; Pilecki, [Raport 1945], PUMST, BI 874, p. 103; Pilecki, [Raport W], AAN, 202/XVIII/1, p. 23.

8 Pilecki, [Raport 1945], PUMST, BI 874, p. 103; Albin, *List*, p. 198; Machnowski, "Sprawa," p. 127. Edward Ciesielski arrived in Warsaw in December 1943 and likely brought news of his latest exchanges with the camp.

9 Pilecki, [Zamiast], Materiały, vol. 223c, APMA-B, p. 1.

10 Szpakowski, Interview, January 31, 2017; Pilecki, Akta sprawy, Protokół przesłuchania Tadeusza Sztrum de Sztrema, Materiały, vol. 223a, APMA-B, p. 398.

11 Pilecki, [Zamiast], Materiały, vol. 223c, APMA-B, p. 1.

12 Pilecki, [Raport 1945], PUMST, BI 874, p. 103.

13 Abramow-Newerly, Interview, October 2, 2017.

14 Abramow-Newerly, *Lwy*, pp. 153–56; Marrus, *The Nazi*, Part 5: "Public Opinion and Relations to Jews"; Abramow-Newerly, Interview, October 2, 2017.

15 Pilecki, Interview, July 11, 2016.

16 Pilecki, Interview, July 11, 2016.

17 Klukowski, *Diary*, p. 257.

18 Fieldorf, Zachuta, *Generał*, p. 277; Kuciński, *August*, p. 77.

19 Pilecka-Optułowicz, Interview, May 17, 2016.

CHAPTER FIFTEEN

1 The figure of ten reports includes Witold's oral and written accounts described in this book. The number may have been higher taking into account other members of his organization who left the camp bearing his instructions.

2 On June 12, 1944, Emanuel Scherer and Anzelm Reiss went to the Polish minister of the interior requesting that the underground attack

Auschwitz and other camps. In July, John Pehle of the War Rescue Board dismissed the idea of a land attack on the basis that "the apparently deep-rooted anti-Semitism" of Poles would prevent the attack from occurring in "good faith." It's not clear whether he was responding to the debate in Allied capitals or had drawn his own conclusions. Fleming, *Auschwitz*, p. 255. Komorowski didn't entirely dismiss the proposal of a ground operation. It made sense to have a force ready in the worst-case scenario that the Nazis decided to liquidate the camp and kill everyone in it, but he remained skeptical that a force could be moved into position.

3 Pilecki, [Raport W], AAN, p. 79. At the end of July, Komorowski dispatched a courier to Auschwitz to contact what was left of the camp resistance to develop a plan, which included blowing up the crematoria and gas chambers in Birkenau. The courier, a member of the so-called Silent Unseen, was shot and captured in September and subsequently interned in Auschwitz, where he died.

4 Richie, *Warsaw*, p. 164.

5 Davies, *Rising '44*, loc. 8673.

6 Bartoszewski, *1859*, p. 696; Korboński, *Fighting*, p. 345; Korboński, *Fighting*, p. 345.

7 Richie, *Warsaw*, p. 133; Davies, *Rising '44*, loc. 2598; Pilecki, Akta sprawy, Protokół przesłuchania Witolda Pileckiego, Materiały, vol. 223, APMA-B, p. 73.

8 Davies, *Rising '44*, loc. 2598; Richie, *Warsaw*, p. 136; Richie, *Warsaw*, p. 179; Iranek-Osmecki, *Powołanie*, p. 427.

9 Nowak, *Courier*, p. 240; Walasek, Interview, May 19, 2016.

10 Forczyk, *Warsaw 1944*, p. 38, cited in Richie, *Warsaw*, p. 193; Nowak, *Courier*, p. 240; Walasek, Interview, May 19, 2016; Walasek, Interview, May 19, 2016; Hałko, *Kotwica*, p. 22; Walasek, Interview, May 19, 2016; Sierchuła, Utracka, "Historia," pp. 216–17.

11 Nowak, *Courier*, p. 240; Davies, *Powstanie '44*, p. 329.

12 Richie, *Warsaw*, p. 244.

13 Sierchuła, Utracka, "Historia," pp. 216–17; Zakrzewski, Interview, October 17, 2016; Richie, *Warsaw*, p. 425.

14 Sierchuła, Utracka, "Historia," p. 6; Richie, *Warsaw*, p. 222.

15 Ibid, p. 218.

16 Ibid.

17 Sierchuła, Utracka, "Historia," p. 7; Pilecki, [Raport 1945], PUMST, BI 874, p. 104.

18 Sierchuła, Utracka, "Historia," pp. 216–17; Remlein, [Wspomnienia]; Korboński, *Fighting*, p. 370.

19 Richie, *Warsaw*, p. 269.

20 Walasek, Interview, May 19, 2016.

21 Sierchuła, Utracka, "Historia," p. 218; Walasek, Interview, May 19, 2016.

22 Ibid, p. 222; Ibid.

23 Walendzik, Interview, October 12, 2016.

24 Bartoszewski, *1859*, p. 772, p. 787; Osęka, "Zabawa," p. 64.

25 Zagórski, *Seventy*, p. 205.

26 The exact figure of the dead is unknown but lies somewhere between 130,000 and 150,000 civilians and 17,000 uprisers. Heydecker, *Moja*, pp. 230–38.

CHAPTER SIXTEEN

1 Ostrowska, [Wspomnienia 1], p. 9.

2 Ostrowska, [Wspomnienia 1], p. 9; Ostrowska, [Wspomnienia 2], pp. 5–6; Zakrzewski, Interview, October 17, 2016; Bednorz, *Lamsdorf*, p. 24.

3 Kisielewicz, *Oflag*, p. 57, p. 111, p. 109; Wołosiuk, "Znałem," p. 1.

4 Kisielewicz, *Oflag*, p. 54, p. 170; Ollier, email, August 16, 2001.

5 Ibid.

6 Pilecki, Akta sprawy, Protokół rozprawy głównej, Spis adresów, Materiały, vol. 223b, APMA-B, p. 659, p. 642.

7 Pilecki, Akta sprawy, Protokół rozprawy głównej, Spis adresów, Materiały, vol. 223b, APMA-B, p. 659, p. 642.

8 Pilecki, Akta sprawy, [Meldunek nr 2], Materiały, vol. 223b, APMA-B, p. 555; Pilecki, Akta sprawy, Protokół rozprawy głównej, Materiały, vol. 223b, APMA-B, p. 676.

9 Zaremba, *Wielka*, p. 340; Ostrowska, Zaremba, "Kobieca," pp. 64–69.

10 Orłowska, Interview, November 13, 2018; Applebaum, *Iron*, p. 248.

11 Pilecki, Akta sprawy, Protokół przesłuchania Witolda Pileckiego, Materiały, vol. 223, APMA-B, pp. 14–18; Pilecki, Akta sprawy, Protokół przesłuchania Makarego Sieradzkiego, Materiały, vol. 223a, APMA-B, p. 363, p. 372.

12 Ibid, p. 190; Ibid.

13 Pilecki, Akta sprawy, [Meldunek nr 2], Materiały, vol. 223a, APMA-B, p. 555.

14 Pilecki, Akta sprawy, Protokół przesłuchania Witolda Pileckiego, Materiały, vol. 223, APMA-B, p. 78; Heuener, *Auschwitz*, p. 69.

15 Heuener, *Auschwitz*, pp. 66–69.

16 Cyra, *Ochotnik*, p. 157; Pilecki, Akta sprawy, [Tragedia kielecka], ASS MON, vol. 4, pp. 62–63; Applebaum, *Iron*, p. 217. Pilecki, Witold, Akta sprawy przeciwko Witoldowi Pileckiemu/innym Tragedia Kielecka, Materiały, vol. 223a, APMA–8, pp. 542–43.

17 Pilecki, [Zamiast], Materiały, vol. 223c, APMA-B, p. 5.

18 Ostrowska, [Wspomnienia 1], p. 12.

19 Pilecki, Akta sprawy, Protokół rozprawy głównej, vol. 5, ASS MON, pp. 25–26.

20 Ostrowska, Wspomnienia, vol. 179, APMA-B, pp. 155–56; Pilecki, Interview, July 20, 2018.

21 Pilecki, Akta sprawy, vol. 5, ASS MON, pp. 107–17; Pilecki, Akta sprawy, Protokół rozprawy głównej, Materiały, vol. 223b, APMA-B, p. 691.

22   The Serafiński family also begged Cyrankiewicz to intervene and bring to the court's attention Witold's work in the camp. Cyrankiewicz replied that the matter was in Bierut's hands.

23   Pilecka, [List do Bolesława Bieruta], date unknown, ASS MON, vol. 5, p. 194, in Cyra, *Rotmistrz*, pp. 190–91.

24   Stępień, Wspomnienia, vol. 179, APMA-B, pp. 176–77; Płużański, *Obława*, p 181.

EPILOGUE

1   Incredibly, the state prosecutor who'd sought the death penalty against Witold, Czesław Łapiński, still worked as a military lawyer and briefly tried to block access.

2   Edek Ciesielski published the first memoir about Witold and the early camp underground in 1966. (Edek, sadly, died of a stroke at the age of forty in 1962.) Over the course of his research, Edek had reached out to Kazimierz Rawicz, leading to a fascinating exchange of letters between the men. It appears they made a research trip together to Auschwitz, where they were able to access a copy of Witold's W report. Ciesielski, [List], July 6, 1958. Ciesielski's letters were accessed courtesy of Marek Popiel. Cyra found a key to the Report W and was able to decipher the names that Witold had coded. In 1991, Report W was published, with a biography of Witold (*Biuletyn TOnO*, 1991/12).

3   Levi, *Drowned*, p. 11.

PHOTOGRAPH & ILLUSTRATION CREDITS

Photos ©: cover fence: Lukas Rozhon/Alamy Stock Photo; 3, 5: Courtesy of the Pilecki family; 7: John Gilkes; 9: Courtesy of the Pilecki family; 11: United States Holocaust Memorial Museum, courtesy of the Julien Bryan Archive; 13: Courtesy of Marek Ostrowski; 16: Narodowe Archiwum Cyfrowe; 19: John Gilkes; 20: Courtesy of Marek Ostrowski; 28, 30, 31, 33: Courtesy of the Pilecki family; 44: From the collection of Mirosław Ganobis; 46: John Gilkes; 53: Courtesy of the Stupka family; 61: From the collection of Mirosław Ganobis; 64: Rainer Höß/Leibniz Institute for Contemporary History (IfZ); 81: Courtesy of Anna Komorowska; 100-101: John Gilkes; 107: Courtesy of the Sławiński family; 109: Yad Vashem; 111: Jack Fairweather; 114: Courtesy of Anna Komorowska; 118-119: John Gilkes; 126: Courtesy of Ewa Biały; 128-129: Beata Dejnarowicz; 130: Courtesy of the Stupka family; 140-141: Yad Vashem; 156-157, 167: John Gilkes; 180: United States Holocaust Memorial Museum, courtesy of Albert Barkin; 201: Courtesy of Marta Goljan; 203, 204, 205: Jack Fairweather; 208-209: John Gilkes; 210: Courtesy of Maria Serafińska-Domańska; 211: Jack

INDEX

Page numbers in *italics* refer to illustrations.